"*Trusted Healers* is a must read for everyone who cares about their own well-being and that of their families, coworkers, and community members. Through the lens of the public health crises in modern times, such as the AIDS pandemic in Africa and the broken physical and mental health culture in America, Dan provides a sobering look at what happens when a person or a society abdicates responsibility for their well-being. He then provides a look into a brighter future at what is possible when a culture embraces health and accepts responsibility, awakening the ability to live our lives with much more control over our well-being."

—**David Folk**, Co-Founder and CEO NEXT Integrative Minds
Life Sciences, Limited

"Everybody can have an aspirational view about something. He has that and can deliver the inspiration and perspiration to go along with it. Dan doesn't always follow the outline. He colors outside the picture a lot to get the job done."

—**Nick Donofrio**, IBM executive vice president of innovation
and technology, and General Manager of Healthcare (Ret)

"*Trusted Healers* demonstrates that social injustice and social inequities invariably impact health and healthcare. First, we have got to accept and believe that. Then we can do something about it."

—**Nwando Olayiwola, MD**, Chief Clinical Transformation
Officer Rubicon MD

"There's a reason Dan Pelino has gathered some of the brightest and most powerful minds in healthcare to help us understand where we are on this journey and what the future will look like. Powerful societal questions need to be addressed by every culture. By following the amazing decade-long crusade of Dr. Paul Grundy around the world, the answers emerge."

—**Glenn D. Steele, MD, PhD,**
healthcare reformers

D1288296

Trusted Healers:
Dr. Paul Grundy and the
Global Healthcare Crusade

by Dan Pelino with Bud Ramey

© Copyright 2019 Dan Pelino with Bud Ramey

ISBN 978-1-63393-684-3

Review copy: this is an advanced printing,
subject to corrections and revisions.

Published by

◿ köehlerbooks™

210 60th Street
Virginia Beach, VA 23451
800–435–4811
www.koehlerbooks.com

in association with

Everyone Matters, Inc

everyonemattersonline.com

Everyone Matters, Inc., is a social impact enterprise founded in 2015 dedicated to ensuring that everyone has equal access to citizen-based services, healthcare, and education. Within this context, all people have the right to dignity and respect, to be who they are without being shamed or demeaned, and to thrive within their own unique individuality.

FOREWORD BY PATRICK J. KENNEDY

TRUSTED HEALERS

DR. PAUL GRUNDY AND THE GLOBAL HEALTHCARE CRUSADE

DAN PELINO

WITH BUD RAMEY

VIRGINIA BEACH
CAPE CHARLES

DEDICATION

In every journey, a story is revealed, its path shaped by
countless advisors, influencers and encounters.
Trusted Healers presents such a journey, and we dedicate
this book to everyone who answers the call.

Why do we do what we do?
Because *everyone matters.*

• • •

With the publication of *Trusted Healers*, Dr. Paul Grundy honors
the memory of Randy and Kathy MacDonald.

• • •

Bud Ramey honors the memory of the *Familiar Physician*, Dr.
Peter Anderson.

CONTENTS

PART THREE—INNOVATION INSPIRES THE JOURNEY

GUIDES AND RESOURCES

FOREWORD

By Patrick J. Kennedy

The fight for mental health parity is deeply personal to me because I am one of the millions afflicted. I have always hoped sharing my story would inspire a deeper understanding of the challenges of mental health, substance use, and recovery. Patients, families, caregivers and healers sharing stories about what I call the "common struggle" is key to changing how the world views these illnesses of the brain.

Many of the inspirational characters in this book came to leadership in the field of brain health very deliberately. I did not. My sixteen years in Congress leading a crusade against the health insurance industry's discrimination in mental health and addiction coverage was initially triggered by selfish cruelty.

When I was a teenager struggling with bipolar disorder and self-medicating, I was sent to inpatient care at a rehab facility. I trusted I was in a safe environment where I could get treatment and heal. Instead, a young man with me in rehab sold my story to a supermarket tabloid for $10,000. His goal was to embarrass me just as I was heading into reelection for a seat in the Rhode Island House of Representatives. He outed me in the most hurtful way—violating my privacy, and stealing my chance to tell my own story, in my own time. Many thought this callous, public display of my illness would end my career in public office.

Instead, I won reelection and later went on to become one of the youngest US congressman in history at age twenty-eight. It was comforting and humbling to know I could survive politically, despite being bipolar and suffering with addiction.

While I worked on many issues during my sixteen years in Congress representing Rhode Island, those most important to me involved mental health and substance use. When I had other embarrassing incidents associated with my illness, I chose to address them publicly, even when my advisors and family members warned against it.

I often joke that in some strange way, I am grateful to the fellow who sold my story to the *National Enquirer*. Being exposed by him at a young age meant I would never really be able to hide my illnesses again; it elevated my personal commitment to protect the millions of people who, like me, struggle with mental health and substance abuse.

In 2008, my father, Massachusetts senator Ted Kennedy, and I worked with our Republican partners, Senator Pete Domenici and Representative Jim Ramstad (who, like me, was in recovery), to deliver the first piece of legislation that could really protect the medical rights of people with brain diseases—the Mental Health Parity and Addiction Equity Act (MHPAEA). It was the crowning achievement of my legislative career, and the last of many crowning achievements of my dad's storied career.

The act was not perfect. We recently celebrated MHPAEA's tenth anniversary with an event in the Kennedy Caucus Room of the US Senate. We discussed how far we still have to go to make the words on the pages of that bill a reality for those suffering with mental health and addiction. Regardless, the act remains a beacon of hope for everyone who has these brain illnesses, for everyone who treats these brain illnesses and for everyone who loves someone with these brain illnesses. So, essentially, almost every American.

The Parity Act was also extremely personal to me, for reasons outside the public eye. My father always loved me, but he never really understood my suffering or my illnesses. He would often say all I needed was a good, swift kick in the ass. But in his last years, as he struggled with cancer and we fought to get the parity bill enacted, I think we had a breakthrough.

At least, it felt like a breakthrough to me. Suddenly, my dad seemed to really be encouraging of me for being candid about my struggles and using that openness to fuel political leadership. "Keep doing the work you are doing," Dad would whisper to me in private moments.

Passing that bill has been my greatest accomplishment as a public servant. Having my father's understanding that my being open about my illness was my strength—not my weakness—was the greatest moment between us. It's a feeling I hope everyone with these illnesses experiences as we work to treat brain diseases and heal our great nation.

I left Congress in 2011 to save my own life as I continued combating my own chronic illnesses. Those closest to me wondered if I would survive. But as fate would have it, I was saved by love. I met a wonderful, compassionate public-school teacher, Amy, who would become my wife and supported me while I committed myself fully to recovery. And it was as we fell in love that I came to understand my part-time job in Congress—offering political leadership and lived experience to the cause of mental health parity—should become my mission in life.

With that vision in mind, I founded the Kennedy Forum in 2014, dedicated to fulfilling what I started during my congressional stint, which is the realization of parity and the end of the insurance denial of these illnesses. During the early days of the Kennedy Forum, we convened thought leaders and policy experts to chart the course of how we could improve mental health and substance abuse care in this country and achieve health equity through the implementation and enforcement of the Federal Parity Act.

It was during these early convenings that I befriended Dan Pelino, who had generously volunteered his time to help us establish benchmarks and standards for parity. Working closely with Dan, I formed a respect for his knowledge and passion in working to resolve these complex issues and breaking down the barriers that pervade this space.

Because of my belief in Dan's mission, I am honored to introduce you to Dan's important book, *Trusted Healers*, which illuminates the thinking and leadership of Dr. Paul Grundy.

I first met Paul in early 2006 at my congressional office as he was about to launch his crusade for the *medical home*. *Trusted Healers* provides candid, powerful stories of mental health and substance use in America, as well as a journey through the cultural taboos and tribal customs that inform, and sometimes prejudice, the thinking of Americans about these subjects. These stories have a common theme; they all occurred when nobody wanted to listen. These stories now convey messages we all need to hear.

Dan and *Trusted Healers* co-author, Bud Ramey, make a compelling case that things improve once a culture overcomes its inability to see the truth and recognizes the tragedy awaiting it if it does not. Changing culture takes patience and persistence as we see in *Trusted Healers*. But while we have certainly made strides in the US legislatively, our collective will to change has been almost stagnant.

We must recognize societally—not just in healthcare—that mental illnesses and addiction are treatable. When those who are disenfranchised receive care, they also receive hope, and that hope becomes the vanguard of transformation.

My wife, Amy, and I hope our children will have the support and guidance to manage and conquer all mental illness just the same as they would any physical illness. We want a world where our children will not know a distinction between mental health and physical health—their conversations will simply be about their health.

With *Trusted Healers*, Dan and Bud provide a compelling narrative that helps all of us achieve that reality.

Patrick J. Kennedy is a former congressman (D-RI); founder,
The Kennedy Forum; co-founder, One Mind; commissioner,
President's Commission on Combating Drug Addiction
and the Opioid Crisis.

While serving Rhode Island's first congressional
district, Patrick J. Kennedy fought to end discrimination
against mental illness, addiction, and other brain diseases.
As lead sponsor of the groundbreaking Mental Health
Parity and Addiction Equity Act (MHPAEA), Kennedy
continues to champion the Federal Parity Law, which
provides millions of Americans with access to insurance
coverage for mental health and addiction treatment.

He founded the Kennedy Forum, a nonprofit
organization that aims to achieve health equity through
parity by advancing evidence-based practices, policies,
and political will. Along with Stephen Fried, Kennedy
co-authored a personal narrative, the New York Times
Bestseller, A Common Struggle, *which ends with a detailed*
roadmap to achieve health equity in the United States. In
2017, Kennedy served on the President's Commission on
Combating Drug Addiction and the Opioid Crisis.

Dan Pelino and Dr. Paul Grundy

LISTEN TO
THE WHISPERS

I vividly recall meeting Congressman Patrick J. Kennedy in the Cannon House Office Building in Washington, DC. It was 2006, and Dr. Paul Grundy and I were together, working on the launch of the *medical home* crusade. We were preparing for an ambitious journey that crossed continents and would last a decade.

Later, I had the honor of sharing the stage with Patrick at the 2016 State of the Union in Mental Health and Addiction address. During my remarks, I quoted a Native American proverb attributed to both the Dakota and Cherokee nations. It brought to mind wisdom shared by elders. I imagined a gathering around the evening campfire, a time when such great wisdom is reverently passed from one generation to the next.

"Listen to the whispers, so we won't have to hear the screams."

I imagined campfire listeners nodding in agreement with the ranking elder in the warmth of a special moment. The fire snapped. Sparks flew upward. There was silence.

This powerful proverb resonated with our audience of mental health champions as well, because we are a nation that struggles with listening to *whispers*.

On her final regular television show on May 25, 2011, Oprah Winfrey talked about her greatest regrets.

"Whispers are always messages, and if you don't hear the message, the message turns into a problem. And if you don't handle the problem, the problem turns into a crisis. And if you don't handle the crisis, disaster. Your life is speaking to you. What is it saying?"[1]

She's right. Now we have the greatest public health crisis of our time with substance abuse, addiction, depression, and suicide. We're paying the price for not listening to the whispers.

Of all the things broken in our healthcare system, perhaps mental health treatment and substance abuse are the most troubling because we as a culture have stigmatized these illnesses.

We hear the *screams*. This book is about listening to the *whispers* of the wise.

Every person's healthcare could be described as a journey. We like using that metaphor.

So, too, every nation's healthcare could be depicted as a journey.

In developing *Trusted Healers,* co-author Bud Ramey and I traveled throughout the US and abroad to retrace the steps of Dr. Paul Grundy, who spent a decade crusading for better healthcare. In these pages, we observe several nations with innovative approaches to healthcare. We also acknowledge that America's healthcare journey has been quite bumpy. By reminding ourselves of where we have been, we can see a better way forward.

We know that many of our healthcare sins have been self-inflicted either through ignorance or indulgence. Early Americans, for example, took a healthful dram for breakfast. Whiskey was a typical lunchtime tipple. Ale accompanied supper, and the day ended with a nightcap. Continuous imbibing clearly built up a tolerance as most Americans in 1790 consumed an average 5.8 gallons of pure alcohol a year.[2] In early America, alcoholism—also known as dipsomania— had a serious impact on communities. Women and children might be in physical danger if the man of the house began drinking. If he became ill or lost his job through drink, there was no social safety net to support or protect his family. In 1862, the US Navy abolished the traditional half-pint daily rum ration for sailors, and in the same period support for Prohibition, banning the manufacture and sale of alcohol, was overwhelming.

By the late 1800s, dipsomania, or alcoholism, was being treated as a disease.

The first arrest for driving under the influence of alcohol was in 1897.

On January 16, 1919, the Eighteenth Amendment, which set Prohibition into law, became part of the Constitution.

In 1955, the Breathalyzer was patented.

Today, Americans drink an average of 2.3 gallons of alcohol a year compared to 7.1 gallons in 1830.

And then there's our history with tobacco.

Most Americans born into the generations following the post–WWII baby boom have gone their entire lives aware that smoking can cause lung cancer. But this fact was not always well known. The tobacco industry intentionally camouflaged smoking's effects and even promoted it as stylish. Societal consequences of that charade were dire.

Prior to the 1900s, lung cancer was a rare disease. But by the turn of the century, we faced rapidly increasing lung cancer rates. New technology allowed cigarettes to be produced on a large scale, and advertising glamorized smoking. Many movies featured lengthy cigarette smoking scenes. Smoking ads were everywhere: "LSMFT (Lucky Strike Means Fine Tobacco)"; "More doctors smoke Camels than any other cigarette;" "Chesterfield: smells lighter, smokes lighter"; and "The Marlboro Man."

The military got in on it too, giving cigarettes to soldiers during World Wars I and II, and continued to do so until 1975 in field rations.

Cigarette smoking increased rapidly through the 1950s, becoming much more widespread. Per capita cigarette consumption soared from sixty-four per year in 1900 to 4,345 per year in 1963.

And lung cancer went from rare to more commonplace. By the early 1950s it became "the most common cancer diagnosed in American men," wrote American Cancer Society chief medical officer Dr. Otis Brawley in an article published November 2013 in *CA: A Cancer Journal for Clinicians*.[3]

The creation of that landscape-altering report began with a letter sent to President John F. Kennedy in June 1961. Leaders from the American Cancer Society, the American Public Health Association, and the National Tuberculosis Association urged Kennedy to form a national commission on smoking to find "a solution to this health problem." Kennedy asked his surgeon general, Luther Terry, to tackle this.

These two behavioral crises provided a rhythm for healthcare all the way into the new millennium. What new health and behavioral crises lie ahead, challenging us?

⌒

Forty years seems like a long time. It's a generation. *Forty years* was used by the ancient Hebrews figuratively to mean *a long time*. The number *40* is used in Scripture many times in various ways.

It was forty years from the tragic assassination of Martin Luther King, Jr., to the election of President Barack Obama.

It was forty years from the Academy Award for Best Picture for the silent movie *Wings* to the first steps on the moon of astronauts Neil Armstrong and Buzz Aldrin.

It took forty years from the opening in 1830 of the Baltimore and Ohio, America's first railroad, until the golden spike was driven to symbolize the opening of the Transcontinental Railroad.

And forty years passed from the development of the nation's first electronic medical record in 1960 until the modern *Age of Healthcare Information* arrived.

Consider taking a closer look and comparing the construction of the Transcontinental Railroad with America's burgeoning healthcare information network.

Railroad track had to be laid over 2,000 miles of often difficult terrain, including mountains of solid granite. Before the Transcontinental Railroad was completed, travel overland by stagecoach cost $1,000, took five or six months, and involved crossing rugged mountains and arid desert. ($1,000 in 1860 represents $30,265 in today's dollars.)

Railroad meeting

The alternatives were to travel by sea around the tip of South America, a distance of 18,000 miles, or to cross the Isthmus of Panama, then travel north by ship to California. Each route took months and was dangerous and expensive. The Transcontinental Railroad made it possible to complete the trip in five days at a cost of $150 for a first-class sleeper. It took six years to complete.

The first spikes were driven in 1863, during the Civil War, and on May 10, 1869, at Promontory Summit, Utah, a golden spike was hammered into the final tie. The ceremonial 17.6-karat-gold final spike is now displayed in the Cantor Arts Center at Stanford University.[4]

In healthcare, the first electronic medical record was developed in 1960. Forty years later, worldwide healthcare stood at the door of the millennium and at the threshold of the *Age of Healthcare Information*.

Some would argue that the global pace of change has now quickened.

That may be true in many areas. But even though medicine and healthcare leaped across large chasms at the turn of the millennium, even though technological advancements are as powerful and lasting as any the developed world has achieved, healthcare still clings to its own rhythm and pace to create cultural change.

Throughout the nineteenth and twentieth centuries, our culture was immersed in unhealthy behaviors. Yet, life expectancy crept up. In 1900, it was in the forties. In 1950, life expectancy had risen to the sixties. By the millennium, expectancy was in the seventies. But it was a struggle. It took Prohibition to slow down our drinking pace. And cigarette makers were finally reeled in by a federal government that could no longer ignore cancer wards filled with patients suffering with lung diseases. Regular exercise was on the rise, but not for most.

Slowly, surely, citizens of the developed world embraced a different idea about taking care of themselves.

Healthcare information technology helped get us on the right course. Healthcare morphed and expanded into not only medical treatment for diseases, but preventative care and improving lifestyles with diet and exercise.

Information sparked this change. We learned how many of us were dying of cardiovascular disease and lung and other cancers. We saw it every day. We lost friends to an early death. This bad news was in the newspapers. On TV. On the radio. The *screams* finally began to yield to the *whispers* as the health railway was engineered.

We knew how to build it, but we did not know for sure how long it would take. We could not know the difficulties ahead. There would be obstacles, as the railroad faced rivers, mountains, and deserts. Like the builders of the Transcontinental Railroad, we would blast our way through.

With time, technology, and perseverance, we unleashed the full power of the *Age of Healthcare Information* into medicine.

Our doctors can now see our entire health record without opening a three-inch-thick paper chart. We can keep track of what works and what does not work, what we have done and what we have not done.

Information flows, which leads to better healthcare decisions. The pace has quickened, keeping up with rapid medical discoveries and advancements. These innovations profoundly impact how caregivers are updated and educated.

Just as the Transcontinental Railroad united East and West, the movement from *healthcare* to *healthy living* unites caregivers and patients. Today, electronic medical records are being used by 96 percent of providers in the US.

The word *prevention* has exploded into our medical lexicon. And we have data to buttress preventative care. Gifted physician communicators have translated clinical research into compelling information on good health and prevention. Real-world research and convincing presentations have drawn millions to embrace wellness.

Anne Altman

Anne Altman, retired general manager of IBM US Federal Government and Industries, who worked with Paul at IBM for many of her thirty-five years there, makes a keen observation.

"Throughout time, healthcare by healers changed. With the *Age of Healthcare Information*, we have access to untapped knowledge about ourselves. At the outset, everybody wrestled with how to manage that information. Who would be responsible, who would be the keeper? The answer became obvious—the *medical home*. It is actionable. That's where all this should reside, with the *Trusted Healer*," Anne says.

Patient information and data empowers caregivers. Clinical protocols are at their fingertips. Diagnostic information reaches the doctor instantaneously instead of days or weeks later. With this advent, medical care advanced. Rural and suburban doctors suddenly had many of the tools and data previously available only in cities. Results were encouraging as patients became healthier. Medical interventions, now based on accumulated evidence, improved.

The acceleration of the speed and volume of information changed everything. Healthcare systems changed. Outcomes changed. People's behavior changed.

We learned that maybe we have a say in how long we live, how we can best avoid disease. This new freedom helped us pause, relax, and ask ourselves some core questions about life:

How can I be most productive for my family and community? How can I live a healthier and happier life?

For the first time *health* became part of our culture's definition of prosperity, and that cultural shift gives hope that we as a country and a world can achieve even more. The movement from *healthcare* to *healthy living* has already changed the world.

Five powerful events happened almost simultaneously:

- Led by Patrick J. Kennedy, we committed to equal clinical attention for mental and behavioral health and opioid addiction. Brain illness is no longer relegated to the sidelines of medicine. Children will grow up with new tools to learn how to navigate society, relationships, disappointments, tragedies, and victories. Gradually, the stigma we created in the twentieth century will dissipate.

- Led by Dr. Paul Grundy, we decided that primary care must be the heartbeat of medicine. The *medical home* model of care solves a crisis in cost, quality, and physician morale. It also gives us an opportunity to have a *Trusted Healer* of our own. No longer limited to just a doctor, the *medical home* brought us the concept of team care. Everyone practices "at the top of their license," which means assuming every responsibility they can within their credentials, and everyone benefits.

- Led by Dr. Glenn Steele and his team at Geisinger Health System, we discovered evidence-based medicine. The clinical world turned upside down. By highly disciplined evaluation of outcomes and care processes, we selected *best practices*, an evidence-based way of delivering care that was proven to have much better results at lower costs.

Dr. Mehmet Oz and Dr. Mike Roizen

Dr. Michael Roizen and the Cleveland Clinic used the new wealth of information to demonstrate best health practices in diet, exercise, stress management, and life management. Dr. Roizen and Dr. Mehmet Oz shared these findings with the people on television and in best-selling books around the world. People began to awaken. Millions accepted responsibility for their own health.

- Escaping a culture boxed in by racism and bias, led by a series of powerful national leaders, a movement guided by the belief that *everyone matters* began.

The speed with which innovations develop has become prodigious. Now, we not only get immediate data, we also receive insights. Our car's navigation system tells us how to get there but can also advise us to take a different route to save twenty minutes. That's insight. Our phones are intuitive. The speed of change is mind-boggling. Everyone has access to a universe of information.

We are advancing the technology to assemble, aggregate and present all of the information needed about the patient's history at the point of care. The more data that is available, the more we can learn about you—expressly for you. We can mine data as if prospecting for gold.

That is the promise in healthcare and the *Trusted Healers* approach. We can move toward understanding our genetic makeup. We can apply more knowledge to the foods we eat so we perform at our best in every way. We can now keep up with the worldwide information explosion in healthcare and digest and offer usable, reliable information to the *Trusted Healers* at the point of care.

And there is so much more we can learn about ourselves.

An end to the *Age of Healthcare Information* has been reached. Mindful and appreciative of the past, we welcome the birth of a new *Age of Healthcare Intelligence,* one where there is a promise of personalized and precise medicine and care.

This is a really big deal.

The Transcontinental Railroad changed our notions of mobility and exploration. The *Age of Healthcare Intelligence* is changing the capabilities of our *Trusted Healers.* Never has so much been developed, so fast, by so many, that can affect every man, woman and child on earth.

This is the golden spike for healthcare.

$$\rightleftharpoons$$

Trusted Healers offers a view of healthcare from the inside out. We embark upon a journey with a front row seat to societal change, to new principles of cultural leadership and to a new threshold in healthcare.

Societal shift starts with this crucial question: How does a culture change? From sincere, trusted leaders, someone who falls in love with the question.

Leadership is the second major tenet of *Trusted Healers.* On our journey ahead, we will view the approach of leaders who have *aspiration,* who create *inspiration* and who have the *discipline* to run the long race. We will see leadership in action, in diverse cultures. These leaders do not grapple for a handhold. They confront complexity and confusion. They lead, and they return to the citizens with simplicity and clarity.

These leaders make the issues come alive, championing causes that matter, and we will see the power of trust which results from a high level of integrity in thought and action.

The third tenet of *Trusted Healers* comes in the final chapters where powerful societal questions about healthcare are asked. To get to these questions, we will illuminate healthcare past and present. We begin to see clearly the path ahead. It's magnificent.

First and foremost, we must enable access to healthcare. Developed nations with assured access to care get rewarded for that with significantly longer life spans and happier people. By having access, we gain and nurture information, allowing for the management of cost and quality and the creation of actionable patient information. That vital knowledge, innovatively developed with new technologies, provides intelligence, which drives personalized precision medicine, creates better care, a higher quality of life, and illuminates for that society that *everyone matters.*

A child born today in a developed nation (one that has solved access to care) could expect to live to be 110, according to Dr. Mike Roizen.

So, what will happen in the next 110 years? What will a child born today experience?

We have some predictions. We will take you on a tour of the *continuum of care* where the medical system is a tool of the individual; you will have the entire continuum of care under your control and have guidance available at the time of need, all in collaboration with your *Trusted Healer.* You will be empowered rather than subjugated. The rails for this journey of healthcare liberation are already laid. The builders have joined the tracks together with the golden spike.

This is now *our* journey toward a much brighter healthcare future. All aboard. Let's have some fun with this. Let's explore it. Understand it. Not just watch the scenery go by. Be awed by where we have been. Be delighted with where we are going. Get ready for a ride that will change the way you look at your healthcare.

Let's begin our journey.

This book is your ticket.

INTRODUCTION

TRUSTED HEALERS

D r. Paul Grundy often leads with this question when he keynotes major international medical conferences: In every society, who would you say holds a high position of trust?

"It's several people," he begins. "It's family. It's somebody who could give you guidance on what happens to you in your afterlife. It's somebody who you turn to when the chips are down. We all know instinctively that we are going to get sick; we all know we are going to die. We try to deny that, but we know it.

"There arises the power of that person in that position in society, the traditional healers, *Trusted Healers*. In every culture on earth, the healer and the preacher are held in highest esteem," Paul says.

You may not know of Dr. Paul Grundy, the world's most powerful advocate for the *Trusted Healers* and godfather of the *medical home* concept. In 2018, he retired as IBM's global director of healthcare transformation.

Paul set his IBM mantle aside, but his work advocating for global healthcare reform remains robust, as does his legacy.

The global societal sea change quietly happening over the last decade continues to be instigated by Paul. The primary care *medical home* crusade led by Paul and IBM, glimmering subversively for years, has found its time thanks to the continuous devotion and credibility of this fascinating physician and to the believers who listened and affected change.

John F. Kennedy asked individuals to step up; Ronald Reagan admonished communists to join the free world; Winston Churchill vowed never to surrender. We are reminded of these most powerful anthems of change.

"I have a dream . . ."

"Ask not . . ."

"Tear down . . ."

"We shall fight on the beaches . . ."

We invoke two more words to precipitate a healthcare revolution that can transform society:

"Trusted Healers."

Sounding the *Trusted Healers* mantra has been part of Dr. Paul Grundy's crusade to transform healthcare, which has awakened millions of people to the vital importance of having a familiar physician. For more than a decade, I had the honor to work with Paul as he championed the *Trusted Healer*s and the *medical home.* This quirky, genius, fearless, rumpled, visionary doctor served on my elite team for over a decade at IBM. I was so taken with Paul's work and medical care vision that I decided to assist Paul in carrying it forward after we both left the company.

For me, the concept of personal healthcare seemed so simple on its face, but it is so antithetical to how modern medicine has evolved. Paul's inspiration is very much a back-to-basics approach but with a modern-world application.

Paul's aspiration, his vision, calls for every citizen to have a *medical home*, a delivery model that ensures that we receive the necessary care when and where we need it, in a manner we can understand, by a *Trusted Healer* and care team that invests the time in getting to know us, standing by us over the years—physically, virtually, emotionally, and spiritually. We will share much more about the *medical home* in the pages that follow.

Under Paul's vision, your *Trusted Healer* glances at your chart and knows all about you, asks about your family, helps you make good medical decisions, and creates a medical partnership based solely on your needs and how you want to lead your life. The relationship with your healer is intimate. Your healer serves your interests—not those of an insurance company or hospital. Your doctor's success is yours as well. It can be easily proven that better medical decisions result from such a powerful relationship.

Trusted Healers do not offer a single solution or point of view on what to do about our broken US healthcare system. We all know the temper of our times is strident and divisive. We have been pitted against each other and our institutions, and the entire developed world, regardless of payment system, faces real challenges with healthcare. Most nations must brace for the impact of people living longer—they will need more care. Costs continually increase, and the population is growing. Immigration issues challenge healthcare systems around the world as refugees flee by the millions to countries offering a better life, which includes healthcare. Vitriolic debate frequently challenges the "social contract" between government and citizens.

Medicine, especially primary care, is treated as a commodity. Doctors are often reduced to mechanics, meeting a patient-load quota. Insurance companies decide levels of care or, as Patrick J. Kennedy so rightly points out, no care at all. Medical systems are overburdened by these insurance companies and hospital systems driven by profit goals. Burnout among doctors, nurses and care teams continues to be crushing. Healthcare journals report surveys citing that over 80 percent of healthcare organizations are experiencing serious burnout.

In the midst of this, Paul, IBM and scores of conscientious providers around the world strive to re-instill patient trust in medical care. In the world of providing medical care, *everyone matters.* Paul inspires nations toward this philosophy and understands the discipline it takes to effect change over time. Effecting change is both an immediate and long-term goal. One day we will all receive better healthcare because of this brilliant Quaker physician who has made a global impact in improving patient care. His crusade may be peaking at just the right time. And a lot of people around the world are pulling for us.

Trusted Healers will leave you with a new understanding of the pace of change in healthcare, why we behave the way we do, and what we have in common with other cultures. As Patrick Kennedy says, "You will never look at healthcare the same way again."

We are on a positive glide path. There has never been a time with more innovations coming forward in every discipline of medicine. America, like many other nations, stands at the threshold of change in primary care.

Yet, in the US, we are just cracking the door to the crisis in mental health and opioid addiction. We have a completely broken mental health culture and, as a result, a completely broken mental healthcare system. Patrick explains that we are in the biggest single public health crisis of our time. Our cold silence has created a layer of protective ice over America's heart. Just look at us. Discard the blinders. Take a look at the numbing, frigid impact of our cultural code of silence about mental health. It's not apathy. It's cultural. It's taboo. It's tribal.

We in America have become so aloof about this that we evolved our own American code of silence, a *don't ask, don't tell* attitude about anything to do with mental and behavioral health. Addiction and depression, suicide, drug and opioid abuse, alcoholism, dementia, bipolar disorder, the entire spectrum of brain disease is still verboten to discuss among an entire generation—largely my generation, the baby boomers.

We now know that opioid addiction destroys people of all walks of life. Americans commit more suicides than murders. Most of the

2.3 million federal prisoners have some form of behavioral illness.
Urban children struggle—40 percent drop out before high school
graduation. America has over two million gang members.

Patrick's crusade for mental health parity and a solution to
substance abuse and the opioid crisis has a believer in my dear
colleague, Dr. Paul Grundy, who openly discusses his father's mental
health struggles in the following chapters.

While serving in Congress, Patrick helped Paul begin his *medical
home* advocacy. Paul thinks in terms of a completely holistic primary
care *medical home*. He proclaims it from podiums all over the world.
Part of the concept acknowledges that no approach to healthcare
is complete without an open, honest discussion about diseases of
the brain.

⌒

What is the *medical home?*

A *medical home* provides access to your *Trusted Healer* when
you need it, anytime day or night. This new model builds upon and
improves on old-style primary care, which decades ago had been
patient-centered, comprehensive and personal. The refined version
advocated by Paul builds into that model team-based, coordinated
care that is accessible and focuses on quality and safety. All over the
developed world, vast numbers of *Trusted Healers* are once again
finding joy, practicing under the *medical home* model.

Not unlike the difference between a horse-drawn buggy and a
powerful sports car, this approach provides a big departure from the
typical twentieth-century medical office.

When we complete this global transformation, the table will be
set for solving other big issues which today look an unbridgeable
distance away. Evidence is already mounting that the *medical home*
is our path forward.

Early pilot programs demonstrated better patient satisfaction
and significant overall cost savings for practices that adopted the

medical home model of care. These early experiments showed a 36.3 percent drop in hospital days, a 32.2 percent drop in ER use, and a 15.6 percent decrease in total cost.[5]

In 2018, Blue Cross Blue Shield of Michigan designated approximately 4,630 physicians in 1,700 practices across Michigan as patient-centered *medical homes*. An updated, actuarial-certified analysis concluded that over nine years, the Blue Cross PCMH care model has led to $626 million in avoided costs.

"Physician practices that earn Blue Cross Patient-Centered *Medical Home* (PCMH) designation provide team-based care that's centered around each patient's individual needs," says Amy McKenzie, MD, medical director at Blue Cross Blue Shield of Michigan. "So they're coordinating and tracking, keeping a watchful eye on conditions and getting patients the care they need at the right time. This leads to better outcomes, and often prevents the need for high-cost emergency or inpatient care."

For example, in comparing Blue Cross PCMH-designated practices to non-designated practices, data from 2018 show Blue Cross PCMH had a 27 percent lower rate of adult hospital admissions for common conditions that respond to office-based care.

Blue Cross-designated PCMH practices also had a 16 percent lower rate of adult ER visits and a 26 percent lower rate of pediatric ER visits for common chronic and acute conditions, such as asthma.

"The commitment to this program from physician organizations and physician practices has created a sustained, measurable transformation in primary care across the state," says Dr. McKenzie. "There are PCMH-designated physicians now in eighty of eighty-three Michigan counties. If you live in Michigan, you have access to this outstanding model of care.[6]

My colleague and co-author, Bud Ramey, creator with Dr. Peter Anderson of the landmark book *The Familiar Physician*, joins me in sharing the commentary of experts around the world who have learned from Paul.

Bud and I devoted the better part of a year to travel throughout the US and abroad to document Paul's influence across continents. We surrendered to our curiosity, following in Paul's footsteps, interviewing people from his past to discover how Paul ticks. We viewed his life through his colleagues, his friends, and world leaders who embrace his message, among whom he has become a celebrity. What we saw was not only an innovator, but a thought leader who inspires others.

He very likely has traveled more air miles than any physician in history as he returns again and again to monitor progress and serve as an inspiration for his colleagues in dozens of nations. In some ways, that makes this work, *Trusted Healers*, a tribute to him. But that's an upshot of espousing his vision. You need to see the man and hear how he is viewed by colleagues to fully appreciate the embrace of his vision and, by extension, his accomplishments. This model of healthcare works everywhere, and his presence around the world has left lasting impacts.

We hope you will be enlightened by discussions with a cadre of health providers and administrators from around the world. This cross section of leaders whose careers intersected with Paul's produces a fascinating and revealing picture of Paul's unique style and courage. Through their eyes, we tap the pulse of worldwide healthcare. These are trusted voices, people who we look to for guidance through their wisdom, experience, and knowledge and who demonstrably care about their area of expertise. Their agenda is set with pure intent.

Of great personal interest to me, we will also see just how to transform cultures and societies—vital lessons we learned at IBM.

Patrick Kennedy reminds us that "the ultimate *medical home* addresses the social determinants, which everyone in medicine knows, and has always known, are the key factors to medical outcomes."

Jeremy Hunt, MP   Professor James   Dr. Doug Henley   Dr. Michael Barr

                Kingsland OBE

In these pages we will hear from United Kingdom secretary of health and social care, the **Honourable Jeremy Hunt, MP** (now secretary of state), who meets with us in Parliament and credits Paul for helping him change the trajectory of healthcare in Great Britain to begin to regain the magic of the general practitioner, or *GP*. Paul has been instrumental in achieving "that quiet revolution and momentum," Jeremy Hunt notes. Paul praised their *Trusted Healers*, or GPs, for their full attention to mental health and the whole person, the "magic" of the British healthcare system.

Professor James Kingsland OBE, England's BBC radio doctor and one of the most famous physicians in the UK, takes us on an inspiring tour of British universal care.

Dr. Doug Henley, executive vice president and CEO of the American Academy of Family Practice, shares the great pride he takes in his team's work over the last decade. This true statesman, along with *medical home* champion **Dr. Michael Barr**, estimates that over 20,000 practices in America are now organized as recognized, developing *medical homes.*

Dr. Glenn Steele, one of the most powerful healthcare administrators and reformers in America and a worldwide leader in evidence-based medicine, tells us how the quality of medical care is advancing in huge strides and that one day we will pay for better, safer healthcare based on proven value. Dr. Steele fully agrees with Paul's crusade.

Dr. Glenn Steele　　　Dr. Nwando　　　Nick Donofrio　　　Sean Hogan
　　　　　　　　　　　Olayiwola

"Our concept at Geisinger Health System concluded that you could enable caregiving with technology, you could enable caregiving with the best specialty and sub-specialty expertise, but when you have a continuing relationship with someone, ideally, in your community, who knows you not just as a patient but as a human being—that combination is the sweet spot."

Dr. Michael Roizen, chief wellness officer at the Cleveland Clinic, perhaps the most successful medical writer of all time, and co-creator of the *Dr. Oz Show*, shares powerful evidence for greater longevity and better health being within our reach, as well as a warning. He fears the consequences if Paul's momentum in this transformation fails.

"We won't tolerate rationing by financial means for very long. I worry about social disruption if what Paul Grundy wants to happen does not happen."

Dr. Nwando Olayiwola, chief clinical transformation officer for RubiconMD, champions high-quality, equitable healthcare for everyone. Her words will challenge what you think of America's care for the disadvantaged.

Nick Donofrio, retired IBM executive vice president of innovation and technology, and General Manager of Healthcare **Sean Hogan** discuss the evolution of IBM's bold campaign to transform medicine around the globe. Nick and Sean speak of being "at the center of gravity for changing the world" from a healthcare perspective, and how Paul inspired this transformation.

Dr. Helene Gayle   Tex Harris   Kanav Hasija

We meet with **Dr. Helene Gayle**, who earlier in her career joined Paul to help **Nelson Mandela** with the HIV/AIDS pandemic in Southern Africa. A young Dr. Paul Grundy teamed up with legendary American State Department hero **Tex Harris**, figuring out exactly how the HIV/AIDS pandemic would soon spread in Southern Africa. Nelson Mandela called Paul a "Rolihlahla," a Xhosa name that means "pulling the branch of a tree," but colloquially it means "troublemaker, a good troublemaker." (This is actually Mandela's middle name as well.)

We learn from Paul of new breakthrough technologic innovations by **Kanav Hasija and Innovaccer, Inc.** that are bringing the full-scale power of advanced information technology to our *Trusted Healers.* For the first time, the blind spots will be removed. Caregivers will have all the information they need to fully understand their patients, bringing complete medical experiences, social care actions, and mental health and social determinants directly to the *Trusted Healers'* electronic health record (EHR).

Dr. Ted Epperly, past board chair and president of the American Academy of Family Physicians, and author of *Fractured: America's Broken Health Care System and What We Must Do to Heal It,* warns that the arrival of social unrest has already happened in America.

Unrest changes societies when harnessed by great leaders. Dr. Epperly reminds us that Martin Luther King, Jr., once said that of all the forms of inequality, injustice in healthcare is the most shocking and inhumane.

As a student of leadership and part of perhaps the most revered leadership team in corporate America (IBM), working with Executive Vice President Nick Donofrio, I understand that leadership lives in the people we influence. We all have a story; we all gain understanding of our purpose in life because of what has happened to us and the way others influence us. Paul has certainly influenced me.

His easygoing warmth awakens in people the desire to instigate change, to make something better. Paul's message resonates with thousands of physicians and leaders who have turned it into policy and process. As Paul champions the *medical home* concept, he advocates for every primary care doctor to have a team so that *Trusted Healers* may focus just on "solving difficult diagnostic dilemmas and developing patient relationships."

The power of this simple idea now plays out in many nations, most notably Denmark. Not only is it recognized for the best primary care system on earth, the Danes love it!

They spend significantly less on healthcare than we do, and because their citizens have 24/7 access to care, they have been able to eliminate expensive, duplicated, and inappropriate medical care. Even though they offer a *Trusted Healer* to every citizen, their costs dropped dramatically. Clinical quality improved so much that healthcare leaders from over sixty nations have sent delegations to Denmark to study just how they did it.

Enough time has passed now that we can confidently conclude that building up primary care, making affordable access to care 24/7, and having a personal *Trusted Healer* initiates much better, less expensive healthcare.

Because of his leadership and guidance, Denmark named Paul one of the twelve original ambassadors for Healthcare DENMARK, a gateway for international stakeholders to experience the Danish healthcare system and its innovative healthcare solutions. Princess Mary, Crown Princess of Denmark, anointed him as such.

Paul's accolades are certainly earned. By interviewing the leaders he has influenced, we reveal how he accomplished so much in just over a decade in this crusade. We also present how cultures respond to change in the twenty-first century, how all change is local, and how leadership like Paul's make change possible.

As you'll see, Paul's journey as both a healer and a champion of healers began as a little boy deep in the primitive heart of Sierra Leone as the son of Quaker missionaries. There he learned about different cultures, about deeply held tribal beliefs, and how *everyone matters*.

"The root of that belief system," Paul recalls, really goes back to my growing up in Africa. It goes back to the power of the traditional healer. In my young mind, I didn't see much of anything that they really offered scientifically, yet they were incredibly powerful and incredibly trusted. It comes from seeing people throw chicken bones against a mud hut."

Paul's comment about chicken bones describes a practice that is very much like reading tea leaves in other cultures. Healers carry a small leather "marble bag" filled with dried chicken bones. When they rattle the bones like dice and throw the bones on the dusty ground, they interpret the scatter pattern.

"I think that answer is built into the brain," Paul says. "I think that we have evolved as social animals. We all need people in our lives that we can turn to, we can trust, kind of when the chips are down. That's the premise that I have in the back of my mind. In building a healthcare delivery system based on that human need, I began to realize, why wouldn't we build it there? Build it around a *Trusted Healer*. Why would we build this anywhere else?"

If after reading this book you change the way you think about your healthcare, then we have succeeded in our aspiration for *Trusted Healers*. It is a book about hope, which lives within the ongoing heartbeat of healthcare around the world.

PART ONE

A TRUSTED HEALER

CHAPTER ONE

PRAYING MANTIS

Traditional African religions embrace natural phenomena. The wind can speak to you. A waxing and waning moon has meaning, as does rain and drought and the rhythmic pattern of agriculture.

The traditional healers deep in the African bush called Paul "the boy who could hear the message of the praying mantis."

Perhaps they were whisperers.

The praying mantis is believed by African Bushmen to be the oldest symbol of God—the manifestation of God come to Earth, the voice of the infinite in the small, a divine messenger. At age six, Paul became known among the witch doctors (traditional healers) as a powerful messenger of the spirits. He grew up with his parents, missionaries from Quakertown, Connecticut, deep in the African bush in Sierra Leone.

His father, Reverend Elwin Grundy, was deeply influenced by his work in 1944 with the Billy Graham Crusade and by his connections with Paul's uncle, Henry Cadbury. Cadbury accepted the Nobel Peace Prize in 1947 on behalf of the Religious Society of Friends, and would become Paul's role model.

Paul's father became a faith healer there. They lived among the tribal natives, stared down devil dancers and warlocks, and preached the Gospel. Paul awakened to the role of the healer. He saw the power of the spirit world and how his friends and neighbors relied in times of need on those who had the power of healing.

"Probably a healer from his youngest days," says Anne Altman, the IBM top executive who worked closely with Paul and I. "Paul has the personality of a healer. He's so generous with his time and talent. He fundamentally believes we all are on earth to make a difference. Paul was born that way. He's a gift to society."

Ralph Crandall, PhD

Paul's best friend since childhood, his first cousin Ralph Crandall, PhD, now retired, served as the executive director emeritus of the New England Historic Genealogical Society. They grew up together. Ralph, six years Paul's elder, watched his young friend come and go from Africa missions twice. The Grundys and the Crandalls embraced the faith of the Rogerine Quakers, a group of pacifists since the 1670s. Quakers played a major role in the abolition movement against slavery in both the United Kingdom and the US. They were among the first whites to denounce slavery in the American colonies and Europe, and the Society of Friends was the first organization to take a collective stand against both slavery and the slave trade, later spearheading the international and ecumenical campaigns against slavery.

Paul and his best pal Ralph

"They moved there, and Paul had some of his formative experiences in Africa. I can remember, even now, his fearlessness. He wasn't aggressively bold, but inquisitive, not afraid of anyone. Being much more reserved than Paul, I could not help but notice that he was a leader, even then," Ralph recalls.

"If he found someone that interested him, he went right up, whether the person was five years old or eighty, and started talking.

He has a natural curiosity and fearlessness and it makes him unique as a person."

In Africa for two missionary tours, the Grundy family lived a spartan life in a house in a village at the mission station. But even when Stateside, Paul and his family were impoverished in his younger years, at least by Western measures. His father could work well with his hands, did a lot of trades for essentials, and had lots of ambitious plans for their life in America. But partly because of a lack of formal education, he never really followed through.

The Grundys' first three-year Africa mission occurred in the winter of Paul's fourth year. As a Rogerine Quaker, Paul's father felt called to independent faith missionary work. The family traveled from their home in Connecticut aboard a slow ocean cargo ship, stopping frequently, including several weeks in England, which they spent with relatives.

The Grundys arrived to a dilapidated, abandoned mission station in the Port Loko district. His father recorded the arrival in his memoir:

> People were coming from the houses and towns or villages very close to us, or even as far as thirty-five to forty miles away, and they came bringing chickens, ducks, sheep, and goats, whole stalks of bananas, or maybe a fifty-pound bag of peanuts or rice. Talk about a grateful and caring people, these Timne [sic] people were it.

Settling into the African culture was seamless for Paul. At such a young age he had very few preconceived notions.

"I guess knowing the local people, growing up speaking their language, playing with their kids, grounded me socially," Paul remembers. "Where I grew up, many worshiped the supreme God through consultation or communion with lesser deities and ancestral spirits. The deities and spirits were honored and kept supportive by sacrificing animals and offerings."

In Sierra Leone, the African religions believed in a cyclical nature of reality. The living stood between their ancestors and the unborn.

Homeschooling for the boys began to look quite promising, but Paul's brother Wayne, two years his senior, was sent to a missionary boarding school in Kabala, which was far from home. Paul would attend that school later. Until that point, the brothers had been inseparable, living amid a humble but fascinating culture.

Rev. Grundy described their life in the bush.

> Did you know that a big part of being a missionary family is just living an ordinary life and doing the ordinary things that ordinary families do? Our lighting system was candles and kerosene lamps; our running water consisted of paying the school children three pennies per bucket for running to the river to get it.

After Paul finished the first grade, the mission furloughed the Grundys, sending them back to America. Paul celebrated his seventh birthday aboard an English merchant marine ship. Arriving at the port in New Jersey, looking down from the ship, Paul started crying. His parents asked him why.

"Because everybody's white," Paul lamented. "To me, adults are white, and my friends are mostly people of color. I'm not going to have any friends here!"

Rev. Grundy bought a car and in 1958 drove the family to California on Route 66 to the Quaker community in Santa Ana. There, they reunited with relatives, the Crandalls, and other families in the historic Quakertown Church congregation there. The Crandalls had lived near the Grundys and also attended the Quakertown Church in Connecticut. Their moving to Santa Ana influenced Rev. Grundy's decision to resettle there. Paul started the second grade in Santa Ana and started to hang out more with Ralph Crandall, his lifelong best friend. Paul was bigger, stronger, wiser, and better equipped to hang around with his older best friend.

The Quaker experience, the world travel, and his inquisitive nature began to shape this young boy. He had already developed values that would guide his life. One sentiment that resonated within Paul, part of his DNA, has been the credo that *everyone matters*. His experiences in Africa and immersion in the Quaker faith instilled within him the Eight Laws of Social Change:

- Individuals and groups must share a common purpose or intent—consensus.
- Individuals and groups may have goals but must not be attached to *cherished* outcomes.
- The goal may not be reached in the lifetime of the participants.
- Accept and be OK with the idea that you might not get credit for the success of a goal.
- Each person in the group must have equal status in spite of any hierarchies.
- Members must forswear violence by word, thought and act.
- Private selves must be consistent with public postures.
- People are not exploitable resources. People are what make change happen and the most important element.

Other Practices
- Do not seek to defeat and humiliate opponents. Instead, seek to make friends and awaken a sense of shame over injustice.
- Do not go after individuals but rather the evil systems that victimize both the oppressed and the oppressor.

- Avoid internal violence of spirit. Refuse to hate your opponent. An "eye for an eye" leaves everyone blind.
- Love offers creative understanding and seeks nothing in return.
- Love your enemies—this transforms the soul of your opponent.
- Have faith in the future, believing the universe is on the side of justice.
- No lie can live forever.

Ralph Crandall's mom tutored Paul after school, laying much of his moral foundation and education. She had been a teacher in a one-room schoolhouse until she married.

Paul was a bright boy but struggled with reading, so much so that he failed second grade, twice. He would later be diagnosed with dyslexia. Mrs. Crandall helped Paul overcome that weakness. She was patient and persistent. For over a year, they practiced reading aloud. After his tutoring sessions, Paul was free to go outside and explore with his best buddy, Ralph.

"We went through the neighborhood and collected cans and soda bottles. I think I used the money I made to buy ice cream cones, or whatever young boys do with their money. Paul saved his money and took it home to his mom," Ralph recalls.

"I really relate to David and Goliath, the whole story of how leaders come out of adversity. Severely dyslexic, my brain seems framed in different ways. I knew I would be figuring ways around it, getting past those hurdles," Paul recalls. Paul never viewed himself as an underdog, and by third grade he knew that he related to the world differently because of his reading struggles. He called himself a misfit.

"I had to find a way to use my brain to figure a way around the misfit part. In the third grade, they would haul you up into a reading circle and make you read *Dick and Jane*. I couldn't read out loud.

I had difficulty with that."

Paul must have frustrated his teachers because he tested off the scale for intelligence. He was pegged as an underachiever, lazy and unmotivated.

Rev. Grundy liked California but wanted to return to missionary work in Africa. The call finally came, but he delayed the return because his wife was pregnant.

After David Grundy's birth in the late summer of 1959, they set off again on a slow English merchant marine boat, stopping in every port up the coast of Canada and all along the coast of Africa. Paul enjoyed the journey and felt more comfortable and accustomed to the way of life on the second mission trip. Encounters with the traditional healers would take on a different energy and importance. He looked forward to living among the Temne because he loved them and understood their customs.

Upon their arrival, Paul enrolled in the missionary kids' boarding school, Kabala Rupp Memorial School. One former student recalls this school on *Facebook*:

> The school was way in the bush. I mean really, really in the bush. There was a huge rock we had to climb up and a bridge that consisted of two wooden planks. It sounds like a movie but it was real . . . at night the drums would start and my roommate told me all kinds of stories about devils and human sacrifice; those drums made me tremble.

Paul's dyslexia became even more pronounced at Kabala Rupp.

"Sitting in the back of the class, with the *C* section of the Encyclopedia Britannica open on my desk, my teacher came back and whapped me," he remembers.

"Stop looking at pictures," she protested. When she looked down and saw no pictures on the pages she asked, "What are you doing?"

"Reading," young Paul replied.

So she skeptically thumbed back two or three pages, asking Paul, "What was the tomato production in 1955 in California?"

Paul gave the correct answer, in detail. He could read and recall, but not read aloud.

"I don't have a photographic mind, that's for sure," Paul says. "But I read and see things very differently than most people. I have a really hard time seeing single words out of context. I would read concepts, not single words, and I would see it that way."

Paul remembers that he scored in the ninety-ninth percentile on math and sciences, but only in the seventeenth percentile for verbal skills. The language tests would have one word to match another word, which played directly to Paul's weakness. Paul played to his strength, instead, delving into the sciences and deciding to become a doctor.

"At the start of the rainy season in 1961 in Sierra Leone, we enjoyed a visit from two missionary doctors, and I got to help them when they did surgery," Paul recalls.

The missionary doctors taught Paul to assist with handing them the surgical instruments during operations. Paul, at age ten, scrubbed up, donned gloves and a mask, and fell in love with medicine.

"International medicine, actually, which led me later to Johns Hopkins, Division of International Health," Paul says.

⌐⫘

The family had frequent encounters with the mystical natives. Paul's dad describes one such encounter.

Coming down the trail from Bir de Bana was the strangest looking procession of devil dancers. In the lead was a man with a sharp machete in one hand and a rope in the other, leading the most hideous looking creature I had ever seen.

That creature, he says, was the porra devil, possibly the most feared thing in the country at that time.

His body was draped with what looked like several kinds of animal skins, and on his head was a huge mask that must have weighed at least fifty pounds. Around the outer rim were at least six to eight human skulls; while up and over the top there were all kinds of other hideous things topped off with a long, pointed horn.

Rev. Grundy suddenly found himself alone on the trail, because "the two men that were with me had skedaddled, disappearing into the dense bush." It was custom for the person of lesser status to step off of the path and let the one of greater status pass.

He stood his ground.

There were so many lessons for Paul and his family about differences in culture and perspective from white America and Europe. These Africans had a different way of seeing the world, opening young Paul's mind to seeing the world more broadly and, perhaps, more organically.

The Grundys' second stint in Africa ended abruptly. Paul's brother Wayne contracted rheumatic fever. Doctors urged the family to get back to the States for his care, cutting the mission trip short.

Returning from Africa to California, the Grundy family struggled. Rev. Grundy tried various construction and development projects, trying to use his design skills, but all failed. Ralph Crandall notes that at this time Paul seemed unfocused and sort of lost. He got in trouble at the junior high school, from a prank gone wrong. Paul was very interested in chemistry and made some things that went boom at his home. After law enforcement finished with him, his school principal took him under his wing, realizing that Paul was a bright, exploring spirit.

"I guess the misfit in him took over for a while. Something innocent, but nonetheless, he got in trouble," Ralph says.

In the eighth grade, tragedy struck.

Older brother Wayne and his best friend, Mark, went to explore the Grand Canyon. On the way to their destination, there was a terrible car crash. Mark was badly hurt, and Wayne was killed.

Wayne's death devastated Paul. This tragedy was one of those watershed moments in Paul's life, dividing everything into a *before* and an *after*.

"We all noticed it at the time. Paul changed literally overnight," Ralph says.

Paul became a different person, very focused and much more daring. At fourteen, he started taking skydiving lessons. At the same time, he became much more responsible to his family, while watching his father continue to struggle professionally.

"We feared that maybe Paul would be having a mental breakdown. I remember being concerned. Very concerned," Ralph recalls. "When I say life changing . . . as starkly changing as you can imagine—night and day. He goes from being a lost soul to being extremely focused. He went from getting Ds and Fs to straight As. I don't think he ever got a B after Wayne's passing. He could have chosen to be angry, become inward, behave very differently, or perhaps behave more like his father, but he didn't do that. He went out and met the world. He decided to make a difference."

His father, crushed by Wayne's death, decided that it was God's punishment because he had left the ministry. He became more estranged from his family and even mentally unstable. Paul stepped in to fill the void, and, Ralph says, "started living by faith."

In his memoir, Paul's dad recalls the moment he told Paul to take over responsibility for the family's future.

Starting today, a lot of the decisions that Mom and I may have had to make for you, you are going to have to start making for yourself, but remember this. They better be good decisions.

According to Ralph, Paul eventually realized that while he had his father's wonderful outgoing personality, without structure or formal education he might suffer the same fate and not accomplish anything significant.

After middle school, Paul attended high school in Hemet, California. He got an after-school job at a restaurant and other jobs as well, Ralph says. Despite the hardship, Paul never abandoned his family, faith, or goal of becoming a doctor.

"He never wavered from that," Ralph says. "He willed his way to becoming a doctor. Absolutely set on becoming a doctor."

Paul became a person who had a global vision, Ralph says. He could see the context of whatever situation he encountered. More intuitive, he learned to read it much better than others.

"Different, fearless, loyal, with capacities that the rest of us didn't have—we all saw these qualities in his early youth," Ralph says.

High school years were challenging. His family moved around. He attended six different high schools. His father's mental health impacted everything in the family.

Paul attended Southern California College, a small Christian Assemblies of God school, now Vanguard University. Learning to cope with his dyslexia, he became class valedictorian with a dual major in chemistry and biology.

"I have often wondered how he accomplished getting into medical school," Ralph says. "At the time, I was finishing up graduate school. I helped him with his [medical school] resumes because he couldn't spell. He must have had a very persuasive interview. Paul can be very persuasive."

Paul explains how he got in:

After his second year of undergraduate work, he accepted a Joint Center of Graduate Studies summer internship with the Atomic Energy Commission in Washington State at the Hanford site (a former Manhattan Project reactor) on the Columbia River. This worked well since his family had relocated to Washington by then.

"I seized the opportunity to do research in the department that used the electron microscope," Paul says.

Scientists used the electron microscope to work on the recently-brought-to-earth Apollo moon rocks.

"I worked on a process of getting those rocks really thin so we could look at the crystalline pattern through the instrument," Paul recalls.

Paul's work earned him the *EXa Luna Scientist Medal* from the international association studying the moon rocks. That accolade piqued the interest of the interviewers at University of California Medical School in San Francisco, where Paul had applied. The admissions team was intrigued by Paul's "high score" on mathematical and scientific reasoning IQ exams and the admission exams, while acknowledging his dismally low verbal scores. His dyslexia was viewed as a disability.

One of the faculty interviewers had served in the Peace Corps in Sierra Leone, three miles from Paul's house there, which led to a lively interview. Only nine out-of-state students were accepted out of thousands of applications at UCSF that year. Paul was one of the nine.

"That year, UCSF assembled the most diverse class in history—50 percent women, 50 percent men, with open welcoming of disabled candidates. I had dyslexia, and one of my classmates was blind," Paul says.

The personal relationships he established with his Vanguard professors as a young, curious, ambitious chemistry and biology major helped Paul hit the ground running in medical school. UCSF gave the disabled students all the accommodations to succeed. The dean gave Paul permission to use the hospital's physician dictating system to do his reports orally. His professors helped him spell. And the neurological professors asked Paul to allow them to study the anatomy of his brain using an MRI. They found profound differences, similar to those noted in Einstein's brain.

"Paul did very well in medical school," recalls Ralph, who remembers visiting Paul there, noting that reading and testing was still very hard for Paul. He would go vomit before the exams, so keyed up about the challenge.

Paul earned his degree, and then went on to earn a second degree from UC Berkeley in public health and a post-doctoral fellowship in international health at Johns Hopkins.

"All desire and belief in himself," Ralph says of Paul. "Look where he began. He's unique, at once brilliant, bold almost to the point of daring, but innocently so. Not aggressively daring, but he has a great capacity for reading situations, for reading people, understanding what is needed in particular situations.

"Most of us have one or two gifts and things that we can do, and we try to ride those to whatever career we have and how we interact with people. But Paul has so many gifts in so many different directions. With most folks, it's all about ego, accomplishment. But with Paul, it's about the project or the idea, or the person. It's about what he wants to do for the world. He doesn't care about himself. In some ways, he's still innocent. He's fearless," Ralph adds.

The boy who could hear the message of the praying mantis had grown into a troublemaker—a good troublemaker.

CHAPTER TWO

TROUBLEMAKER

As Paul finished his medical education, one of his teachers, Dr. Peter Budetti, was quietly planning a White House-sponsored, clandestine medical student exchange trip to Cuba. First Lady Rosalynn Carter wanted to use medical diplomacy to nudge open the door with Cuba. Paul volunteered to join the effort, which led to an ongoing student exchange and a continuous dialogue that advanced relations between Cuba and the US.

"I call it the Cuba Caper because of the need to stay off the radar with these trips," Paul recalls.

At the time, Paul was still in school, a recipient of a US Air Force Healthcare Professions Scholarship. Even though he understood the importance of the chain of command, he never went through official military channels, and instead worked with the Carter White House independently.

When in Cuba, police rounded him up for questioning on more than one occasion, yet he always talked his way out of such difficulty, showing his medical credentials and just being himself.

From 1974 to 1985, Paul served as a medical officer in the US Air Force. His career involved teaching and attaining advanced degrees, with assignments abroad in Korea and Saudi Arabia, followed by a State Department career that began in Yemen.

Captain Paul Grundy's first duty station abroad was Korea from 1979 to '81, where he served as a flight surgeon and chief of hospital services. Paul became a progressive force in global public health, publishing highly acclaimed articles for international medical journals.

During Paul's Air Force assignment in Korea, parking spaces at the base were limited. Paul had no place to park his car and could not find a sympathetic ear. In the middle of the night, dressed in black, tiptoeing in the dark like Inspector Clouseau, Paul visited the parking lot for the generals and top officers. He painted one extra set of lines right next to the first parking space, labeled for the commanding general, and there he parked his car for his entire assignment.

While in Korea, Paul found the love of his life, Hyewon. They got married and moved back to the States together. He continued his advanced medical education at Johns Hopkins School of Public Health in Maryland for a year, shaping himself as a top authority on international public health. While a physician in residence there, his first son, Eugene, was born. Paul then taught at the Center for Epidemiology at Brooks Air Force Base in Texas from 1982 to '83.

This experience prepared him for stepping directly into the most dangerous hotspots and pandemics in the world. One of those hotspots emerged while he was assigned to Saudi Arabia.

Paul was assigned by the Air Force to help with the medical preparations for one of the most dramatic humanitarian efforts made by America in decades. Called *Operation Moses,* the November 1984 covert operation rescued thousands of people of color, Ethiopian Jews ("Beta Israel" community or "Falashas"), from starvation and flew them to Israel. They were being persecuted mercilessly in the refugee camps.

The US gathered an alliance—the Israel Defense Forces, the Central Intelligence Agency, the United States embassy in Khartoum, mercenaries, and Sudanese state security forces. The alliance agreed to a covert airlift and met with Mossad and Sudanese representatives to facilitate the operation. The Israeli base for the operation was cleverly disguised as a holiday resort on the Red Sea, where Paul set up medical facilities for the refugees.

The operation rescued 18,000 Jews. The dramatic secret escape caused an outrage in the Arab world[7] but was applauded at home. CIA director George H. W. Bush sent a personal letter of thanks to Paul for his work on the mission.

Paul used his diplomatic and medical skills to work closely with the Saudis to eventually enable complete access by all personnel to every Ministry of Defense hospital and dental facility in the entire Saudi kingdom. That ended the need to airlift very sick Americans from Saudi Arabia.

⁓

Following his USAF service, Paul joined the Department of State and took on another tough assignment—medical attaché to the US embassy in Yemen, Sudan, and Djibouti. It was July 1985, the year that Paul's son Joe was born.

Top Yemini officials relied on Paul for medical evaluation and treatment. Ambassador William Rugh, in a key evaluation of Paul, noted that Paul performed as "a superlative medical practitioner with a warm, reassuring bedside manner that the fictional Dr. Marcus Welby would envy. If I were in the US, Paul's blend of skills and sensitivity would be exactly what I would want in my family doctor."

From Yemen, Paul wrote a letter to his colleague serving as medical director for the Department of State in Washington. Here we find how Paul's fine-tuned sense of humor colored his professional life:

> One arrives at the main entrance to the hospital on a wide dirt road cobbled with discarded plastic water bottles and cans. Patients besiege the main gate, some

coming from distances of two or three days by every means of transportation.

Every male over the age of about twelve has an eight-inch curved knife (jambia) tucked under his belt, carrying an AK-47 or similar automatic weapon.

It should be pointed out that the guards at the gates also carry AK-47s and the fun begins when the patients have to be disarmed before going in.

Diplomat Tex Harris had become the State Department's toughest negotiator. Tex and Paul would link up in Africa, but first, Tex would face down a genocide.

Before their career paths merged in South Africa, Tex was given a special assignment to go to the US embassy in Argentina to investigate vague rumors of genocide in that nation. Tex worked for the Carter administration under legendary assistant secretary of state for human rights Patricia "Patt" Derian.

In 1984, Bill Moyers aired a television documentary report on Tex Harris on CBS's *Crossroads Argentina*.[8] Here is how Moyers introduced Tex:

> His job was to tell the truth to Washington about what was going on. And that got him in trouble. Trouble with the military junta. At least twice, armed men threatened him and his family.
>
> And it got him in trouble with his superiors at the American embassy.
>
> Democracy finally returned last year to Argentina. After eight years of military rule the people threw out the junta and elected a civilian president.
>
> Some of them also talk about erecting a statue to the tall Texan from Dallas.

His name is F. Allen Harris, but he's simply called
Tex. Tex Harris.

Not many Americans know he is a hero. But back
in Argentina, they know.

Tex spoke about how people were tortured routinely and killed.
Thousands had disappeared, Tex said, mostly from Plaza de Mayo in
the city. Tex took to the streets and interviewed mothers searching
for children who had been detained by the military regime. He
handed out cards, asking the mothers to come into the US embassy
and explain what happened to their family members. It began slowly
and then became a torrent.

The US government leadership at the embassy tried to muzzle
Tex, not wanting to impair diplomatic relations between Argentina
and the US. Tex had documented 10,000 disappearances through
meticulous record keeping. Embassy colleagues called him crazy.

Tex's efforts went largely unrewarded and unacknowledged as he
was reassigned to various low-profile posts in the State Department.

"I was penalized for not being a team player. For seven years, my
career was paralyzed," Tex says.

Like Paul Grundy had in Saudi Arabia, Tex Harris cut his teeth
on some of the most dangerous State Department assignments on
the planet. The wall between white and people of color in South
Africa awaited both men.

⁓

Tex got his orders to go to South Africa just as Dr. Paul Grundy
received orders to report there as first secretary of US embassy for
medical affairs, Pretoria, South Africa.

Before Paul and Tex arrived, events set the stage for major change
in South Africa. Violence was widespread as apartheid was challenged
by the world. Anti-apartheid revolutionary Nelson Mandela was about
to be released from prison.

Paul quickly noticed the caste system in South Africa upon his arrival.

"I remember moving in to our house," Paul says. "People of color were domestic help and actually needed a pass to get into the neighborhood. The neighbors saw us and came over with a huge bowl of spaghetti, knocking on the door. When they saw my Korean wife and mixed-race kids, their eyes bugged out of their heads. But when I showed them Hyewon's ID [South Africa identified Koreans as white], suddenly everything settled down, and the neighbors relaxed about the racial invasion."

The family also encountered personal tragedy. Paul's son Eugene lost his closest friend to violence.

Later, as an adult, Eugene wrote a powerful letter to his deceased friend, Ronald, which describes the violent nature of the conflict the family lived with in South Africa:

When my father sat me down and told me you had died, I could not believe it. My mind refused to register the possibility that you were actually gone. The notion of the finality that death imparted was incomprehensible to my young mind. Yet when I went to school a couple days later and saw that your chair was empty, I knew that I would never see you again. Suddenly the faces of my peers became clear to me and the sadness that everyone felt began suffocating me. I couldn't take it.

I remember, my friend, getting up from my chair and leaving the class without a word. The teacher knew how close you and I were, Ronald, and as I walked out, she didn't say anything either. I went to the office, called my father, and asked him to pick me up. When in the car I demanded to know by what accident you had died. My father thought for a few minutes, looked out the car windshield, and then told me you did not die of an accident, that you were killed. He said that you and your whole family was murdered because your father was a member of the ANC, and when he saw that I didn't understand, he told me that you died because of the color of your skin.

Paul served as the regional medical officer, based at the embassy in Pretoria, responsible for insuring quality care for American personnel and evaluating all the medical services in the southern part of Africa.

He evaluated the doctors and hospitals and authorized them to Medevac people to Germany if needed. He also noticed something alarming.

Paul heard stories about antenatal clinics with enormous incidence of HIV viruses in pregnant women. The husbands of these expectant mothers were away working in the mines. Prostitutes seized upon the lonely, love-starved men, setting up camp nearby. Doctors were seeing a 60 percent infection rate among young, pregnant women in those areas. The pattern was alarming.

As Paul prepared to probe further, a tall Texan limped into Paul's office offering a huge smile and a heavy handshake. He had a ruptured tendon.

"Hi. I'm Tex Harris."

Tex stepped in as counsel general in Durban, South Africa. A bond instantly formed between a man who risked his neck to stop genocide and the person who, as a boy, could hear the message of the praying mantis.

People working closely with Paul noticed that he often had a sixth sense. He could visualize scenarios and puzzle together seeming disparate events. The first vision Paul had on his assignment in Africa would have worldwide consequences. It was, as he described, "more as a feeling at first—a visual came to me of trucks, of a highway. Of flowing commerce."

Paul recalls the moment.

"Interestingly, I just kind of saw streams of this epidemic flowing, visualizing. I see it. I guess the way my cortex operates. Sometimes, I have a clear picture in my mind of what's coming. I am really lucky in that regard." The neuroscientists at medical school studying Paul's brain when he was a student noted that Paul has "a billion-dollar mind, the kind of thinker that comes along once in a century."

Einstein himself often claimed that he would think visually rather than verbally. Rare parietal lobe patterns, observed in Einstein's brain (now in 240 different slices mounted on slides), were visible on Paul's MRI examinations by medical school faculty.

Whatever Paul's gift entails, it was in high gear as he puzzled together a frightening pattern of disease spreading in Africa. Tex became Paul's wartime consigliere (Tex would use the term "disciple") and joined Paul in a campaign that had a nasty parallel with Argentina's genocide. The people most in need of listening were not listening. And people were dying because of that. Embassy staff did not believe the scope of the epidemic or the direness of the threat.

But Tex believed it.

"I saw by the look in his eye that this discussion made a huge impact on him. He wanted to do something about it," Paul recalls.

Tex took immediate action. Coming from a similar religious upbringing as Paul, Tex possesses that same instinct to buck conventional thinking and rescue the afflicted.

"When you see something wrong, something in your heart, you are controlled internally by that inner voice, repeating 'You need to do something, you need to do something,'" Paul explains.

They would have powerful experiences here, slamming head-on into the discovery of the dark truth of how one of the deadliest pandemics of the century spread.

CHAPTER THREE

PANDEMIC

A t Paul's urging, Dr. Helene Gayle, who was leading the Centers for Disease Control work on international AIDS efforts, came to South Africa to see what the US government could learn about how the AIDS epidemic was evolving there. She arrived in 1988 and joined with Paul and Tex to form the earliest US-led campaign to halt the HIV/AIDS pandemic in Africa. For decades since, she has battled this plague in an array of high-profile leadership roles.

Her resume is expansive and includes serving as president and CEO of CARE, a leading international humanitarian organization; twenty years with the Centers for Disease Control, working primarily on HIV/AIDS; directing HIV/AIDS and global health programs for the Bill and Melinda Gates Foundation. Just prior to taking the helm of the Chicago Trust, Dr. Gayle led the McKinsey Social Initiative (now McKinsey.org), a nonprofit that leverages relationships across the public and private sectors to create, test, and scale new ways to address the world's most pressing issues.

Born in Buffalo, NY, she earned a BA in psychology at Barnard College, an MD at the University of Pennsylvania and a master's in public health at Johns Hopkins University. She holds fifteen honorary degrees and faculty appointments at the University of Washington and Emory University.

We interview Dr. Gayle in Chicago where she serves as president of the Chicago Community Trust. She has a lot to say about the resistance and denial she faced in South Africa.

In her office overlooking the Chicago skyline, pictures of her with Nelson Mandela stand behind her desk.

"When you think about traditional societies and what perpetuated the human species, in particularly the agrarian societies, men having more than one woman and many children may have served a purpose," Dr. Gayle says. In Africa, having multiple partners—something that may not be suited for today's society—helped perpetuate the spread of the HIV virus to pandemic levels.

"Behavior change always follows behind societal change," Dr. Gayle says. "Today, having multiple partners carries major risks. Women's lack of control over sexual interactions puts women at particular high risk of HIV or other sexually transmitted diseases."

Paul and Tex discovered that for themselves and sounded the early alarm about the spread of HIV/AIDS. They recognized that in South Africa, the ruling whites did not want to take seriously the threat of a pandemic because it did not impact heterosexual whites. The people of color did not want to hear that their sexual customs were the problem, and they distrusted everyone, calling the spread of HIV/AIDS a CIA plot. Paul's instincts told him how serious the threat could be.

Paul "saw" the streams of this epidemic, and he brought Tex Harris to a house of prostitutes in the port of Durban to show him how one of the most dreaded pandemics on the planet spread unchecked. Many of the men were commercial truck drivers, moving from the port town bordellos inland to other communities where they spread the virus.

"Like Dante's Inferno," Tex hisses as he describes the scene.

Tex recalls that these ladies appeared as the unhealthiest, most emaciated, HIV/AIDS prostitutes you could imagine. "Sad. We went there and talked with these women."

The streams of this epidemic in Paul's vision became clearer.

Prostitutes as young as fourteen lined many of the towns' main streets, including Lyantonde and Livingstone and ports like Durban. Some would rendezvous with truckers passing through or parked on the outskirts of these towns. At the ports, truckers usually waited days for their cargo to be unloaded and the customs papers signed, passing the time by visiting prostitutes. The prostitutes would be paid as much as six times more if they did not use condoms. Some would see twenty or more men a night.

There are forty-three transport corridors and nineteen ports on the continent of Africa.

South Africa's first reported death from AIDS occurred in 1983. Three white males developed AIDS that year. By the time Paul and Tex arrived in 1987, the disease was exploding beyond Central Africa where 20 percent of the adult population was infected. Over five million people carried the virus.

Paul and Tex met with an array of traditional government leaders, mining companies, trucking companies, big businesses, clergy, doctors, health officials, traditional healers, and educators. Slowly, they built a coalition of believers in the true extent of the crisis.

There was an answer to the horror, Paul and Tex preached. It was safe sex and abandoning centuries of tribal customs of multiple partners and nonmedical cures rooted in cultural beliefs.

Paul visited the capital city of Lasaka, in Zambia. One of Tex's best friends served as the ambassador in Zambia, and he organized a meeting with the African National Congress (ANC) leadership. The ANC was founded in 1912; its primary mission was to give voting rights to people of color and mixed-race Africans and, from the 1940s, to end apartheid. Today, the ANC remains the dominant political party in South Africa, winning every election since 1994.

"So, I had the chance to interact with the ANC and at the same time, with the government of South Africa. Ambassador Genta Holmes arranged for me to meet with the foreign minister, and I began sharing what we were seeing," Paul recalls.

A survey was taken, revealing that in the village of Lilongwe, men were having sex on average ten times a week with five different partners—men and women.

In his retirement, Andrew Winter, Paul's senior administrative officer in Pretoria, prepared an oral history that recorded key moments in Dr. Paul Grundy's journey.

"Paul came back from a trip to Lilongwe and he was devastated. He came into my office and said 'Andrew, it's hopeless.'

"I said, 'What's hopeless?' He said, 'AIDS in Africa.'"

USAID and European Union counselors repeatedly traveled to Africa to help educate labor leaders about how the modern labor system worked. The program provided the first opportunity for Paul, Tex, and Dr. Gayle to meet and engage Nelson Mandela. Their bridge to Mandela was Walter Sisulu, another historic leader of the liberation movement in South Africa. Sisulu had spent twenty-six years in prison. The government released him in October 1989, just ahead of Mandela's release from prison.

Dr. Gayle recalls the way they met Sisulu.

"We went to Sisulu's house. Which seemed unusual. But with Paul, you do unusual things. On a walk in town, Paul said, 'There's Walter Sisulu's home. Let's see if he's home.'"

Sisulu answered the door and graciously welcomed Paul and Dr. Gayle into his house. The trio briefed him about the HIV/AIDS pandemic for over an hour. Sisulu, though hardened by a quarter century of brutal imprisonment, exhibited a real concern and wanted to help find solutions.

The second time Paul met Nelson Mandela occurred right after the Zambia visit.

"We all agreed to start a conversation hosted by the World Health Organization between the ANC and the South African government," he says.

During their meeting, Mandela eagerly asked Paul and Dr. Gayle for news and information about his colleagues, friends and their families. Mandela still was under house arrest at the time and had limited contact with the outside world.

Mandela said something to Paul he will never forget.

"Mandela looked me in the eye, and pretty much in these words said, "You have your own personal magic, Paul . . . you have the instinctive ability to empathize and really, really care about other people whose lives, at any instant, might be totally and tragically impacted. People see that and want to follow you . . . people with your magic are a rare gift."

After the meetings with Mandela, Paul organized a third meeting, this time between Mandela and a US diplomatic delegation that included Health and Human Services secretary Louis Wade Sullivan, and about a dozen others. They met at the Cape Town home of US ambassador Bill Swain. Sisulu came as well as Mandela, Dr. Gayle recalls. Mandela would make himself available to everyone there.

From her Chicago high-rise office overlooking the city, Dr. Gayle describes that vital meeting. Sitting with us is Dr. Paul Grundy.

"I just remember seeing this guy and feeling electricity. You literally shake his hand and you feel this electric current going through your body. And he's just incredibly charming and vibrant. His wife, Winnie, stood by his side, still there, still part of his life. We had a wide-ranging conversation about lots of issues."

They discussed HIV/AIDS, and the politics of tackling the problem.

"We learned that while we could help, we needed to meet with playmakers in secrecy," Paul says. "South African leadership did not want to be seen as collaborating with Americans at that time."

As an African American, Dr. Gayle interacted with people of color in South Africa more openly. Paul and Tex had to be more discreet because of distrust between the races and apartheid. She would be the spokesperson for the US, advocating interventions at the bordellos and for a public education campaign.

"I stayed behind the scenes, organizing it all, out of the limelight. I met with Mandela to organize it, trying hard to fire up the American leadership's attention. I wanted our government to take a grip on this," Paul says.

After the reception at the US ambassador's home, Mandela pulled Paul aside and called him a troublemaker, a good troublemaker.

A lot of people, particularly the people of color, would at the time go to a regular doctor as well as a "witch doctor" to cover their bases. Politeness would dictate use of the term "traditional healers." In open markets, witch doctors would be there selling their cures and administering advice.

Trying to better bridge old methods with new medicine, Paul and Tex organized a meeting between several hundred traditional healers and Western medicine folks in Pretoria. The Zulus wore their beaded Sangoma headdresses, which was an intimidating scene. The presentations by the medical community fell flat on this audience. The witch doctors did not like what they were hearing. For a while, it seemed the gathering would not have a positive outcome.

Paul, as usual, listened intently to everyone, not saying a word. Just when the conversation about HIV/AIDS seemed to fall apart, Paul stood and the room went silent.

Many in Paul's position would have felt a sense of menace and isolation. Not this man. It became his finest hour.

Paul's knowledge of local tribal culture was deep and wide. He knew that in African theology, the world is divided into two big pillars—the belief system of sacrifice and appeasement, and reincarnation. A Supreme Being watches other spiritual beings below. The spirits who have passed away interact with society. You need to appease the spirits of those who have died—otherwise, they could do you harm. Paul understood this from being immersed in this culture as a child; the tribal healers at the meeting recognized he understood this from a very deep, primal level, as did they.

"Consider this," Paul said to the silent crowd of healers and the frustrated group of Western practitioners. "Humanity has so angered the Supreme Being that he has placed a curse, a curse that once placed cannot be removed."

The witch doctors gathered among themselves and started asking questions.

"The healers believed they could remove HIV/AIDS with the right *juju*, because for them, everything results from a curse," Paul explains.

"The next day, I got a call from the head of the South African Traditional Healers Association saying that the wind must be speaking to me. That's what the healers think," Paul recalls. "I became a formal advisor to them. We created an acceptable traditional and spiritual methodology through which the healers could accept the use of condoms, safe sex, cleanly incorporated into their belief system. That wonderful relationship lasted for my entire remaining time in South Africa."

~

In his last years, increasingly frail, Nelson Mandela became one of the most important and effective campaigners against HIV/AIDS, a difficult issue to take on because it pitched him into opposition with his own government.

Believing that public confrontation would be unhelpful, he chose his words carefully; they were no less powerful for that. But the delicate balance of governing required an "extreme consensus" at first, and the nation's newly elected leaders were not at all in sync with the HIV/AIDS solutions. Mandela explained that as president of South Africa in 1994, he did not feel empowered enough to act on the AIDS epidemic.

Paul recalls that National Public Radio (NPR) aired a segment when Mandela died, interviewing one of his biographers. The reporter asked his biographer what Mandela thought was his biggest mistake. The biographer replied that Mandela became emotional, saying words to the effect that "I didn't listen enough to Dr. Helene Gayle and Dr. Paul Grundy when they told us how bad the HIV/AIDS epidemic would get."

"They lost so many lives unnecessarily," Dr. Gayle says. "Some people wouldn't think of it that way, because it's just a disease, or whatever, but when you think about the toll, and what has happened since then, and how hard it's been to get it under control—I think it does expose some of the challenges of how a country moves from a liberation struggle to governing."

Paul says that medicines were available to dampen a fatal disease and that lives could have been saved by quicker acceptance of aid and cooperation with world health authorities.

Summing up the experience of working with Paul in Africa, Dr. Gayle looks at her old friend at the doorway to her high-rise office and smiles. "Paul hasn't changed at all."

CHAPTER FOUR

INFECTIOUS PERSONALITY

About the same time that Nelson Mandela prepared to speak out on HIV/AIDS, Paul was assigned by the State Department to Moscow as counsel for medical affairs, and shortly thereafter kicked open some long-closed doors in the Kremlin.

Dissolution of the Soviet Union accelerated decrepitude within that empire. Paul was assigned to evaluate the medical capabilities of the new satellite nations being created from the USSR's collapse. Each new nation would eventually have a US embassy, and medical contingency planning for those staffing the new offices was paramount.

In mid-August 1991, an unsuccessful coup against Soviet president Gorbachev triggered the Soviet Union's demise. The formal end would come some months later on Christmas day when President Gorbachev hauled down the Soviet flag from above the Kremlin and signed his formal resignation.

One week after the famous coup, Paul, after weeks of little cooperation with the USSR medical authorities in Moscow, bullied his way into the once-private VIP Kremlin Clinic near Moscow University. He convinced them that since their entire bureaucratic structure was crumbling, it would be in their best interests to look toward the foreign community for patients and hard currency support.

Paul tells the story of how, as it turned out, that bold move made it possible to save the life of Jim Collins, then-deputy chief of mission.

Collins was US ambassador to the Russian Federation from 1997 to 2001. Before his appointment as ambassador to Russia, he served as ambassador-at-large and special adviser to the secretary of state for the newly independent states. He was deputy chief of mission and *chargé d'affaires* at the US embassy in Moscow from 1990 to 1993, the period during which this story takes place.

Jim's day began by getting Ambassador Bob Strauss and his family installed in Spaso House, the ambassador's residence. Jim retired for the evening as normal only to awaken with a chest pain that Paul, having been called, quickly diagnosed as a life-threatening collapsed lung requiring rapid emergency treatment.

It was the moment of payoff for all Paul's persistence with the Kremlin Clinic. An ambulance was summoned. Paul and Jim were whisked to the clinic, where Jim received emergency treatment, for which he recalls having to interpret between Paul and the Russian surgeon.

At that time, the best healthcare facilities were reserved for Kremlin leadership. They had excellent facilities and medical talent, but none of these facilities were available to normal Russians, much less outsiders such as American diplomats.

"It's just a fact that Paul's foresight and persistence in opening up for embassy personnel this network of quality, dependable medical care in an extremely difficult foreign culture within weeks of his arrival changed the life of everyone at the embassy and was little short of miraculous," Jim says. "When I became ill, newly arrived Ambassador Bob Strauss, was, needless to say, more than concerned that the deputy he had counted on to get him set up and established had deserted him for the hospital."

Paul knew he would be concerned.

"The first thing I did when we got to the VIP Kremlin Clinic was to notify Ambassador Strauss that Jim was in the hospital and in a bit of medical trouble," Paul recalls. "The ambassador got on the phone with President Gorbachev, let him know the situation, and made clear his expectation that all would be done to assure Collins' full recovery. From that point on the bells and whistles got turned on in the clinic."

Jim was admitted to what was known as the Louis XV Suite, a luxurious six-room wing reserved for the most senior communist party officials or visiting heads of state. His care was put in the hands of the Soviet Union's top thoracic physician, and he recovered beautifully. Moreover, the day it all began, September 28, 1991, Ambassador Collins recalls, was the day of his last Marlboro, a personal benchmark that remains a lasting tribute to the "Grundy effect."

With the successful treatment complete, all, including Jim with his newly mended lung, breathed a sigh of relief.

"I was, needless to say, impressed by Dr. Grundy's quick diagnosis of my medical problem, but not nearly as impressed as I was by what he had made possible in getting me into the clinic. His ability to access, interact with, and get an extremely secretive, labyrinthine Russian VIP system to run like a Swiss watch was impressive," Jim says.

⌁

Though it had been five years since the April 1986 Chernobyl accident, Paul anticipated post-Chernobyl environmental concerns in Minsk as his health unit carried out extensive monitoring throughout the region. Chernobyl is considered the most disastrous nuclear power plant accident in history, both in terms of cost and casualties. It is one of only two nuclear energy accidents classified as a level seven event (the maximum classification) on the International Nuclear Event Scale, the other being the Fukushima Daiichi nuclear disaster in Japan in 2011.[9]

Seeing that medical diplomacy could affect international relations, Paul spearheaded a drive for an American-Russian hospital in Moscow. Having the VIP Kremlin Clinic available to international business personnel made the prospect of bringing American industry and government personnel to Moscow a lot more palatable.

Paul pulled projects together and made it look almost effortless, one colleague notes, "like a master violinist playing a piece of well-rehearsed music."

Paul's role of counselor for embassy medical affairs involved many challenges in trying to smooth the way for establishing US embassies in the fifteen newly created nations. He immediately visited each new state to evaluate its medical capabilities.

His survey revealed a decline in health attributable in part to air and water pollution, contamination (largely from nuclear accidents or improper disposal of radioactive materials), overcrowded living conditions, poor nutrition, alcoholism, smoking, and, in part, to a lack of modern medical equipment and technology.

Paul encountered an underfunded system of socialized medicine. Seven levels of "doctors" existed in these republics. VIPs received the best facilities and care. Nurses would never dream of taking a blood pressure reading or giving an injection to the powerful, as that was the purview of doctors. Basic medical care, available to most of the population free of cost, suffered from quality measures we consider low by Western standards.

Paul found some of the poorest conditions in Tajikistan and Turkmenistan, bordering Afghanistan. A resident epidemiologist advised that the region had the highest rate of anthrax in the world.

In Armenia, Paul found violence and civil unrest, and acute lead poisoning from bullet wounds. There was "very little, if any usable primary care," he concluded.

This tour of the miserable healthcare he witnessed in the fallen Soviet countries gave him an even broader global perspective of failed medical systems. Despite its shortcomings, Paul found that healthcare in the former Soviet Block for VIPs was much more hands-on than the more corporate US system. He sent this example to the State Department leadership:

> With a sore back in the US, we would throw some pills at you and tell you to rest. In the VIP system here, they would offer you physical therapy, ultrasound therapy, and hydrotherapy three times a day for one week.

Paul's unclassified communiqués described the conditions.

> For a cold we would tell you to go home, take Tylenol and stop bugging us. Here they may very well put you in a machine which blows some unknown mist into your sinuses, followed by a sauna, then a sinus massage.
>
> In the VIP system, 170 doctors and a staff of two thousand take care of only eight thousand blessed elite. This healthcare system requires a certain sense of adventure, as it certainly is different.
>
> In Moldova, the health association has three sanitariums for rest and recuperation, all with hydro baths, physical massage, water massage, mud massage, exercise therapy, sports therapy, sauna, dance hall, movie theater and excellent food.

In Uzbekistan, Paul found the sanitarium just outside of town on the former first secretary estate. He describes this spa as a restful facility done in marble, stained glass and oriental tapestries, set in a pomegranate and apple orchard.

"In the former Soviet Union, this was the place to go when ruling the people got too tough," Paul says.

Paul notes that after an appendectomy, the VIP Soviet system insisted on keeping you in the hospital for two weeks. There, you would enjoy daily electric stimulation for wound healing and perhaps hyperbaric oxygen therapy. This would be followed by one to two weeks in the sanitarium for recovery. In America, Paul quips, "we would have kicked you out after three days and sent you back to work after five to seven days."

Paul tells an amusing story about a VIP American visitor to Moscow—actress and political figure Bess Myerson, the first Jewish Miss America, visiting the homeland of her parents, both Russian Jewish immigrants.

An elder from the Mormon Church, a physician, showed up, seeking a place to care for his young missionaries. So, Paul introduced this doctor to the head of the Kremlin Clinic hospital. The hospital team needed somebody to teach them English. They agreed that he would come and teach English two days a week at the hospital.

Meanwhile, Bess Myerson badly injured her leg and showed up in an ambulance at the front gate of the US embassy, wanting to know where to get care.

"So, we end up getting her into this VIP hospital," Paul said. "I happened to be on the floor with the Mormon physician, helping to teach Russian doctors a little English. We heard the fussing and walked into her room. She had the recovering deputy ambassador with the collapsed lung in the bed next to her."

Paul introduced her to an American doctor who worked in this hospital. Her eyes brightened. She looked up at him and said, "God must have sent you."

He took his little Mormon nametag out of his pocket, clipped it on, looked at her intently, and said, "How did you know?"

Ambassador Collins noted in a formal review of Paul's work that Paul seemed happiest when he found a way to improve morale or efficiency. "Extremely ingenious," he said of Paul. Jim added, "Sometimes the agency whose pocket he has so neatly picked gets upset afterwards. Paul should continue to artfully pick their pockets but should probably restrain his glee."

Everywhere Paul served, he defied expectations and amplified the standards, and still found time to be a misfit.

⌇

Over nine years of service from 1985 to 1994, Paul evolved into the top medical officer in the State Department. He learned everything about the Russian healthcare system, using that knowledge to promote Western healthcare, including the Adventist Health Center and the American Medical Center, which supported not only the US embassy, but more than one hundred American businesses who said they would not be there without it.

Ambassador Thomas Pickering, Paul's boss in Moscow, who would become US ambassador to the UN, notes that Paul created better healthcare and services for the US embassy and the American community overseas, increasing American business support for US programs in Russia.

Paul also organized the Clinton/Yeltsin health initiative, a 157-million-dollar bilateral initiative in Russia, again setting new benchmarks for American medical diplomacy.

This would be Paul's last assignment for the State Department. He finished his career as a minister counselor, the highest rank for a doctor and the equivalent of a three-star flag rank in the military. The Department of Defense and the State Department rolled out the awards and medals:

- 1993 Department of State Superior Honor Award for handling the crisis surrounding the two attempted coups in Russia.

- 1992 Department of State Superior Honor Award for work done in opening up all the new embassies after the fall of the Soviet Union.

- 1991 Department of State Superior Honor Award for work on the HIV/AIDS epidemic in Africa.

- 1987–93 Four Department of State Meritorious Service awards for outstanding performance in the Middle East and Africa.

- 1985 Department of Defense Superior Service Award for outstanding service addressing HIV/AIDS.

His leadership with the Adventist Health Center in Moscow led Paul to accept the role of medical director for the organization for three years. His work there sharpened his nonprofit health system experiences and his occupational medicine skills.

In 1997, he again thirsted to work with different cultures and joined SOS International, providing and coordinating care and medical assistance for hundreds of multinational corporations. As the medical director, he built and staffed new clinics for corporate international businesspeople in China, Burma, Cambodia, and Vietnam. His work took him to Asia, Europe, and Africa. IBM, expanding internationally, became one of his primary clients.

After three years with SOS, Paul learned that both his parents were ill. The strain of separation had grown painful. He decided it was time to get a job in the States.

One call to IBM and Dr. Paul Grundy had a job—before he even boarded his plane home. He would first go to San Jose and shortly thereafter settled in Rochester, Minnesota, with Big Blue. As fate would have it, things at home were getting very interesting.

CHAPTER FIVE

A CRUSADE

I BM chief executive officer Ginni Rometty rallied Big Blue to help tackle what she saw as one of the world's largest challenges.

"Our moonshot will be the impact we will have on healthcare. It has already started. We will change and do our part to change the face of healthcare. I am absolutely positive about it. And that, to me, while we do many other things, that will be one of the most important," Ms. Rometty said in 2015 on PBS.[10]

At the dawn of the new millennium 2000, IBM and the entire technology sector stood at the threshold of major technological breakthroughs in the practice of medicine worldwide. The current structure of medicine was at a breaking point.

The CEOs of many US corporations felt the sting of rapidly rising medical costs. IBM wanted to get a handle on why US health expenses were so shockingly high when compared with what the company paid for healthcare in the 173 other nations in which it operated.

One of the most troubling aspects to America's broken healthcare system was the perfect storm descending on primary care. Baby boomers, now entering their sixties, streamed into their doctor's office with very complicated health issues. Primary care doctors faced longer workdays, less reimbursement, a hectic pace, and a new EHR system chewing up time with their patients, disabling personal care.

During the 1970s, it was recognized by policymakers that there would be a shortfall of primary care doctors in the coming years. A wave of coming retirements was expected to cause a physician shortage. The outlook was bleak for the profession. The Physicians Foundation finished up an enormous physician survey, which included over 85 percent of all practicing doctors, and found that 60 percent of physicians "would retire today if they could." Eighty percent said medicine was in decline.[11]

Crossing the Quality Chasm: A New Health System for the 21st Century, prepared by the Institute of Medicine's Committee on the Quality of Health Care in America, concluded that merely making piecemeal improvements in current healthcare systems would not be enough.

The report concluded that tens of thousands of Americans die each year as a result of preventable mistakes in their care, and its authors laid out a comprehensive strategy by which government, healthcare providers, industry, and consumers can reduce medical errors.

At the time, healthcare costs in the US accounted for 16 percent of the country's gross domestic product (GDP), and per capita healthcare spending was (and still is) approximately twice that of other major industrialized countries. Bringing state-of-the-art care to all Americans in every community would require a fundamental, sweeping redesign of the entire health system, according to the report by the Institute of Medicine (IOM).[12]

Given that the US system's performance was no better than that of other countries, the IOM concluded that much of the money spent on healthcare was unnecessary or wasteful. The IOM report also concluded that information technology, including the internet, held enormous potential for transforming the healthcare delivery system, which "today remains relatively untouched by the revolution that has swept nearly every other aspect of society."[13]

At the time, the IBM executive team agreed that action was needed. The conversations centered on "what was right" and "what was wrong" with healthcare, not only in America, but also globally. The problem was deeper than just high costs.

IBM general manager of healthcare Sean Hogan took part in the efforts to launch a health industry initiative at IBM. We meet with Sean near the company's worldwide headquarters in Armonk, New York.

"IBM had deep expertise in supporting industries such as banking, airlines, and telecommunications. Yet at that time, while we had a significant role with transaction processing, such as claims, we had no significant presence across healthcare. For such an information-intensive industry, we believed there was a role for IBM to play," Sean says.

IBM believed new technologies could help healthcare advance with software and transaction-processing capabilities. Information technology advances made it possible to gather data used to measure quality and good performance.

As the executive team examined the issue, it became quite clear that IBM could help advance healthcare around the world. Healthcare analysis and process improvements could become a major business for technology companies such as IBM. Everyone was aware that the delivery system was broken, and IBM had analytic tools to help identify why and to suggest fixes.

"But this was an industry that did not spend much money on technology," Sean says of healthcare providers. "Information technology investments at the time were very low. Healthcare was a fragmented, highly specialized industry and hard for IBM's model to reach.

"We believed that the industry should invest more in technology, but just because we believed it, well-intentioned as we might be, it did not mean the industry would be ready to invest. And they weren't!"

IBM's most fundamental challenge was how to "make a market."

What IBM did know was that healthcare costs were not sustainable in the US, and that IBM was not the only worldwide corporation concerned about that. "We knew we had to do something differently," Sean says.

~~

Retired IBM executive vice president of innovation and technology Nick Donofrio, who guided IBM's innovations through four decades, decided that a focused effort was needed—a new department, focused on global healthcare transformation—and he put me to work.

"I assigned Dan because he was a non-traditional choice as he was not a physician or academic PhD; he was an integrator, change agent and market visionary," Nick says.

Paul had recently joined IBM's Human Resources Department, working with Senior Vice President of Human Resources Randy MacDonald, assigned to employee health and well-being. They knew him when he helped IBM build clinics abroad. He was a doctor, a diplomat, and he was, well, different.

That ended up being a perfect match. Randy, who was Paul's greatest champion, knew the power of the combination, Nick says.

While we knew the buyers of our technology well, we did not yet have a connection or relevance to the community of people who actually deliver care. Having Paul on the team created clinical relevance for IBM. Paul's vision was to give medical stakeholders a voice.

As time passed, Nick and others of us noticed that Paul did not emulate the typical executive. He wore blue jeans with a coat and tie, his hair often in disarray. Because of his dyslexia, he sometimes misspelled words. He was, in many ways, a breath of fresh air and diversity in our otherwise button-downed IBM universe.

The team embraced a budding movement known as "patient-centered care." Yet this was not the way the healthcare field currently functioned. We would design everything for the *patient*. It seemed so obvious, but US healthcare was based almost entirely on the desires and needs of physicians, healthcare organizations, and insurers.

The concern about quality arose more from fear and anecdote rather than from facts. There was little systematic evidence about quality of care in the US. There was not a national system, and few local systems, that tracked the quality of care delivered to Americans. More information was available on the quality of airlines, restaurants, cars, and VCRs than on the quality of healthcare.[13]

There were pockets of high-quality care in organizations with salaried physicians such as Mayo, and Cleveland Clinic, but there was little accountability for value in US medicine outside of risk-bearing integrated systems like Geisinger and Kaiser that included both the care and the healthcare plan under one umbrella.

The opportunity for improvement was immense. We soon discovered that our healthcare suffered from waste, which many thought accounted for 30 percent of all costs—wastes from overtreatment, poor care coordination, failures in care processes, administrative complexity, pricing failures, and fraud and abuse.[14]

IBM saw the potential for information technology to address these inefficiencies, but the industry itself was not structurally motivated to do so.

"If you are content with the current fee-for-service model, then you are focused on volume and not quality or outcomes. If you are not investing to unlock value, you really don't care about the things that modern technology can do. So, for our strategy to work, we needed wholesale industry transformation. We set out with a goal of transforming healthcare," recalls Sean Hogan.

Paul envisioned a new way of organizing primary care, which he had been following for years, called the *medical home.*

The *medical home* was first used in 1967 by the American

Academy of Pediatrics as an ideal for the care of special-needs children. The first to pioneer the new care model was Hawaiian pediatrician Dr. Calvin C. J. Sia.

Under the *medical home* idea, which the American Academy of Pediatrics adopted as a formal policy statement in 1992, "the medical care of all infants, children and adolescents should be accessible, continuous, comprehensive, family-centered, coordinated, compassionate, and culturally effective."[15]

In 2002, leading medical researchers Dr. Kevin Grumbach and Dr. Thomas Bodenheimer of the University of California, San Francisco, encouraged more general adoption of these principles.[16] Pediatricians were already using this idea all over the country, improving access to the children's *Trusted Healers*. Dr. Sia attached the slogan "Every Child Deserves a *Medical Home*" to that movement. Dr. V. Fan Tait, a pediatric neurologist and chief medical officer of the American Academy of Pediatrics, always gently reminds Paul that pediatricians had been doing the *medical home* model for years!

The more Paul looked at it in the context of addressing the primary care crisis, the better it looked. He did not invent the *medical home* model of care. But the crusade Paul put together would transform the world of medicine. He gave it voice, definition, structure, and made it real.

Before investing into a long-term campaign for global change, any initiative had to be relevant to the business, and potentially beneficial. For IBM, that translated to selling technology aimed at improving healthcare delivery to big companies.

Doctors and small physician practices were not a target market; technology buyers resided in large corporations and government. But Paul's vision changed that paradigm. There was now great potential for big companies to assist smaller medical practices with better analytics and practices. This means that life sciences fields could become fertile ground for technology giants. IBM's management team began to recognize that Paul's *medical home* could apply not just to IBM's healthcare cost containment efforts, but also to its broader business interests.

⸺

Healthcare is a big, complex system with lots of stakeholders.

Paul not only figured out the best solution for the primary care crisis, he assembled stakeholders to orchestrate change. For those healthcare organizations comfortable with their level of financial success, it would be a message they perhaps did not want to hear.

Paul helped primary care providers see that the *medical home* concept would improve quality, reduce costs and alleviate burnout. The healthcare industry needed to embrace technology, to use its tools. It was a catalyst for change, but not the entire answer. What Paul prescribed was not about marketing technology; it was about transforming the way an industry operated. Paul provided the voice of this movement, and IBM furnished the facts to bolster the case.

IBM could point to evidence that care systems with a strong role for primary care across the Atlantic were less expensive and more effective. Paul's study of powerful *medical home* systems in Europe helped convince healthcare leaders that there was tremendous value here and this could not be ignored. Real change was possible, and it made sense for all.

We on the IBM executive team working with Paul anticipated that he would help our company and others lower healthcare costs. What IBM did not expect is that he would ultimately play a role in a worldwide transformation of primary care.

⸺

A consensus around fixing healthcare had to be achieved. That required unification, a platform, a meeting place. Paul's plan was to first bring together all the primary care doctors, who were clearly divided into four different associations.

They also needed the buyers of healthcare to weigh in. They needed to find a way to ask the nation's top business leaders, who were paying for a broken healthcare system with inconsistent quality care and costs out of control, to join a reform crusade. This was also about the same time that the *medical home* was awakening in military medicine.

Paul taught that healthcare should not be approached with a silo mentality. Rather, it was an ecosystem built around the *continuum of care* and needed to be approached as such.

The silo approach was driving primary care doctors into the ground. They were more like traffic cops assigning lanes than care providers. They wrote prescriptions and referrals, treating patients episodically during sickness or crisis instead of working to avoid disease and keep patients healthy.

Paul understood this disconnect and sensed the possibilities. Healthcare is about treating and caring for patients, but it is also a business that needed to run more efficiently for the sakes of patients and doctors. Paul looked for opportunities to bring in the business-practice leaders with the doctors. IBM was a huge purchaser of medical services for its worldwide labor force, so Paul saw the opportunity he was looking for.

He had been serving as a representative of big business on a committee of ERISA (the Employee Retirement Security Act of 1974) to protect the interests of employees enrolled in benefit plans. IBM belonged to several major business organizations. As he attended these meetings, he got to know some of the most powerful business leaders in the nation, forming a powerful consortium to back the *medical home* concept. There he also met Edwina Rogers, previously a health policy expert in the White House. Her influence in Washington with policymakers and around the world in business pushed the idea forward.

"This was the moment when the frustration about healthcare costs was bubbling up among the biggest corporate leaders, and it became a major topic of discussion among business organizations," Paul says.

The four different primary care associations—family practice, internal medicine, pediatrics, and osteopathic care—totaled a combined membership of 660,000 doctors in all. The first item of business was to draw up that new covenant, which they called the *Joint Principles of the Patient-Centered Medical Home.*[17] This became a vital component for the future of primary care in America.

The four powerful primary care physician organizations recognized the power of the *medical home* and got on board right away because it would potentially be a lifesaver for their struggling, overwhelmed practices. The fact that all four of the associations endorsed a new approach to practicing medicine for the common good was a primary factor in the success of the entire crusade.

～

Most healthcare insurance in the country was bought and paid for by large corporations on behalf of employees. The other big buyers of healthcare included the Veterans Administration, the Department of Defense, the Federal Employee Health Benefits Program, Medicare, and Medicaid. Each organization needed to have a hand in the reform movement. So a common platform was needed, a new organization that focused on the transformation of primary care.

Paul seized the momentum and set about to create an exchange of excellence with the best healthcare providers in the world. This initiated a worldwide dialogue about the vital importance of *Trusted Healers* and a *medical home.* Other nations, particularly Denmark, had based their healthcare around robust primary care and sported a widely acclaimed medical system, both from a quality of care and a cost standpoint. Others could learn from that experience.

In 2006, business and primary care joined together and created this platform for change. All the stakeholder organizations had a seat at the table—the primary care associations, insurance companies, equipment manufacturers, pharmaceutical companies, hospitals, health systems, mental health, long-term care, the Veterans Administration, Department of Defense, US government employees, Medicare and Medicaid . . . everyone.

Because of the highly collaborative nature of their work together, they named this powerhouse organization the Patient-Centered Primary Care Collaborative (PCPCC). It works fine until you try to roll these letters off your tongue.

Here's what they agreed to do together:

- Advance an effective and efficient health system built on a strong foundation of primary care and the patient-centered *medical home.*
- Facilitate improvements in patient-physician relations.
- Create a more effective and efficient model of healthcare delivery.

They did not have to wait for everyone to come to a full consensus, as occurred with Mandela's experience in South Africa. The founders achieved it from the outset and hit the ground running.

Patrick J. Kennedy, then a House representative from Rhode Island, helped launch the organization with a keynote address. The PCPCC created an open forum where healthcare stakeholders freely communicate and work together to improve the future of the American medical system. The collaborative developed model language for health reform proposals to include the patient-centered *medical home* concept.

At IBM, Senior Vice President of Human Resources Randy MacDonald boldly committed to the effort. As a healthcare consumer, IBM wanted better choices. Randy's message to the world's largest was that they were paying too much for poorly organized healthcare of questionable quality and accountability.

Among that group of major corporate leaders, Paul and Randy found like-minded businesses that were also feeling the pain of US healthcare costs. Many responded enthusiastically to the need to transform healthcare in America, beginning with the backbone of medicine—primary care. Health insurance providers were forced to listen, and act.

With the weight of big-name companies behind him, Paul had put the *medical home* on a trajectory that would cross continents.

⁓

According to the *Joint Principles of the Patient-Centered Medical Home*, developed and maintained by a number of professional societies, the five main features of a successful patient-centered *medical home* published on the PCPCC website include:

- Providing comprehensive care by considering the patient as a whole person and supporting both mental and physical health with a coordinated-care team.

- Taking a patient-centered approach to care delivery by developing meaningful relationships with the patient, her family, and her caregivers that considers the patient's socioeconomic and cultural values and preferences.

- Employing care-coordination strategies by harnessing health information exchange, EHR interoperability, and population health management analytics. This ensures that patient health information is accessible and usable at all care sites across the healthcare continuum.

- Ensuring the accessibility of services by offering extended hours, alternative sites for care during emergencies, improving the scheduling process, or making use of technologies such as *telehealth*, *mHealth*, and home-monitoring devices. (The term *mHealth* refers to use of mobile and wireless technologies to support the achievement of health objectives.)

- Focusing on care quality and patient safety by using evidence-based medicine, clinical decision support tools, healthcare analytics, and best practices. This will provide a safe, high-quality, satisfactory experience for each and every patient.[18]

Few would argue with such aspiration. But the practical-minded obviously would want to know how we will pay for it. Only a decade earlier, the healthcare field had watched the Health Maintenance Organization (HMO) effort blow up.

"There were many reasons HMOs, for the most part, did not succeed. Some, like Kaiser, thrived. Others did not because of pushback from the physicians they attempted to manage," Paul says.

"All in all, the HMO movement did not have the clarity of data to be able to manage a population. They focused on costs. On risk. But they had no data on what to do and how to make it the right thing for the patients."

The PCPCC began tackling that, gained traction, and nearly a thousand members signed on. An entire industry united. Everyone wanted the broken system to be fixed.

Many of the largest companies in the world validated the movement. They all piled on, stipulating that they too wanted a *medical home* option for their employees. They enlisted through the various employer groups to which IBM belonged and made convincing presentations. They began demanding the service and, together, re-shaped the buying process for healthcare.

Paul also engaged regulators, federal agencies like the VA, the Centers for Medicare and Medicaid and private insurers and physicians to get on board. Everyone said it needed to change. Yet, no one was ready to take the first steps.

Paul created that change, seeing things from the lens of the different groups. He communicated well with doctors because he was one. He communicated with business leaders, because he was one. He communicated with global leaders, because he was a trained diplomat and a person immersed in world culture.

He found a receptiveness in doctors and healthcare leaders who wanted to perform better. The system they operated under was only paying for volume—episodic transactions—not health and health outcomes. Employers had been buying access to medical networks, and paying dearly. So when the *medical home* model was introduced, doctors experienced higher personnel and management costs to enhance the delivery of care. While thousands of doctors loved the new model of care, without some relief from the increased costs, many were in no hurry to transform.

Cost hikes ran downhill as traditional insurance providers passed all cost increases to the funders of healthcare. This impacted the employers, the government, taxpayers, and individuals.

So, to offset the costs, insurance plans managed their costs by increasing co-pays and deductibles. As early as 2006, the consuming public began to feel the pain of high costs at the point of care. By shifting the costs, it was the employees, uninsured individuals, and small companies who lacked negotiating leverage who were getting crushed. That pain is still felt today.

The Henry J. Kaiser Foundation noted the seriousness of the problem. It released a study that revealed the lack of integrated, efficient systems for electronically storing and transmitting health data. Not having that capability resulted in service duplication, misdiagnosis, and high transaction costs. The failure to use that technology limited the data available to study the effectiveness of treatments.[19]

So, a market emerged for electronic systems, but there was not a distinct role or need for *scale technology and services* for the *medical home* model. If a market was going to buy and pay for a new service or offering, it needed to come with a set of principles and standards for what it delivers.

Paul would often say, "The way to herd cats is to move their cheese!"

Creating a model and standard for *medical homes* by using information technology to measure and to document value would be the cheese used to coax healthcare delivery into patient-focused healthcare business.

The VA, Medicare and Medicaid, and the Federal Employees Health Insurance Program studied what Paul prescribed and joined the *medical home* movement. Planning at commercial insurers began as they decided to offer *medical homes.* Their customers—the employers—wanted to buy that.

Big healthcare organizations and health systems that had an interest in delivering better care came on board, such as Kaiser Permanante, Group Health, and Geisinger Health System. At Geisinger, Dr. Glenn Steele began re-engineering healthcare, basing much of their evidence-based protocols on the structure of a solid *medical home.*

Bridges to Excellence (BTE), the nation's largest effort to reward physicians for delivery of high-quality care, announced its support of the *medical home* approach in 2008 by launching its own BTE *medical home* program.

Paul's ideas made their way to regulators and policy makers. They needed to get on board if employers and doctors and insurers were, in fact, all agreeing that the *medical home* produced better patient health at less cost. Paul knew that governmental leaders love policy that sits well with all their stakeholders.

∽

If you're going to pay for it, then you need to measure it, and for that you need data and analytics and technology. Several healthcare organizations began setting up to accredit, or recognize, *medical homes* that fulfilled the requirements. To do so, big insurance plans invested in new processing platforms and information technologies. They either offered technology services, analytics and exchanges to their network, or required these things from them.

CHAPTER SIX

ROAD SHOW

D
r. Paul Grundy is often called the "godfather of the *medical home*," not because it's his brainchild, but because he was a provocateur who articulated both the clinical and business cases for organizing medical care in a new way. Paul did not expect this accolade, but as the movement became real, its deepest believers wanted their champions, and he was chief among them.

Paul grabbed the attention of audiences and left them with something to think about. He began a whirlwind campaign to speak to every primary care conference in the nation. (Every state has several such meetings each year.)

Ultimately, he understood, the individual physicians must understand the *medical home* and be willing to risk a lot of work, time, and talent to change almost everything they do.

This seemed to be how the message spread over the years: Doctors struggling with their practice heard about the *medical home* crusade a few times, from different quarters, and it piqued their interest. Many heard Paul speak at their regional or statewide conference, and then someone they knew transformed his or her practice into a *medical home*. And they noticed those caregivers had never been happier.

Dr. Peter Anderson

A great example of how Paul's crusade for the *medical home* reached America's primary care doctors is the story of Dr. Peter Anderson, a Virginia family practice physician who reached a crisis point of burnout in his career and, thankfully, went to hear Paul's presentation to primary care doctors in Charlottesville.

"Hearing him speak in 2007 at the Virginia Academy of Family Physicians enthralled me," Dr. Anderson says. "After going to lectures and conferences for years, I finally heard somebody from the academic world articulate the value of the doctor-patient relationship in a non-refutable way." (Dr. Anderson always refers to any physician who does not have an active practice as of "the academic world.")

Dr. Anderson knew that primary care was an undervalued, disenfranchised piece of the equation. When he saw that Paul was working to get big employers into the equation, since they pay for more than half of all healthcare bills, he got very interested.

Eleven years later, Dr. Peter Anderson vividly remembers Paul's presentation in Charlottesville. Paul shared some research that IBM conducted with its own employees.

- They had 20 percent less mortality.
- They had 30 percent less cost.
- They were much happier.

This came from having a physician they knew.

"That's what made me fall in love with the *medical home*. The first tenet of the *medical home* sets the structure our culture desperately needs, that every patient deserves a personal relationship with a *Trusted Healer*," Dr. Anderson says.

"I hated medicine. I was ready to quit. I had to innovate, which led to me developing the Team Care Medicine model in my practice. My staff was trained to do all the non-physician work. This, among many other benefits, allowed me to have the access with my patients that they needed."

This new model of care delivery allowed Dr. Anderson the ability to hire additional staff and truly function as a high-performing *medical home*. Becoming the first fully accredited *medical home* in Virginia, his practice evolved into the most profitable, productive, and best-quality practice in Virginia's largest primary care medical group.

The switch flips when clinicians across the nation discovered that the *medical home* is good for doctors, patients, staff, and that they can significantly improve the bottom line.

Dr. Anderson observes that primary care has navigated a landscape where more expensive urgent care centers are the "favored child." Almost 40 percent of primary care has gravitated to urgent care centers, just because primary care offices are inaccessible at that moment of need. The benefits of having a long-term *Trusted Healer* relationship are interrupted by poor access resulting from an outdated model of care.

"If primary care is not accessible, it becomes marginalized, instead of being the backbone of healthcare," Dr. Anderson observes. He published a landmark book, *The Familiar Physician,* and sent it to thousands of healthcare executives in America in 2015.[20]

"I know as a practicing physician that I can give better care than anybody in an emergency room or urgent care center because I know the patient. Not because I know more; because I know the patient. I know that I am the best doctor for my patients in terms of quality and cost effectiveness. I am their *Trusted Healer,*" Dr. Anderson says.

Dr. Anderson notes that the innovative genius of Paul, besides pulling the four associations of primary care together, was in bringing business to the table—"the unconnected piece of this puzzle." The people who paid the bills started having a part in the decision-making process. Dr. Anderson saw Paul's bringing business into the solution as the game changer. "That's a critical piece. It changed everything."

When invited, Paul spoke anywhere in the world, keynoting almost every major medical event, and he kept a bag packed for any opportunity. This intense speaking tour lasted a decade.

The *medical home* evolved as Paul championed the advancing role of the nurse-practitioners, physician assistants, and registered nurses working to free up the doctor to practice medicine. Doctors all over the world embraced the concept of the *Trusted Healer*, recognizing that the healer can be a key member of the team as well.

Transforming primary care to enable that team to work at the "top of their license" became a life goal of Dr. Anderson. In 2012, he retired from the active practice he loved to help train physician practices in team care, something that was never taught in medical school. His consulting group, Team Care Medicine, demonstrated how physician groups could provide six or seven-day-a-week access, offer after-hours care, keep up with medical record demands, as well as set time aside every day for urgent appointments, allowing patients to see their known and familiar physician.

Dr. Anderson watched this *medical home* transformation unfold for hundreds of practices, as doctors regained the joy of the practice of medicine, helping physicians and the care team to end their burnout crisis and improve patient care.

Looking back, aspects of the *medical home* concept were not always accepted at the same pace, notes Katie Capps, who has guided the information and public relations for the PCPCC since inception.

From her Health2Resources offices in Northern Virginia, Katie reflects on the twelve years she has supported the organization with

Katie Capps

Paul, carrying this banner from day one. Katie's promotional and organizational strategies created a real movement. Her strategies pulled this group of like-minded thinkers together.

"A lot of this was flourishing through chaos," Katie observes. "Amid this chaos, we heard Dr. Paul Grundy's sobering voice: 'Here is *true north*; this is the problem; there is a solution. We need to refocus on what will guide us to these solutions.'"

The *medical home* movement, which started as a group of forward-thinking physicians and business leaders, responded to Paul's "steady illumination," as Katie describes it. Katie thinks IBM's reputation as a buyer of healthcare, as opposed to a provider of equipment and services, created the traction.

"When Paul spoke to our assemblies, he presented a point of view of someone who had a responsibility to purchase care on behalf of a population—buying healthcare for employees."

Paul gave a speech at an *Economist* event explaining that healthcare transformation must have three dimensions to it: reimbursement redesign, patient-centered benefit design, and care delivery inclusive of *medical home*. His vision offered a financial mechanism, a value proposition, and a differentiated delivery model.

Paul's efforts with the *medical home* engaged the industry in a constructive dialogue on how to deliver better quality, more affordable, individualized, and person-centered care. By offering a solution that appealed to stakeholders, he propelled the industry to make steps toward meaningful, transformative change.

Katie notes that Paul's integrity and authenticity brought to life a formula for success. No one ever felt like he imposed something into this situation. He just described what he could see. He spoke in a manner business leaders could understand. And he spoke in a manner that clinical people could understand.

"One word I would use to describe Paul would be *Sherpa*," Katie says. More than a mountain guide, a Sherpa leads someone on a path, she explains; when people started traveling up mountains, they found people living in those areas that could guide them, taking them through the twists and turns, dangerous passages, keeping them out of harm's way.

"Paul guided this tentative bond between the buyers of healthcare and the deliverers of healthcare, a sensitive union, through the twists and turns that arose as the movement matured," Katie says.

She adds that there is a second definition of Sherpa—someone a ruler sends to represent them, to a meeting or as their ambassador, so to speak.

Different cultures welcomed his message. Paul took his crusade abroad. He found rapid and enthusiastic traction. He created an exchange of sorts, inviting world healthcare leaders to America to see what we did well in healthcare. In turn, US leaders visited other developed nations to see how the *medical home* idea and robust primary care impacted healthcare there. He gained the confidence of the Parliament in Denmark, creating a center of excellence diplomacy where we shared our best and brightest, and Denmark did the same. Other nations called on him for advice continuously.

"He guided the developed world to the value of the primary care physician, the *Trusted Healers,* as the key to a safe journey through a dangerous and confusing medical experience," Katie says.

As with any major change initiative, planners often seek to achieve early or quick wins at the outset to create momentum. Paul and the leadership team at the PCPCC focused on the worldwide crusade, journeying to all points of the compass as well as setting a goal of making those small, persistent, and sometimes painstaking wins happen as soon as possible.

Looking around a PCPCC meeting in these early days of the crusade revealed an assembly filled with dedicated leaders in business and healthcare, eager to get going. Who, though, was ready to be first to act to create value and improve quality?

Paul knew that the conversion of the US doctors to the *medical home* would be slow and deliberate until the current system of reimbursement fully changed. It is costly; additional staff must be hired. It's hard work. The practice can never fully stop to retool things. Management of that change required some outside guidance. Then the bigger dominoes began falling.

The primary care organizations that could most easily achieve the *medical home* transformation were the big healthcare systems and the governmental healthcare programs. The integrated healthcare systems had been developing large primary care practices for over a decade. The decision to transform these practices to the *medical home* was economically within reach for most. Paul walked the halls at Walter Reed, Bethesda, San Diego, the Pentagon, Congress, and the White House. He visited leading health systems and medical schools.

So, while it may take some time and effort to gather believers at the federal or corporate level, once it's decided, it's done. The change could be debated and then executed with a signature.

The first giant player in US healthcare to lead the way was the Veterans Health Administration, the largest integrated healthcare system in the nation with over nine million patients that receive care in over 1,100 health facilities.

Most don't realize that we do indeed have socialized medicine in the US; the government owns all the VA facilities, hires all the staff, and pays all the bills. That's a socialized system.

Joanne Shear, now retired from her role as clinical program manager at the VA, guided that organization through the enormous task of transforming their primary care into the *medical home* model. Joanne remembers her first impressions of Paul.

Joanne Shear

"Who is this guy? He looks like the Nutty Professor. He always wears jeans. He may have a tie and a coat on, but always in jeans. Who is this doctor? People who know him call him an icon, an amazing person, a thought-provoking person, an international figure—and VA senior leadership afford him that level of respect," Joanne recalls.

Paul met with the VA team many times. In 2009, he keynoted their annual conference, presenting his *medical home* vision.

"Paul also brought people in from all over the world who showed us better ways to take care of patients," she says.

A SNAPSHOT OF HEALTH INSURANCE IN AMERICA

156,199,800 . . . . .Employer

20,525,500 . . . . .Non-Group

62,152,400 . . . . Medicaid

42,802,800 . . . . Medicare

4,588,200 . . . . Other Public

27,400,000 . . . . Uninsured

Source: 2017 Henry J. Kaiser Family Foundation[21]

He put her in touch with key executives at other organizations, like the armed services, Kaiser, Geisinger, Intermountain Healthcare—all pioneers in the *medical home* movement. Joanne notes that the VA would not have gone down this path without Paul. "We believed in it with our hearts."

"Just listen to him," she told colleagues. "This is how we want to practice."

Kicked off in 2010, a huge transformation project began, and 8,000 care teams transformed into patient-centered *medical homes*. Paul recalls the moment it all changed at the VA, when the exploration into transforming primary care came to a beautiful conclusion.

"One of the most exciting moments of my life takes place in the Executive Office Building next to the White House, where President Barack Obama signed the executive order to mandate the *medical home* model in all Veterans Affairs, military medicine and governmental employee medical coverage."

When Paul describes this moment, we see that this really had an impact on him. With one signature, the *medical home* became a part of the healthcare future for millions of beneficiaries. Paul recalls that the ceremony included the leadership of primary care in America. In attendance were the physician and business leaders who worked to get us there. It was truly an inspirational moment.

The transformation of the VA occurred from the bottom up. Over 200 people from across the country participated in the planning and implementation of the *medical home* model. Paul stayed with the VA for the entire journey, calming the waters. He spent a lot of time on Capitol Hill talking about it, calming impatient folks who wanted to see results immediately.

The nature of measuring healthcare involves time. If you are going to measure the quality of care of stroke patients, or heart patients, or people fighting addiction, it may be years before enough time passes to draw meaningful results.

"Paul changed the face of healthcare in the United States," Joanne says.

In 2009, the Department of Defense issued HA Policy 09–015, preparing the launch of the *medical home* throughout the Military Health System. By 2010, the *medical home* launched for the entire Federal Employee Health Benefit program—the largest employer-sponsored US program, providing healthcare benefits for over eight million employees, retirees and family members.

Paul continued counseling and helping Ireland, Canada, England, Denmark, Norway, Australia, China, Singapore, and the United States reshape their healthcare around robust primary care. Each nation has proceeded at their own pace, within their cultural traditions and tribal traditions.

⌐═⌐

American healthcare still has an iron grip on a financing system based on volume—not value. This inhibits the full potential of the developing *medical home* model to nurture *Trusted Healers*.

Why? When we compensate a practice for excellence, prevention, and value, it incentivizes physicians to fully implement the full *medical home* model. It provides resources and funding to accomplish it, especially the mental health component and prevention programs. Increased reimbursement creates thorough chronic disease monitoring. It enables carefully planned community and social services connections, and greater daily access to the care team.

As private insurers come to understand the benefits of quality care they will, for their own economic reasons, offer *medical homes* to employers. This will be a slow transformation because it is initially risky and expensive. These massive companies have boards of directors and millions of shareholders to satisfy.

Large insurers usually follow Medicare's decisions closely, but the entire reimbursement system must change from volume-based payment, and that is not yet where it needs to be.

But a tipping point has been reached. We can see that change on the horizon as evidenced by leaders like Dr. Glenn Steele, who has proven at Geisinger Health System, beyond the shadow of a doubt, that evidence-based medicine, reimbursing for value not volume, can drive higher quality and lower costs.

⌐═⌐

During the last five years of Paul's career at IBM, the international awards and recognition began to multiply. Primary care practices throughout America steadily embraced the developing *medical home* model. The *medical home* national accreditation program grew exponentially. Thousands of grateful *Trusted Healers* began to climb out of a very deep hole and regain their love for the practice of medicine.

Paul became one of the most decorated and honored physicians in history. See *Notes* in the back of *Trusted Healers* for the entire list.[22]

And he did one thing that everyone who knows Paul would have predicted.

He retired from IBM in 2018, took his wife, Hyewon, on a long-awaited, two-week vacation to Egypt, and then jumped right back into the transformation efforts he nurtured while leading the global transformation initiative. He took his road show to more than fifty cities on five continents to continue championing primary care. In less than nine months, he traveled to New Zealand twice, Ireland and England eight times, made three trips to Denmark, two trips to the United Arab Emirates, three to Saudi Arabia, four to Australia, and went to Singapore and Canada. In the States, he shuttled back and forth to Ohio, Colorado, Nebraska, California, Iowa, and to Chicago, New York City, Washington, DC, and other cities as needed. He was bringing healthcare reform to the people.

CHAPTER SEVEN

IT'S PERSONAL

B right ideas are candy to Paul, and few have been sweeter than Denmark's deployment of idle firefighters and rescue teams. Instead of waiting around the station for the next call, they visit frail elderly, evaluating their well-being, responding to the next rescue call from wherever they are. It is precisely this kind of effort—this simple but cutting-edge approach—that Paul mines and then spreads like gold dust in the wind.

Just as Paul loves Denmark's healthcare innovation, Denmark loves his worldwide advocacy. In 2014, Mary, Her Royal Highness the Crown Princess of Denmark, presented Paul one of the most prestigious honors in the world of healthcare. The princess is patron for Healthcare DENMARK. Paul became one of twelve experts and thought leaders from around the world so honored.

"With his reputation as a healthcare transformation and integrated care advocate, we are proud to have him as a Healthcare DENMARK ambassador," says Hans Erik Henriksen, CEO of Healthcare DENMARK.

Hans, a former IBM executive who has benefited by Paul's friendship and leadership for over a decade in Denmark, confirms that over sixty countries have taken interest in the Danish healthcare system, and that the tipping point has indeed been reached for a tremendous worldwide emphasis on the *medical home*. (They call them *primary care homes* in Western Europe.)

Hans Erik Henriksen

"A lot of the delegations we receive wish to know how we have developed primary care as we strive to do as much care as possible outside of the hospital. Around the world, the challenges of changing demographics, people living longer and getting more chronic diseases—the solution to that is not to build more hospitals. That is not sustainable from a Danish perspective," Hans says.

"Our solution is robust *primary care homes* that emphasize early detection of chronic diseases, and we place a high value on prevention, avoiding extensive surgeries and interventions later. Having Paul as an ambassador really helps. He makes a major difference around the world with his advisory relationships and guidance."

Paul does not offer any nation a full prescription of how to solve its problems. He asks questions. He suggests a better way, and then proves it. The rest is up to the culture. Then he repeatedly returns and restates the solution, until listening turns to action. Great ideas or innovations are fodder for him to spread and encourage even more breakthroughs.

Paul is unpretentious. He thoughtfully asks questions to help national leaders make good decisions. And sometimes, when he is asked a question, he has been known to say, "That is not the right question."

Paul also understands that reform comes from the bottom up, not the top down. Instead of waiting for the insurance world and our elected government to catch up, Paul focuses on the grassroots by helping *Trusted Healers* implement change at the point of care.

Paul prescribes building on bedrock a comprehensive network of primary care throughout the country. Putting patient health more fully in the hands of primary care decentralizes the control now held by corporations, insurance companies, hospitals, and healthcare networks. He envisions a day when sickness prevention is at its highest form with a *Trusted Healer* for every citizen. He sees a day, as Patrick J. Kennedy calls for, with full physical and mental health and addiction support staffed by a fulfilled, productive team that loves the practice of medicine.

Once such pillars are in place, we can easily move to universal care because we will have eliminated most of the waste, duplication and inappropriate use of our healthcare system. Paul understands that this evolution will take time and persistence. Cultures are slow to change, especially those dictated by powerful corporations serving their own interests.

In quiet moments, Paul tells stories that personalize the healthcare crusade. Reform is, at its core, about people. His reasons for advocating for a *medical home* are personal.

"I almost lost one of my best friends because the doctors treating him did not coordinate medications and he almost passed away from a drug interaction. That, and my father spent more money on end-of-life medical care than he made in his entire life. It was unnecessary. Hundreds of thousands of dollars spent for the last two weeks of life. Where was the *Trusted Healer*? Where was the *medical home*?"

Paul and his good friend and colleague John Crawford, IBM's European Healthcare leader, meet for coffee at the outside patio of the IBM South Bank Headquarters in London overlooking the Thames River on a sunny summer afternoon.

Later that afternoon, Paul has an appointment at Parliament with Jeremy

John Crawford

Hunt, who for six years as secretary of state for health and social care worked to transform England's primary care with Paul's regular guidance and counsel.

Sipping their coffee, Paul and John explain worldwide healthcare evolution.

"There's really three systems in the world actually," Paul says.

"Four if you count cash-paying-only healthcare," John adds.

Paul explains that after World War II, the only entity that could really build and run hospitals was government. So, Lord Beverage designed what is known as the Beverage Model in England, in which the government owns and runs the hospitals.

England became an example of mixing public and private healthcare. Every citizen was given the right to have public care of high quality, but some opt for care through the private sector. While bearing expensive insurance premiums, British citizens with private insurance can get faster care, a wider range of specialist treatments and more creature comforts, like private hospital rooms, and have the policy pick up any expenses not covered by the NHS. Nice, but fundamentally unnecessary.

Scandinavian countries adopted that same model. Denmark would be the extreme of that model, but there is basically no private care in that country because the public care is so good.

Paul notes that an even earlier model emerged out of Germany, named for the Prussian chancellor Otto von Bismarck, who invented the welfare state as part of the unification of Germany in the nineteenth century. Despite its European heritage, this system of providing healthcare would look familiar to Americans. The Bismarck model provided an employer-subsidized health insurance model.

That model was adopted in the US during World War II when there was a labor shortage and wages were frozen, Paul says. "And so government allowed insurance to be purchased for you or by you. That model is in most of Central Europe, Germany, Holland, France, Austria, Switzerland, but with exacting cost and price controls."

Another idea emerged out of the prairies in Canada after World War II, called the Douglas model. They call it *medicare,* in which the government provides care through taxation, but they do not own the private-sector hospitals. Canadians, for the most part, love it, but complain about elective surgical wait times and a weak preventive care emphasis.

President Johnson adopted that model, calling it the same name, *Medicare,* for Americans over age sixty-five, Paul says. "So, if you are under sixty-five in the United States, you have the Bismarck model [employer sponsored]. If you are employed, you have the Douglas model once you turn sixty-five, as predominate insurance provider [Medicare].

"If you are one of the ten million in the Veterans Administration, you have the Beverage model, where the government owns the hospitals [England, Ireland]. If you are poor, or under-insured, you become Medicaid or self-pay, frequently the only form of healthcare available in third world countries."

In his book *The Healing of America,* T. R. Reid, summed up the matrix of American healthcare better than anyone:

> It may be possible to provide fair and cost-effective healthcare for all while maintaining separate systems for the elderly, for the poor, for veterans, for renal-failure patients, for military personnel, for Native Americans, for working people, for members of Congress, and so on. It may be possible, but no country has ever made it work. That fragmented approach to healthcare clearly hasn't worked in the United States, which pays more and gets less in return than the rest of the industrialized world. And no other developed country wants to try it.

"So, we have all four systems and we have never had the political will to decide on any one of them," Paul says. He called it the "road-you-are-traveling" system. "What happens in most parts of the world is that if you are on a road going in one direction, you tend to stay in that direction. In World War II, government runs basically everything. So, they come out of the war and that's the road they are on. It wasn't an ideological thing. It was just the road they are on."

⌐⌐

In fairness, it's important to acknowledge that while every developed nation except the US has a universal healthcare system that provides care to everyone regardless of income, consumers in these nations demand changes all the time. Every nation shapes its care delivery differently as its population and economies grow. Griping seems normal, everywhere. All universal healthcare systems face cost pressures. But the happiest nations are those with robust primary care, where people know their *Trusted Healer.*

"The very happiest people are the British, the Danes, the Scandinavian nations, the French, the Germans and Singaporeans. Americans usually show up on surveys as the unhappiest, yet many profess that we have the best healthcare anywhere. That may be so, for some," John Crawford says.

Ask the hardworking US laborers who cannot afford to use the insurance they pay for every month because of high deductibles and co-pays how happy they are, or the hourly employees who cannot afford insurance at all and have to find a free clinic for care, choosing between food and the pharmaceuticals.

Paul and John explain the Scandinavian phenomenon.

"All the Nordic countries are kind of broadly similar in the way they think about things, like social equity. Equity through education, healthcare, aging—they pay quite a high price through taxation [Denmark is approximately 55 percent], but they also rank very high on the happiness scale," John says.

Most get free education up to the first degree. Medical school is free all the way through, Paul notes. They view higher rates as an investment in their quality of life.

Paul tells the story of sitting next to a lady on a flight to Scandinavia. He asked her what she did for a living and where she was going. She worked in a senior home taking care of the elderly. She loved taking care of old people.

"And I am thinking of my own experiences in the US with nursing homes," Paul recalls. "The nurses and aides endure very low paying wages and thin benefits. Turnover is horrible. Yet she [the elderly caregiver] doesn't have to worry about healthcare, a decent pension or education for her children—all the basics are taken care of, so it's just not as important that she earn a lot of money. She finds joy in her job."

John Crawford adds that the UK also has a pretty good work-life balance. Norway and Denmark also stress this. Those countries vie for the top happiness ranking across most surveys and measurements.

Bidding adieu to John, Paul heads for the London borough of Newham, just east of the center of the city, to a territory called "Ham," which was first chartered in the year 956. Today, the poverty rate there hovers around 37 percent and its residents speak many languages.

Paul next plans to meet with lay member for patient engagement Wayne Farah and several of his associates. In Great Britain, experienced civilians guide the funding stream for health and social care—not governmental officials. Wayne is one of those people.

Paul arranged for his colleague Kanav Hasija to join the meeting as well. Kanav's organization, Innovaccer Inc., develops technology that brings in real-time new information to the primary care physician—data like social factors, insurance usage, and connections with ERs. Kanav wants Paul to show him firsthand the pain the GPs experience in England.

England provides a wonderful crucible to prove new technology being developed by Innovaccer, technology that aims to connect all the data silos in healthcare while making it actionable and valuable. In collaboration with everyone in the care delivery ecosystem, the goal is to save costs and lives by unleashing the right data at the right time.

Healthcare in England is universal. Everyone enjoys excellent care, regardless of social rank. And, in the UK, social care and healthcare are both universal. The Brits would never think of separating them as we do in America. So much of health is driven by social determinants, such as poverty, welfare, living conditions, mental and behavioral health, drug abuse, alcoholism, and family history of violence.

Kanav's technology brings all of this data into its modern healthcare platform. There, it performs a multidimensional analysis of clinical and social data. Using advanced analytics in the same way as Google and Amazon, it pushes the most important insights into the physician's workflow at the point of care.

This is a system that augments the intelligence of the doctor and the electronic health record with more comprehensive insights. Through insurance documents, doctors can see other medical visits by the patient, testing performed, pharmaceuticals, X-rays, social care actions, hospitalizations, previous diagnoses, and so on. This augmented intelligence resides right on top of the EHR, in bullet form to cue the doctor's interest.

"Kanav stands at a historical point of inflection," Paul notes, explaining that Innovaccer is developing this new system based on a whole new way of looking at information, like Alexander Graham Bell did with the telephone.

Great Britain secretary of state for health and social care Jeremy Hunt becomes an Innovaccer believer when Paul introduces him to Kanav Hasija. A big frustration in the UK is the lack of communication between social services and medical services. The system has not aligned. Information is missing. Hasija's new technology proposes to merge the social care systems in the UK with its medical system, potentially providing a more comprehensive medical portfolio on patients.

Paul calls the new system an "inflection point" for the primary care physician, a historic moment in creating the system the *Trusted Healer* needs at the point of care.

Adrienne White

We contact Adrienne White, vice president of growth enablement at Innovaccer, to discuss the significance of this new technology in depth.

Adrienne first met Paul when she joined IBM, about the time Paul and his colleagues formed the PCPCC. Fascinated with what he was doing, she reached out to him to learn more. Soon after, she found herself on assignment with Paul as a product and offering manager in IBM's care coordination solution group. She spent over a year on his intensive tour of *medical homes* all across the nation. When asked about the time she spent with Paul, she says it was the most fun of any work in her life. "So much learning and excitement!"

"When I first joined Innovaccer, I went to India to meet with the formative team there," she recalls. She says that they have been looking for solutions to a key problem in healthcare around the world—the problem that all these different systems of information cannot talk to each other. "It's called interoperability. The doctors are practicing medicine with 40 to 50 percent of the information they need because of this."

Innovaccer seems to have solved this problem, she says. "It's an amazing breakthrough because it enables real-time augmented intelligence, putting Innovaccer at least five years ahead of the field."

"Innovaccer is developing a source of truth for the GP," Paul notes. With a system like this in place, the doctor will have every piece of information needed to serve as a *Trusted Healer* for the patient. "It's a whole new way of looking at it."

⌒⌒

Next up on Paul's jaunt through the UK is the visit with Wayne Farah at his spartan but immaculate offices in Newham East London, the region of the city home to the 2012 Olympics. Wayne has lived in Newham for more than twenty-five years and has experience as a policy officer in local government. He is a local community organizer who has led groups that monitor policing and racist attacks (similar to Black Lives Matter), promote refugee and migrant rights, and deliver social housing.

He runs marathons, which undoubtedly fuels his energy and passion.

We are here to see what pain the GPs feel at ground level. Wayne helps guide the NHS Newham Clinical Commissioning Group (CCG), responsible for purchasing and quality assuring the full range of NHS services for the local community.

"My role is vice chair and non-executive director for patient and public engagement. As a lay person, I seek to ensure that the local community is engaged in their local NHS and that their interests are represented," Wayne says. The CCG represents fifty-two practices for about 400,000 people in the borough; "but we are already at least eighty-one GPs short. The local population is growing fast, and the GP community is shrinking, with almost a third of local GPs approaching retirement age," he adds.

"We operate in a local health economy in financial crisis," Wayne says to Paul and Kanav. Wayne explains that the local health economy is unbalanced. Over 90 percent of the activity is in primary care, but 90 percent of resources are spent in acute care. Local health challenges are those that require primary interventions and care closer to home, but the budgets and incentives don't support the redirecting of resources to where they are most needed.

"This is even more true in relation to prevention," he says. "We love our general practitioners, and they deliver great care, but too often they practice in out-of-date facilities.

"Services and pathways are not always properly integrated, coordinated, or designed around the patients, so patients can struggle to access services, manage their own care, and to comply with treatment plans."

There are over 140 languages spoken by students in Newham schools. There is a ten-year difference in life expectancy between the wealthiest and poorest parts of the borough. The borough "represents the largest urban regeneration project in Western Europe," he notes, "and the vast deprivation here is masked by that."

GPs see about thirty patients a day, budgeting about ten minutes per patient plus telephone calls, home visits and clinics on different days. Patients should have access to health professional in primary care within forty-eight hours. But waits can get much longer to see their own GP, highly valued by those with long-term conditions who need continuity of care.

Most have an automated registration system as you sign in, which lets you know what exam room to go to and when—reminiscent of going to a Division of Motor Vehicles office in the States.

Wayne explains that the data they receive comes way too late to be useful. "We need live data. That's what's most attractive to us about the *primary care home.*"

Kanav nods. He sees the direct connection where his technology could solve a nationwide problem.

"GPs cannot track where their patients are in the system. They make referrals for specialist diagnostics or consultations but don't know where patients are in the system, or what has been done. Patients end up having multiple appointments and tests every time they see a clinician," Wayne says.

"*Primary care home* is attractive because it promotes integration, multidisciplinary work and care coordination. It is led from primary care, with the GP at the heart of the system," Wayne notes.

Wayne says that the primary care givers are over-scrutinized and underappreciated.

He says they need the local health economies and GPs to be given the investment to build the *primary care home* that meets local needs and priorities.

"One size will not fit all," Wayne says, "but nationally NHS often seeks to micromanage. We need some protected space to line up our resources for the *primary care home*. We need a business plan so the organization can be ready when it's our turn. Clinicians are very receptive about the *primary care home* model. They have a long history of working collectively and want to have a go at it."

Wayne notes that GPs know they need to develop local solutions for local communities that deliver prevention, integrated services, and coordinated care closer to home. They need the NHS to support them by helping to redirect resources from secondary to primary care.

The Brits are tough. They wade through frustrations—proud, abrasive, but seem willing to ride it out without anger.

The next stop for Paul is Parliament to meet with Secretary of Health and Social Care Jeremy Hunt. As we ride the tube, Paul tells of how he was summoned by the secretary.

Jeremy was a healthcare heavyweight who was about to have an even bigger footprint in the healthcare crusade. His resume was a ladder to the top of UK bureaucracy. He graduated from Oxford University with an honors degree in politics, philosophy, and economics. He then worked for a management consultancy firm before going to Japan for two years where he taught English and learned Japanese. Upon his return to the UK, Jeremy set up his own educational publishing business, and a charity to help AIDS orphans in Africa, in which he continues to play an active role.

He first became a member of Parliament in 2005, and held a string of positions, which included serving as minister for disabled people, and secretary of state for culture media and sport, and later secretary of state for health.

Paul had given Jeremy a copy of *The Familiar Physician* at a conference he was attending, and the two remained in contact. Paul told Jeremy that he was flying to London to begin conversations about moving toward *primary care homes*.

Jeremy said that he had some legislation in Parliament to do just that.

"And I said, 'Please don't do that,'" Paul recalls. "Let's reach out to the GPs and ask them to tell you how the *primary care home* can improve their practices and then select the most devoted GPs and have them pilot the idea. Then, once proven, let everyone have a go."

In other words, let the doctors make the call. That's the process Paul insisted on in the US. Jeremy agreed wholeheartedly and set about planning the pilots throughout the nation. As we meet with the secretary, the Brits have engineered 220 active *primary care home* pilots throughout Great Britain, led by the National Association of Primary Care.

As Paul makes his way to meet Jeremy at Parliament in July, Jeremy is about to be named secretary of state for foreign and commonwealth affairs.

Part Two

TALES OF
THREE NATIONS

CHAPTER EIGHT

UNLOCKING GPS

J eremy Hunt is tall, probably six foot two or so, and offers, like Paul, a ready smile and a playful wit, so the chemistry between Paul and the secretary is quite warm.

Paul congratulates Jeremy on his latest appointment and introduces him to Kanav Hasija, who is traveling with us.

"So my colleague Kanav is perfecting the use of artificial intelligence, natural language processing, all of the innovations we were developing at IBM when I retired. I recently had a chance to see it in a clinic, actually at the point of care with the doc. Thank God we are out of the *Age of Healthcare Information* and into the *Age of Healthcare Intelligence*," Paul says.

Paul first met Kanav in San Francisco, having just retired from IBM; Paul had asked colleagues to name the most innovative technology they had seen in supporting and taking away the pain in primary care. "Everyone pointed to this new technological leap at Innovaccer, and then introduced me to Kanav Hasija, one of the founders. When I met with him, I was pleased to see that, when he is not on an airplane, he often visits London."

Kanav is Indian by nationality, but he spends some time in San Francisco and some time in New Delhi. His sister lives in London.

"The foundations of our company come from our belief that data needs to be in the right hands, at the right point. Primary care is the right hands," Kanav says to Jeremy. "To take care of the patient and heal the patient. The new technology does not require a change in the EHR. It augments it."

Dr. Paul Grundy, Jeremy Hunt, and Kanav Hasija at Parliament

As the meeting with Jeremy progresses, members of Parliament tap on the conference room door periodically, apparently urging Jeremy to conclude his private meeting with us. There are muffled grumblings outside. His administrative assistant *harrumphs*. Jeremy does not blink.

"And the next big piece is communication between the patient, the healer and insurance. When communication is solved between all of them, concurrently, the patient is benefiting," Kanav explains to the secretary. "So, the data communication piece, in this new age of Google and Amazon and Facebook, why can't it be in healthcare as well?"

"I brought Kanav here to go down to the practice level and see the pain of your GPs, so we can keep them from burning out," Paul says. "Right up at the top of the screen will be the things that the primary care doctor needs to effectively manage that patient, information that they need, way beyond the medical record, which can then engage in social services as well."

"Yes," Kanav says. "I met clinical leaders over the past two days, both from England and Ireland, and I showed them what we do, and they were really excited. They just need the right incentive to use this technology."

When Jeremy asks for an explanation of how this works, Kanav explains that a GP just clicks on the red-and-silver logo in the right-hand corner of the EHR screen to reveal critical information about the patients—Innovaccer insights that are derived from multiple applications (with clinical, financial and social data), effectively connecting the whole system together.

"I was meeting with the doctors from Ireland where in one region, they have one hospital with fifteen GP practices around it. We can bring all their data into one platform. And then communicate all that data back to all the stakeholders. They have never had this before," Kanav says. He explains the value of this medical intelligence from a practical point of view.

"So, this GP doesn't know that the patient that just walks in went to an emergency room twenty times this year. That's bad. This GP doesn't know that this patient also visited three more GPs, which is very risky. All the information the GP doesn't have today, but they need, is something we get to them. And to the insurer."

This is precisely the sort of disconnect Paul has been trying to mend.

Jeremy notes that this very goal matches up with what his colleagues at the National Health Service aim to do and that they have a plan in place to integrate the GP record with secondary care and social care.

"You're presuming to have a platform to make that happen, is that correct?"

"From my perspective," Paul says to Jeremy. "I am really trying to connect the data and put it in the hands of *Trusted Healers* to make it actionable."

Jeremy looks at his stenographer and asks her to make a connection for Kanav.

"Matilda, contact Simon please."

His assistant makes a note to get in touch with Simon Stevens, the top executive at NHS.

"Kanav, I will help you do that. It sounds like a fantastic piece of technology. We will put you in touch with the guy who is precisely in charge of this for NHS England. I just secured money for NHS, and doing the right thing with the technology is one of our big priorities, and now we have got to find it."

"I listened to your last speech," Paul says.

"You have listened to me give quite a few speeches, Paul. I get a rough time . . . from the GP community. They are, as I said, not very happy."

"I have met, in my travels around the country the last few times, some GPs I can guarantee you are much happier than they used to be," Paul says.

"Good. I think they are. I felt, to be honest, the morale issues are more pronounced in general practice," Jeremy says.

Paul responds that GPs face intense difficulties—the pressures come from all directions.

"We need to figure out how to take some of that burden off, help the caregivers become a team with the *primary care home* model, as England now plans—provide complete information at the point of care," Paul says. "There are two things that doctors should be doing with their time: difficult diagnostic dilemmas and relationships. And when I look at your practices, they are spending about a third of their time doing that. You know, two-thirds of the time they are scribing.

That's a ridiculous use of doctors' time."

He suggests the use of medical assistants for more documentation and administrative tasks.

Jeremy nods. "Yes, yes."

Paul offers another powerful resource to Great Britain.

"So, the other thing I am doing is helping a nonprofit I joined after I left IBM, HealthTeamWorks, and frankly I have spent more time both here and in Ireland than I have back in the States. We currently are also helping the Chinese and the Irish," Paul notes.

He explains that this new company has helped put together some highly experienced leaders to help cultures transform their care. This team of experts, pulled from successes in America and abroad, is creating a digital learning experience at the practice level, so as to make it much more affordable to transform to the *medical home* or *primary care home.*

"So, working with Kanav, we really can get to the data, and, working with distance learning with a sophisticated interactive learning center, we are hoping we can brand it with National Association of Primary Care here in Great Britain."

We discuss the next stage in what Jeremy affectionately refers to as *The Familiar Physician* revolution.

"I feel this is something we used to have in this country, but we have lost it," Jeremy says. "The idea that you should have a doctor who knows you and your family and can therefore make, you know, smart judgments about what things are likely to be, and, you know, understanding mental health because they understand family context. All of that really struck a chord with me. And I have been trying really hard to promote it here, but probably with mixed results if I am truthful."

Jeremy learns about this book and its title, *Trusted Healers,* which reminds him of another Grundy-inspired text.

"Well, I was given a copy of *The Familiar Physician* in 2015," Jeremy says, looking at Paul. "And there was a business card inside it with a friendly message from Paul. I was on holiday in California, where I read it. And we had just won the election, so I was back in office, and I was thinking, what's the next stage? I am not a physician. I have no clinical background, which has good points and bad points." One good point, he says, is that "you look at things from the point of view of the patient."

Jeremy says that the general practitioners are beloved in Great Britain and are one of the most notable attributes of the country's National Health Service. "But it had lost its magic." He says to Paul, "What really inspired me was that you seemed [in *The Familiar Physician* book] to be talking about how to get that magic back."

The wonderful thing that primary care doctors have is continuity of relationship with their patients, Jeremy says. They are part of that community. And that's what makes it a magical job.

"So, if you allow your system to deteriorate to the extent that, actually, they don't have those relationships anymore and they are just seeing, you know, forty patients a day at ten minutes a shot coming through, going to work is like being on a hamster wheel. You are really losing there," Jeremy says.

He credits *The Familiar Physician* for helping him to understand the clinical benefits of the *primary care home.*

"What is incredible is that in just three years—to see it has mushroomed. We started with just a few practices and it has mushroomed to 14 percent of the population of England now covered by GPs doing the *primary care home.* And people talk about it. And they don't think it's a foreign concept."

General practitioners, he says, don't think it's being imposed by politicians. They actually think it's unlocking what everyone always wanted GPs to be.

"It's a great lesson how Paul has achieved that quiet revolution and momentum."

The impatient *tap-tap-tap-tap* on the conference room door starts up again. This time, a rather red-faced envoy enters, interrupting our meeting. When the door opens, we see a rather large crowd of members of Parliament with agitated body language, murmuring loudly. The envoy goes to Matilda and whispers something. She *harrumphs*. The envoy leaves. Jeremy pauses and there is some nonverbal communication with his assistant, but then he continues, unfazed.

"We actually have two or three approaches that are taking root," Jeremy begins again, with matchless poise. "It's probably the single thing that is giving hope to general practice, because one of the problems they have is that they are funded through a capitation model. [A capitation contract pays a physician or group of physicians a set amount for each enrolled person assigned, per period of time, whether or not that person seeks care.] That needs to change. Unlike hospitals, where you've got fee for service, we've got payment by results."

What that means, the secretary explains, is that as demand goes up in the system with the aging population, hospitals feel pressure, but they get paid more for the more work they do. By contrast, GPs must absorb the extra work with the funding that they have.

"So, some of the insights in this, about how you can actually reduce burnout, I think this is going to be the key to our recruitment and retention going forward," Jeremy says.

Our time expires. We crack the door and the gates burst forth with rowdy legislators filing into the room. We bid good-bye to the secretary of state for foreign and commonwealth affairs for Great Britain.

Following the meeting, Paul sends a congratulatory message to Jeremy Hunt. He receives a message from Jeremy in response: *Thank you, Paul! But I will miss Health and always treasure the brilliant work we did together.*

CHAPTER NINE

UK HEALTHCARE OK

Dr. Paul Grundy and Professor James Kingsland at the White House

No matter where you travel in the world of primary care in Western Europe, you encounter Paul and Professor James Kingsland OBE, either through their teachings and policies or because they are physically present at some medical conference.

Professor Kingsland and colleague Dr. Nav Chana are the most prominent physician champions of the *primary care home* in England. Dr. Chana is president of the European Association of Primary Care

Partners and immediate past chair of England's National Primary Care Association. Always cheerful, he brings the latest, ongoing, detailed research on the financial impact of the *primary care home.*

Professor Kingsland is president of the National Association of Primary Care, the primary care lead for the Faculty of Disaster Medicine for India and Nepal, and he coordinates the International Forum for Primary Care, of which the NAPC and PCPCC are "founder" members.

One of the highest civilian awards from the queen was presented to him at the queen's New Year 2012 Honours. He was appointed OBE for medicine and healthcare services. OBE stands for officer of the Most Excellent Order of the British Empire, a lifelong title. In June 2018, he was appointed an honorary clinical professor within the School of Medicine at the University of Central Lancashire.

Professor Kingsland is also senior partner in an award-winning general practice in North West England. He devotes his professional time between clinical practice, national advisory roles, and company boards and is the co-creator of the *primary care home.* He is the resident doctor for the late show on BBC Radio Merseyside and has provided a regular live interactive program for the BBC for sixteen years, making him the longest-serving BBC radio doctor, covering the widest range of health issues raised by the listening public.

We interview Professor Kingsland at the 2018 Annual Meeting of the PCPCC in Washington, DC, to hear his assessment of healthcare in the UK and reforms that are needed.

"The reason we love our GPs so is history. General practice predates the National Health Service. So, the generalist, community-based physician predates it by tens and tens of years," Professor Kingsland says.

The people of England have had a love affair with general practitioners for over forty years. The populace considers healthcare to be one of England's greatest achievements. England is one of the lowest-cost systems in the world, with one of the highest satisfaction levels among developed nations.

Great Britain is just now adopting the *primary care home*, incorporating its GP network in the National Health Service. The United States began this process in 2006, so England can benefit from what America has done well and avoid what America has not.

Americans can look across the Atlantic and see what it's like to have a universal healthcare system and take a closer look at challenges under this system of care. If America one day makes the transition, we can take some of the mystery out of the process.

So, how can England's GPs be so beloved and so much in crisis at the same time?

The Brits share many of the same problems primary care doctors face in America—

not enough funding to expand into a full-scale *medical home*, time demands of an ever- growing chronic-care patient population, time demands of the electronic health record, physician burnout, being trapped in a practice organization that is extraordinarily inefficient. Yet, they remain wedded to the GP being the primary care provider.

When the Brits' National Health Service (NHS) was created in 1948, there was recognition that the country needed to retain its best GPs and to create reasonable-sized patient panels for the general practitioner.

"In very round figures, even now we know that 90 percent of all contact within the NHS occurs in the community, with most of that in general practice. Yet less than 9 percent of the total cost of the NHS is invested in that sector, in community services and general practice," Professor Kingsland says.

"Any other industry would say that is the most efficient part of our industry and we've got to beef that up. We've not really done that since the NHS was created."

Professor Kingsland explains that the UK's healthcare costs measure up very well in worldwide comparisons—largely because of the vast number of people who get "finished care episodes" in their community rather than from a hospital-based system, which can cost ten times the amount for the same care.

When we interview him, he has just made a presentation to the powerful group of world leaders called the International Forum for Primary Care, where delegates from many developed nations meet regularly to share the current healthcare situation in their countries. Among his key messages, "The solution is out there. It may not be locked into a single system."

He elaborates, "There is not *the* perfect system. There's never the perfect set of circumstances. I have not found it internationally, and it certainly doesn't exist in the NHS, despite the Commonwealth Fund's *Mirror Mirror* international comparative analysis, which shows the NHS at the top of the pile.

"But if we incrementally build on the experience of what has been successful, what's recognized as the best, we may just develop something that is longer lasting than our reforms to date and something that provides the transformational care that we are all seeking."

Professor Kingsland has been working within and for the British primary care system diligently since the late '80s. He observes that transformation works when you look at it as a process over a considerable period.

"Transformation, actually, is not quick. Ultimately, progressive change is a well-managed set of sequential experiments with the expectation that you will fail at times and that you will need to recalibrate, correct, and then continue. No one gets it right the first time, and you need to keep on testing and prepare for variable feedback.

"If you don't plan to create something in the long term, then you will always try a short-term fix, and then transformation rarely works.

The notion of 'let's just try and change a system completely over a short period of time' is lazy thinking. A multi-year process can be exhausting work, and the teams that do the work must be well prepared for this."

Professor Kingsland notes that forty years have now passed since primary care was elevated to an important sector in the healthcare system with the Alma-Ata declaration, endorsed at the International Conference on Primary Health Care in 1978. That pivotal conference held in Almaty, Kazakhstan, brought together health experts and world leaders to commit to health for all. The Alma-Ata declaration formed the foundation for future global primary healthcare efforts.

The worldwide belief in *Trusted Healers* took another step forward at the Global Conference on Primary Health Care in Astana, Kazakhstan, in October 2018. A new declaration emphasized the critical role of primary healthcare around the world. The declaration aims to refocus efforts on primary healthcare to ensure that everyone everywhere can enjoy the highest possible attainable standard of health.[23]

⌒

When money gets tight, a secretary of state or a government or a system will revert to protecting their preference, and that is usually the hospital sector, Professor Kingsland laments.

"So, if we are hoping for a major cultural shift and behavioral change in healthcare delivery—not least, if we are going to sustain reform—then you need to have payment reform and then institutional reform," he says.

For example, he suggests that the outpatient department in hospitals is an outmoded, probably largely obsolete way of delivering care. Outpatient departments were created in the eighteenth century as a holding place for people entering hospitals. They were never intended to function as service delivery. Yet, they persevere.

"It is an expensive waste of time and money to provide routine follow-ups. As opposed to day-case surgery, which can be a more efficient use of an outpatient environment. So, we need to determine whether in the future we build hospitals with outpatient services or don't have an outpatient department—or downsize it," he says.

Professor Kingsland describes the difficulty with the public perception of an effective care service. When it is suggested that the government is going to invest in more community services, that the range of community care will be expanded, but as a result part of the hospital must close, it is opposed.

"The first person chained to the railings of the hospital saying 'Protect our hospital' is the local member of Parliament. That is followed closely by their most vociferous constituents," he says.

"So, it's very difficult, then, in that scenario, when a secretary of state says, 'We must invest more in primary care.' Often this investment has to be *instead of* rather than *as well as* the current care service."

While the UK still grapples with shedding the old, its neighbor Denmark has become a beacon of modern medicine delivery. So, why hasn't Great Britain adopted more of that nation's primary care strategies and practices?

Professor Kingsland offers the view that the NHS has a "debilitating syndrome." One reason why British culture doesn't adopt and spread exemplars or service developments is that "they are not made here." A new care system designed and created in Liverpool for its residents might work in Liverpool, but it might be difficult to implement in Manchester less than forty miles away.

"Too often our approach to innovation is to keep inventing new models of care rather than adopting and spreading current best practice. Paradoxically, a system created in Denmark might be more readily seen to apply here despite very different healthcare structures and funding," Professor Kingsland says.

The truth is, the UK often knows what works from previous reforms. The problem is overcoming political cycles or the reform cycles that call for changing everything instead of just those parts that are broken. Sweeping reforms scare people and take tremendous political will.

Thus, Paul's advice to his physician colleagues in the UK was to launch pilot programs for the *primary care home* all over the country and let the leading GPs try the experience. It's a bottom-up organic approach rather than a top-down political imperative.

Professor Kingsland notes that England's 220 pilots have, as Paul suggested, created a learning network for the *primary care home* that provides information, tools and support—not funding.

"Our evaluations are showing that it is well received by patients both in improving access and reducing waiting times, so the overall experience of care is improving. Similarly the people who are providing the care are saying they enjoy working in this new environment with a team-based approach, much more than they did in the smaller units. We are also starting to get some early improvement in a range of quality indicators that is quite encouraging," he says.

"The issues we hear about the most in the NHS are waiting times and access to care services. People don't generally complain about the technical competency of their physician. They don't necessarily complain about the interaction they have. What they complain about is how long it takes to get an appointment. And how local it is to where they live."

"NHS England, the governing body for the NHS in our country, is now reviewing the best way to expand this system that clearly is successful and is becoming the preferred model of first contact primary care," he adds.

We ask the professor what he would tell Queen Elizabeth if Her Majesty asked about the state of primary care today in the UK.

"I would say, 'Well, Your Majesty, we've never had a better opportunity to focus efforts to extend care in the community setting . . . certainly since the creation of the Internal Market in 1990, in fact, since we created the NHS.' I would explain that finally, our national focus recognizes that universal health cannot be delivered through a hospital-based system. Our peoples' wishes and needs are for care that is locally based.

"Ma'am, people want to have their complex technical care in the hospital but want most of their care provided by a responsive, local team close to where they live or at home when needed."

Professor Kingsland says he would remind the Queen of the *primary care home*. Lower costs. More efficient. Better response. Better access. Better patient experience. Improved outcomes if you have a good primary care system. Better team satisfaction.

"This may be our last chance to rejuvenate the NHS, ma'am. To make this sustainable, we've got to hold our nerve through probably another two or three political cycles before we get to what we think will be full maturity in this model. We could use your endorsement," he says.

"As you well know, ma'am, 'free at the point of need' healthcare provision in the UK is one of our proudest achievements, post-Second World War. It's the most loved public service that Britain has. Our brand, the NHS, is internationally respected for its ability to deliver care, which is not based on anyone's ability to pay. It's a brand and a name that our current society has grown up with and has high expectations for.

"If we just pay lip service to the expansion of primary care in the NHS and we continue to focus most of our investment on hospital-based services—we may not lose our National Health Service, but we may not be able to continue funding it through income tax alone."

England is in a good position today to move the *primary care home* into full-scale adoption because its version of the *medical home* was developed by utilizing a strong organizational memory and reflecting on what had worked in the past, Professor Kingsland says—not trying harder at what has failed.

"But sometimes we do go around in circles and try to reinvent the flat tire," he notes.

Today, thanks to the strong influence of our international forum, and particularly Paul, we are taking primary care to the next stage, with the *primary care home* fitting into a more international view. Yet, Professor Kingsland cautions, "In its current form, the NHS may be drinking at the 'last chance saloon'—the last chance to strengthen primary care before it potentially falls over. We all are seeing a rapid change from general practitioners working full time just in the last ten years. There has been a huge drift from full-time work to part-time and portfolio work."

GPs are becoming overstretched with the pressures of being self-employed independent contractors, with responsibilities as employers and running a small business, as well as delivering their medical service. There is increasing administrative work and contractual change, which doesn't create the best environment for discussing reform and prompting change.

"As we are seeing a move to more GPs taking salaried positions and changing to sessional work, we are starting to lose some of the efficiencies of the self-employed contractor. We are encountering recruitment problems, on the back of all the increasing demand on the system, low morale and increasing expectations on the service. With the cost of new technology and treatments, societal demographic changes, and the increasing number of people living longer but with more long-term conditions, we have not prepared well or consistently to meet these challenges which we have known about and been discussing for at least the last twenty years."

"Sometimes," he quips, "the more you talk about it without definitive action, the more you could be seen to be admiring the problem rather than dealing with it."

In 2018, for the first time since 2010, the NHS has received guaranteed funding uplifts over the next five years and in particular "ring-fenced funding" for primary and community care services. Prof. Kingsland views this as the perfect opportunity to advance the *primary care home* to its full potential.

Despite austerity budgets, funding challenges and timidity about changing the way healthcare is delivered, "some say we still have the best healthcare service in the world. And yes, we do deliver high quality care most of the time," he observes.

"What we have, and this is significant, is a service that is free at the point of need—not based on anybody's ability to pay. Now, there are always going to be people who occasionally fall through the gaps, are not registered with a GP, fall out of contact with care services or are not adequately provided with the care they need. But it is a relatively small number.

"People who need care do not have to pay for it," he explains. "The NHS is largely a tax-funded system. Having said that, the NHS has always had some modest payments within the systems. Prescription charges, but many with exemptions, anticipatory treatments for foreign travel, administrative support for non-NHS care; and some people may say, 'I paid for the car park in the hospital. Is that a charge?'"

Professor Kingsland explains that the NHS also has some rare charges and cost-recovery schemes, for example for ambulance costs from those causing injury to others. If you have a traffic accident, some charges may apply.

For most health needs, patients get unlimited care from their registered general practice, whenever their GP service is open. The GP contract currently requires daily office hours from 8:00 a.m. to 6:30 p.m. Outside of contractual hours, people then get a free service from out-of-hours primary care or urgent care services. When registered, patients can go as needed, every day of the week, every day of the year—at no cost.

If a GP surgery is closed, there are urgent care centers or hospitals' accident and emergency care—at no cost. If a GP thinks that you need a hospital colleague for an opinion or an operation, they refer you; you're seen as a patient, and you have the procedure—at no cost.

"That is something to savor and not to lose," Professor Kingsland says.

England usually shows up in international studies as one of the lowest-cost healthcare systems per capita in high-income countries.

"I prefer to think the reason why we can do that is because the vast majority of care is managed in the primary care sector," he says. "We use the public research firm Ipsos MORI, which, on behalf of NHS England, does an annual survey, and quite a big sample, of people's experience of general practice."

The survey evaluates the 7,000 or so general practices in the country, asking a wide range of questions about responsiveness, quality of service, quality of healer, access through reception, and overall satisfaction of the service.

"We have over 90 percent of our *customers* say they are delighted with what they receive. Something's going pretty well in general practice, in what is still an evolving service, and it's consistent year-on-year. There's always some variance, but only a small variance in a highly regarded service. The main concern is generally about access, and this is where any criticism usually lies, but it's still pretty responsive."

As one of the most recognized physicians in the United Kingdom, Professor Kingsland's opinions resonate.

"When I am on the BBC, it's a call-in program. You ring the show and ask anything you want to ask," he says. "A lot of the phone calls I get are just qualifying something they have heard in the media or previously discussed with a clinician."

Callers most often cite that they didn't have enough time with their doctor to fully understand their condition, treatment, or medication, he observes. This suggested that primary care does a good job but may be a bit squeezed in the amount of time available to explain things fully.

"It's the demand on the system which often dictates the amount of time that you have with people. And it's interesting that my radio interviews are often just qualifying a bit of information, not asking for a second opinion, never complaining about the service they have had, even though they have called to have a chat with the doctor on the radio.

"It's not, 'I had a bad service, I need somebody else to tell me,' it's 'I had a good service, I just didn't have long enough time and I still have another question and you happened to be on the radio, so I'll ring you.'"

This sentiment seems to be widely shared.

Claire Oatway

We interview Claire Oatway, who agreed to some time with us at the Health+Care event in London.

A knowledgeable and energetic super-practice manager in England, Claire stands at the forefront of implementing the *primary care home* in her practice operation in Plymouth, along the southwestern coast. The viewpoints of a practice manager in transition to the *primary care home* indicate the progress of the transformation.

Claire manages Beacon Medical Group, a super-practice supporting more than 30,000 patients in Plymouth and South Devon. Super-practices often operate from a number of different sites within an area, with staff working across sites.

Claire explains that in 2015, the Vanguard scheme piloting *primary care homes* across the nation was launched, with Paul's help.

"At the beginning, I felt we needed more on this *primary care home* model. I got in touch with Paul and miraculously within twenty-four hours, he arrived. It was a blustery, wintery day in February in Plymouth, and he stayed for a couple of days." Plymouth is a beautiful community with a fascinating history. The first record of the existence of a settlement at Plymouth was in the Domesday Book in 1086. In 1254, it gained status as a town and in 1439 became the first town in England to be granted a charter by Parliament.

After a tour of Plymouth, Paul visited Claire's office and told the staff how technology being developed now would make their jobs easier.

"Ever since, he has been helping us to network with places in the States, and to have conversations and learn things that we never thought we could have," Claire says. "We found ourselves among the first fifteen practices selected for the *primary care home*. We knew that practices like us were grappling with big, knotty problems. So, on one of Paul's later visits, we arranged a closed-door meeting."

Paul heard the GPs express that they didn't know how to talk to the hospital people in one area, and the hospital people in another area were saying they didn't know how to talk to these GPs.

"Paul managed to keep us all going, inspiring the physicians, telling us all, 'You've got all the answers you need.'"

Now, after meeting with Paul, "we feel like we are in a protected space now to be innovative, and relationships are more comfortable. It's really energizing," Claire says. "I am not a clinician, I am a super-practice manager. And I know that trying to disrupt the clinical model is sometimes quite hard. We learned from Paul to bring the evidence to everyone, creating a space where practice managers are thriving, contributing ideas, and communicating with each other."

Ireland's situation, on the other hand, could be described as troubled.

CHAPTER TEN

NO PAIN, NO GAIN

I reland has struggled with a frustrating healthcare system for a long time. The country has a beloved GP system and embraces a form of universal care very much like America's Veterans Health Administration model. But the Irish have not transformed their beloved GPs into a robust primary care core.

Paul has visited Ireland for years, teaming up with a talented group of inspired healthcare and government leaders to advocate the creation of an advanced primary care system for the nation. Doing so would solve most of the nation's healthcare problems, especially hospital overcrowding. Irish news media describe healthcare in 2018 as the worst year in history.

Kevin McGowan

One of Paul's key crusaders for this nation's primary care has been Kevin McGowan, an IBM senior manager in Ireland. Kevin is the strategy and integration manager. He ensures that local operations support and continually transform to meet business needs as a globally integrated enterprise. Kevin also helps with healthcare thought leadership, where he has over eleven years of experience. The company has a relatively small leadership contingency in Ireland, but still encourages them to help the culture at every opportunity.

Kevin works closely with the IBM Watson Health division's development team located in Dublin, which is applying *augmented intelligence* into care coordination. Unlike artificial intelligence, which tries to replicate human intelligence, augmented intelligence works with and amplifies human intelligence capabilities, such as human clinical decision making, when coupled with these computational methods and systems.

He is an adjunct associate professor of eHealth at Trinity College Dublin. In May 2017, Kevin became a member of the IBM Industry Academy, a vibrant community through which the company's most eminent and innovative industry visionaries shape global industry. He has also joined the international panel to the European Association of Primary Care Partners and is a founding member of the Irish branch of the International Federation for Integrated Care. Kevin has advocated for the *primary care home* from the outset, when Sean Hogan, who was leading the IBM healthcare business, put him in contact with Paul.

We rendezvous with Kevin in White Plains, NY, near IBM headquarters, and he immediately begins talking about Paul.

"Sean said that there's this great guy, Paul. He travels the world. He'll help you. So, I just reached out to him, and within a day or two, Paul came over to meet with me and some clinical leaders," Kevin says. "He is one of the most modest people I have ever met in my life."

Kevin says he started sharing Paul's ideas in a series of meetings at Trinity College Dublin's Medical School. Paul was quick to grasp the essence of Ireland's healthcare challenge and instigated a grassroots push to fix it. This group became an advocacy pop-up known as Tomorrow's Health—Connecting the Pieces.

Part of the issue in Ireland, Kevin says, was that past attempts to solve the healthcare dilemma of overcrowded hospitals did not create the desired result; in fact, every year it grew worse. Consequently, the public became skeptical that meaningful change could be achieved.

"So we asked Paul for evidence that we can show our leadership that the *medical home* can really have an impact and that it can be done in a relatively short period of time," Kevin says. "At the time, I was quite nervous about trying to start such a movement with just a small group of thought leaders."

At dinner one evening, Paul sat back in his chair and told Kevin an interesting story. "As usual, he led with a question," Kevin says.

"Kevin, how many people did it take to start the abolition of slavery?" Paul asked.

Unsure, Kevin shook his head.

"Just two people," Paul replied. "Two people sitting down and deciding that they want to do it, and then accepting that they may never see it in their lifetime. They may never get the credit for it. They just started to champion the movement."

Paul provided an example of what can happen when the right people with sufficient determination are in place—the creation of the Anti-Slavery Society by the Quakers in 1823. Founding members included William Wilberforce and Thomas Clarkson. Their efforts resulted in the abolition of slavery throughout the British dominions.

"That was profound for me," Kevin says of Paul's example. "It made me think as a person about what I could do. I could not help but notice that at this moment, there were just two people in this conversation. So I said okay, let's take on this challenge."

Paul got the ball rolling, arranging for high-powered speakers like Dr. Jack Cochran of Kaiser Permanente, and Dr. Craig Jones from Vermont's Blueprint for Health to present at an IBM-sponsored, one-day symposium in the Royal College of Surgeons of Ireland.

"We invited about one hundred and fifty key leaders; about a hundred attended. We made certain we had political leaders as well as administrative leaders in attendance, and we positioned a way forward, drafting our principles document, much like the origin of the PCPCC."

Kevin recognized that an IBM cliché pertained to his situation in Ireland. "One needs a compelling reason to act," he says. That *reason* was clear. "We have an aging population, and the budgets are unsustainable. In Ireland, we have a privately funded and a publicly funded system, so the objective of the government is to move it much more toward publicly funding based on need requirement."

Kevin explains that those with money gain access more readily. For those depending on the public system, there are still contentious issues around wait times for procedures. Paul would hear this firsthand.

On one trip to Ireland, Paul appeared on a national television talk show with consumers of healthcare and government spokespeople. They discussed the impact of the horrible flu season, which strikes every winter like clockwork, fills up the hospitals beyond capacity, and leaves everyone arguing over what to do about it.

Paul told a story he had heard from the taxi driver who brought him to the television studio—a sad tale of the driver's wife's illness and the lack of chronic disease care.

"His wife was forty-seven years old, a mother of three kids, aged eight to seventeen. She was a teacher. She had a stroke because her hypertension was never diagnosed and treated. She went from being a productive member of society, teaching and caring for her kids, to being paralyzed on the right side and unable to speak, requiring around-the-clock care, all for the lack of very basic primary care," Paul told the audience.

For Paul, the story underscored the need for full access to a *medical home.* When the moderator asked Paul for his solution to the hospital problem, he simply said, "You aren't asking the right questions."

"I have never seen Paul tell people exactly how to solve a problem or say that 'this is the way it has to happen.' He just tells good real-life stories that are factually based, but in an interesting way," Kevin says.

"We develop all the policy papers. But we have found it very hard to turn policy into execution," Kevin adds. Paul's stories connect on a human level. They give "the problem" a face. It creates emotion, which creates momentum.

On the radio show, Paul faced the skepticism so rooted in Ireland's past failures to fix its problem.

"People keep saying, 'That's great what you are telling me you've done in the United States, but how do we do that in Ireland?'" the moderator said.

Paul again responded.

"You are asking the wrong question. It's not about how do I do this, or how do I change Ireland. It's about finding leadership in Ireland—that will help you enable that change," he said.

To nurture Irish leadership, Paul suggested that his longtime colleague Joanne Shear, who led the highly acclaimed VA *medical home* transformation in America, come in and help because the Irish universal care system highly resembles the VA model. One of Paul's gifts is matching problems with proven problem solvers. The other is bending the right ears.

Dr. Andrew Jordan, Dr. Paul Grundy
and Chris Goodey

In London for the conference, Paul meets with Chris Goodey, CEO of the Irish National Association of General Practitioners and chairman of the European Association of Primary Care Partners. Chris is traveling with a group of prominent Irish physicians grateful for Paul's support in their quest to solve the healthcare crisis in their country.

"One step forward and two steps backwards for the *medical home*," Chris laments to Paul. Chris and his association have been lobbying the government for evidence-based decisions regarding primary care for five years. Paul coached Chris and his organization with the advocacy effort.

"When Paul is in Ireland, they agree to everything he says. But trying to get it implemented is challenging. It has been over two years and we are still in committee. A snail's pace," Chris says.

He explains that primary care suffers because there is no budget to back up government intentions and policies. By budget time, money has been swallowed up with nothing left for revamping primary care.

"We move from one crisis to the next in general practice," Chris says. "We are so lucky to have an infrastructure of GP, of *Trusted Healers*. It's the jewel in the crown of Ireland. And yet we are systematically destroying the envy of the world. We should be embracing our GPs, but brick by brick we are destroying it."

As an example, he notes that for the last few years "we have seen patients waiting three to four years for a hip replacement and up to five years for cataract surgery."

Paul acknowledges that the Irish people must feel a lot of pain before they make a change. He suggests that maybe they have not felt enough pain yet to demand change. Paul reminds Chris of their experience visiting a low-income community and visiting the GP office in the neighborhood. They arrived about midday and about forty people were queued up outside the door. Paul shook hands with each of the patients, asking how they were doing, were they happy, showing sincere interest in their world. Oddly, they all seemed content.

One patient replied, "Oh yeah, we love Doctor O'Shea. If I am here by two o'clock, I will get in to see the doctor by six."

Chris thinks Paul may be right. "Maybe the system needs to break before it can be fixed."

Chris and Paul talked again at a PCPCC Annual Meeting in Washington in the fall of 2018. Paul heard that Chris was feeling distressed about the inertia in Ireland. Paul stopped Chris in the hotel lobby. He calmed Chris, telling him that it has taken a decade to nurture the *medical home* to where it is in America—that we are on the cusp of success, but have not yet fully realized it. This will take time and persistence in Ireland, he said.

Chris returned to Dublin comforted, set to continue seeking incremental reform and pilot projects to prove the *primary care home* vision.

CHAPTER ELEVEN

JOURNEY TO HEALTH

Every day we hear of new studies that prescribe one thing or another. Take an aspirin a day. Don't take an aspirin a day. Running is good. Running is bad. Certain foods are good, others dangerous. Dr. Michael Roizen, along with his cohort Dr. Mehmet Oz, helps us sort out these contradictions and other vexing medical issues through his books and frequent appearances on network television and the *Dr. Oz Show.*

In his most recent work with Michael Crupain, MD, MPH, *What To Eat, When—A Strategic Plan to Improve Your Health and Life Through Food,* Dr. Roizen reveals how the food choices we make each day, and when we make them, can affect our health, our energy, our sex life, our waistline, our attitude, and the way we age. In his next book, *The Great Age Reboot,* scheduled to release late in 2020 or early 2021, he provides evidence-based guidelines on how we can live to be well over 110.

Anyone would be hard pressed to find a pair of physicians with the impact of Dr. Oz and Dr. Roizen. They write a daily newspaper column syndicated across the world. Dr. Roizen is a former editor of six medical journals, has published over 175 peer-reviewed scientific papers, received thirteen US and many foreign patents, and helped found twelve companies. He is an anesthesiologist and internist who serves as chief wellness officer at the Cleveland Clinic. He is also chief medical consultant to the *Dr. Oz* Show and has authored or co-authored fifteen books including four No. 1 *New York Times* bestsellers. (See a complete list of his works under Guides and Resources at the end of this book.)

Speaking with Dr. Roizen about healthcare or aging is akin to a moral awakening. He may meet with you while walking rapidly on a treadmill in his office, fulfilling his daily oath of 10,000 steps. He lives what he teaches. And it shows. Most people cannot keep up with him.

He has not eaten red meat in decades and is emphatic about diet. He says he is having more fun than ever, changing the way people all over the world view their health.

Like Paul, Dr. Roizen carries his data with him. He has detailed studies that back up his medical predilections. His desk provides a perch for dozens of those studies, residing in neatly stacked displays of academic excellence. And he's much more than an academic. He runs the Cleveland Clinic's Wellness Institute, which is dedicated to helping patients, community members, and employees achieve optimal well-being and a high quality of life, implementing wide-reaching wellness programs that aggressively advocate healthy living and remove possible barriers to this end.

Dr. Roizen's office is located is a beautiful reflective glass building tucked away in the woods on expansive acreage outside of Cleveland. The road that leads to the Institute meanders through woods with beautiful, well-kept landscaping. Parking is invisible to the naked eye, a healthy walk from the Center.

Inside, the atrium features waterfalls, indoor greenery, the visual impact of the forest outside, and silence. You hear the waterfalls when you enter the building. Even though hundreds of people are exercising, doing yoga, meditating, taking classes or being counseled, the building design removes most of those sounds from the environment.

Cleveland Clinic's Wellness Institute breathes *wellness*. So do the people who work there. These seem to be happy, content, friendly, fit employees. Many can be seen outside on the grounds walking.

Dr. Roizen offers a welcoming smile as he paces vigorously on one of two treadmills. Stacks of books and piles of studies occupy every horizontal surface in the spacious corner office overlooking the forest. He looks twenty years younger than his chronological age of seventy-two (his RealAge is 53.8—from his book *RealAge*).

We visit with him to get his take on the current state of the medical health system, and to learn more about the strides he has orchestrated as a practicing doctor and clinician. We learn that he and Dr. Paul Grundy go back aways and how they share a common belief in the old notion that preventing disease and illness is the best cure.

"I met Paul way back when, and I considered him as kooky as possible and he probably considered me that way. I remember hearing him speak at the University of Chicago and attending several of his lectures. I really liked where he was taking things.

"At the time, I most often ran into Paul at a group of healthcare leaders called the Health Education Network [HEN], which could be described as leaders willing to take risks—that's a theme that ran through our meetings, which over time resulted in many subsequently losing their jobs. IBM gave Paul the platform to make a difference, an awesome, brilliant team."

One of Dr. Roizen's many platforms has been his *6+2 normals* program. He piloted this concept at Cleveland Clinic beginning in 2008, and the results have been astounding.

Chronic disease management accounts for more than 84 percent of healthcare costs. If you achieve at least four of the following *normal* measures of good health, as well as two behaviors, you'll dodge chronic disease about 80 percent of the time.

The Six:

- Regain and maintain normal blood pressure. Your target: below 130/85.

- Regain and maintain a normal level of lousy LDL cholesterol. Your target: 100 milligrams per deciliter or lower if you do not have diabetes or vascular disease; below seventy if you do.

- Regain and maintain a normal fasting blood glucose level of 107 mg/dL or below, or HgbA1c below 6.4 mg/dL.

- Achieve the healthy weight for your height. With a body mass index below thirty (obesity) and aiming to get below twenty-eight.

- Have your asthma managed. With many companies, learning and practicing stress management gives more health and a faster ROI. Practice ongoing stress management.

- Have a cotinine level indicating no primary consumption of tobacco products, no smoke from tobacco in your body. Declare yourself a smoke-free zone.

The Two:

- See your primary care doctor so you know your numbers, including blood pressure, lousy LDL cholesterol, blood glucose, body mass index, etc.

- Make sure your vaccinations are up to date. (Boosters are essential to protect you from whooping cough, tetanus, and diphtheria. Everyone needs an annual flu

shot; it decreases flu and lung problems plus lowers
stroke and heart attack risk. Folks fifty-plus need the
shingles vaccine and sixty-five-plus need the vaccine
for pneumonia.)

The Cleveland Clinic adopted this program in 2008, working
in conjunction with primary care doctors of employees and their
dependents.

The program helps employees make good health decisions by
giving them access to free smoking-cessation and weight-control
programs, free fitness center usage, and by partnering folks with a
buddy to build mutual support.

The clinic also took fryers out of kitchens that serve employees
and patients, removed sugar-added beverages, and began to pay
employees (initially with a check, then in reduced premiums) to
achieve the *6+2 normals*. Dr. Roizen says the biggest and most
important measure is "the quality of life enhanced for our employees.
When you meet them, they are fitter, happier, and more energetic
and committed than you would expect."

Cleveland Clinic is a nonprofit multi-specialty academic medical
center that integrates clinical and hospital care with research and
education. Today, with more than 1,400 beds on Cleveland Clinic
main campus and over 4,500 beds in the system, Cleveland Clinic
is one of the largest and most respected hospitals in the country.
Nationwide, it has 60,000 employees.

"When we began, we had 12 percent of our employees
participating with the *6+2 normals*, and now we have 69 percent
participating. That saves us the difference between the national curve
and our curve—$254 million over the last three years," Dr. Roizen
says. Better employee health translates to a better bottom line.

Since 2008, he explains, whereas the national average for cost per
employee has gone up $7,000 per person, the Cleveland Clinic's has
gone up $800 and dropped two of the last four years.

"And that's with only 43.6 percent of voluntary participants achieving six *normals*. You can see in every ethnic group, whether Asian or African American, Caucasian or Hispanic, our trend line is up.

"There's been a 28 percent reduction in unscheduled sick leave, and 63 percent of clinic employees have seen their paycheck go up by between $1,400 and $1,600 annually," he adds. "So, we have constantly made huge efforts that get more people to voluntarily participate.

"One of the keys is doing stress management early on. That's important. In type 2 diabetes, we have partnered with our primary care physicians—as Paul would say, their *medical home*—with outreach coaches, and part of their *medical home* is a coach. We then show the patient all the data."

More benefits to employees of another company we worked with include reversing metabolic disease 50 percent in the first year. (Metabolic syndrome may include increased blood pressure, high blood sugar, excess body fat around the waist, and abnormal cholesterol or triglyceride levels that increase risk of heart disease, stroke, and diabetes.)

Deeply concerned about the national picture in the US, Dr. Roizen's forecast, like everything he does, is based on careful data analysis. The cost of healthcare projections by the Congressional Budget Office (CBO) have been seriously underestimated, he says. They only take three things into account—aging of the population, new technology, and increased access. They do not consider the influx of chronic disease, which is increasing five to seven times faster than the population.

"So, looking at this through the lens of dementia, or type 2 diabetes, or osteoarthritis, this will not end well," he says.

We know how to prevent 80 to 90 percent of chronic disease. Currently, 75 percent or more of healthcare costs are for chronic disease management. Unless altered, healthcare costs will disrupt societies. Federal spending for healthcare programs and Social

Security in America, allowing for aging of the population, cost increases, population growth and the huge increase in chronic disease, means we have six years to change this, Dr. Roizen says.

If the US government would do the same program he has developed at Cleveland Clinic—provide incentives to achieve the *6+2 normals* goals—the cost situation would level off. He forecasts 7 percent of gross domestic product rather than the over 16 percent predicted by CBO analyses.

"America has exported its bad habits: too much stress, too much toxins, but especially too little physical activity and too much food and too much of the wrong food. Our cost destruction of the economy through health needs has crossed the Atlantic and the Pacific.

"The problem with England is the problem with the whole world, if you will," Dr. Roizen says. "England does rationing based on age. And so Paul is really, really needed there. And maybe that's why Paul got more *medical home* pilots going there. The British healthcare system, like ours, is in real crisis.

"America's system is in crisis, but most people don't understand it's in crisis yet. We do not accept that because of the way we have rationed things and the patchwork we have done. Britain has realized it, and that's why the National Health System is in real crisis."

We relay to Dr. Roizen that Paul told a colleague in Ireland not to worry about the slow progress of robust primary care, the reason for which is that Ireland hasn't felt enough pain yet.

"That's right," Dr. Roizen says. "The problem with waiting until you feel pain is that sometimes you make the wrong moves when you have pain. Sometimes you get a narcotic instead of going after the underlying cause. And that's why you pray that a whole mess of people grab hold of *Trusted Healers*. In other words, it can't be Paul alone, or Dan alone, or me, to change the world alone. You need an army. You need a World War II–like effort to transform health.

"Globally, I think we are on a longevity disruptor. I think we will learn how to live well past 110 before the CBO decides that that's a healthy thing for America," he quips. "My CEO retired this year at age seventy-five. The CBO would have said that his last ten years were useless, because after the age of sixty-five, the Congressional Budget Office considers you a cost to the government, not a benefit."

We have gone from 6 percent of people working at age seventy-five to 26 percent of people ages sixty-five to seventy-five working the equivalent of full time. Over the last five years that group has generated $5.3 trillion in economic activity in the United States and $1.3 trillion in taxes, Dr. Roizen says.

He says four things play into our shared future:

"First, we have got to change the age perception, because we will live a lot longer. At the same time, we have a lot less fertility, because people are concerned about being able to support their families, I think.

"Second, an older society clashes with the *care*. As we get older, we need more care. If you look at health as staying healthy vs. interventions in care, we are learning how to make us healthier with interventions, but we are charging a lot more for it.

"Third, if we don't change the influx of chronic disease, we are in big trouble as a society, because we aren't going to be able to afford the care that we require.

"Fourth, technology has grown like crazy. And it's costly."

Paul believes that longevity and health must come together by having a *Trusted Healer* so you can be productive for the long term.

"Or I like the term 'play-span'—able to enjoy your passion, be it work or something else, for longer," Dr. Roizen says. "That's having a younger *RealAge* or inner biological age as you get older by the calendar."

Dr. Roizen explains that if health and longevity lose to chronic disease and cost increases, we will end up with rationing and major social disruption. Rationing healthcare may push some countries to the brink. Rationing in Ireland and Britain may be tolerated because it is age-based. But in the United States, rationing is financially based. And we don't tolerate rationing very well, Dr. Roizen suggests.

"A friend of mine came down with brain cancer. Has good insurance. But the drug he needs has a co-pay of over $1,000, out of pocket. He could not afford it. They told him, essentially, don't come in without the thousand dollars. There is something wrong with this picture," Dr. Roizen says.

"This just isn't right as a society. And so, I called the insurance provider to find out if there a way to get the drug company to move on this. The insurance company said, 'No, but if you appeal to us enough, we'll lower the co-pay.'"

Dr. Roizen shakes his head. "Again, this just isn't right. This patient didn't know how to do that. Horrible. We'll tolerate it for a little while, but that tolerance will not last very long," he says. "I don't think the American people are going to tolerate rationing by financial means for much longer. I worry about social disruption if what Paul wants to happen doesn't happen."

CHAPTER TWELVE

REVOLUTION
IN VALUE

About the same time Paul and his colleagues were forming the advocacy campaign for the *medical home*, Glenn D. Steele, Jr., MD, PhD, prepared to turn the entire clinical world upside down with evidence-based medicine.

Just as Dr. Roizen changed the way we look at personal health and taught that it is not too late to begin a healthier lifestyle, Dr. Steele illuminated the stunning geographic and demographic disparities in the frequency of surgery and wide variability in outcomes.

Dr. Steele has been named to *Modern Healthcare*'s 50 Most Powerful Physician Executives in Healthcare, and among the 100 Most Powerful People in Healthcare. He garnered the attention of the nation while serving as president and CEO of Geisinger Health System, an integrated health services organization in central and northeastern Pennsylvania that was nationally recognized for its innovative use of the electronic health record and the development and implementation of new care models.

Like Paul, Dr. Steele is a member of the National Academy of Medicine. He received his bachelor's degree in history and literature from Harvard University and his medical degree from New York

University School of Medicine. He completed his internship and residency in surgery at the University of Colorado, where he was also a fellow of the American Cancer Society. He earned a doctorate in microbiology at Lund University. Dr. Steele has authored or co-authored nearly 500 scientific and professional articles.

He has since retired from Geisinger and now leads the Health Transformation Alliance, which is comprised of over forty-seven major corporations looking for better ways to pay for the healthcare their employees receive. The alliance resembles the PCPCC, which began with a similar-size gathering of corporations, and is still going strong in its second decade, with a huge and diverse membership championing primary care around the world.

Dr. Steele believes the work that goes into innovating is easy compared to scaling and generalizing.

"You have to prove that the innovation is sustainable, which means there has to be not only an altruistic, compelling intent, but there has to be a business model," Dr. Steele says. "And it has to be a business model that appeals to everyone involved in the re-engineering."

When it comes to providing high-quality care in the most efficient, cost-effective way possible, *ProvenCare®* is the gold standard in the industry. Developed at Geisinger Health System and praised by healthcare leaders worldwide, this pioneering approach provides a blueprint for healthcare executives who want higher levels of care for their patients, greater incentives for practitioners, and smarter solutions at lower costs.

Dr. Steele proved the opposite of what many of us believe; he proved that there is an inverse relationship between the quality of care and the cost of care.

Surgeons and hospitals operate under a financial model that pays them more if they perform more procedures—not by the value or quality of those procedures. They also get paid more if there are complications, suggesting a profound lack of accountability.

At Geisinger Health System, Dr. Steele demonstrated to the

healthcare world that patients have better outcomes, receive better care, and have lower costs when disciplined, evidence-based medicine is applied. His team's accomplishments catapulted him into becoming one of the most powerful and successful healthcare reformers in America. His model involved partnering with insurance companies, physicians, and health systems on behalf of the patient. He formed a partnership with IBM to help roll out his reforms. We meet Dr. Steele in Washington to discuss his experiences working with Paul and his stunning clinical advancements during his tenure at Geisinger.

"Our innovative approach is known as *ProvenCare*, and it's about ensuring that quality, cost-efficient care comes standard," Dr. Steele wrote in his recent benchmark book, *ProvenCare: How to Deliver Value-Based Healthcare the Geisinger Way*. Applied across America, thousands of lives and billions of dollars can be saved by the advanced use of proven evidence-based care protocols and best practices.

The Geisinger team systematically applies national guidelines and results from clinical trials and their own re-engineering studies, parsing the kind of healthcare that works from approaches that do not. They develop reliable healthcare methods that improve quality, maximize safety, and get patients feeling better faster. They offer these proven protocols to healthcare organizations across the nation.

Testament to the success of Geisinger's approach were the results of following new protocols for heart surgery. Geisinger showed a 68 percent decrease in mortality, a 4.8 percent reduction in cost per case, and a 17.6 percent increase in contribution margin (profit).

"I drank the soup," Dr. Steele says.

Dr. Steele became patient number eighty-six in *ProvenCare Heart*. The discovery of a faster than usual resting heart rate, combined with heart issues in his family history, led to his diagnosis and subsequent surgery. Dr. Steele became proof of their success.

With *ProvenCare Perinatal*, Geisinger showed a decrease in C-section rates from 28 percent to 20 percent, and a reduction in neonatal intensive care unit admissions from 9.5 percent to 5.9 percent.

With *ProvenCare Knee*, Geisinger showed a reduction in average acute and rehabilitation time from 16 to 9.9 days.

Geisinger charges patients a flat fee for *ProvenCare* acute and chronic services. That includes a commitment, or "warranty," to cover complications and readmissions for ninety days.

National news media reported the extraordinary results—better quality, higher patient satisfaction, lower costs, higher margins, and the guarantee.

"Paul and I were both totally consumed with trying to change healthcare," he says during our interview with him in Washington. "When I first went to Geisinger, my aspirations were actually limited compared to where we are now."

The first half of Dr. Steele's professional healthcare administration career involved troubleshooting—reviewing cases where patient care was not handled quite properly. Dr. Steele notes that the most important aspect of any kind of initial intervention when someone is really sick is that it is done right the first time.

"I thought that I could prove that we could fundamentally change how we cared for patients in this very unusual environment. Geisinger is unusual in that we own both an insurance company and a provider. We had great credibility in terms of our brand, regardless of whether it was the insurance Geisinger brand or provider Geisinger brand."

Geisinger Health System emerged as one of the most progressive healthcare systems in the country with a path of quality, transparency, and accountability. Dr. Steele based his platform on what matters in healthcare—the measured quality of the care, the outcomes, and the use of best practices. *Evidence-based* medicine.

"I didn't care whether it could be applied anywhere else; I just wanted to know internally that it was possible to create real value by doing away with a lot of the unnecessary or hurtful stuff that usually happens in trying to diagnose and treat the most prevalent conditions, and then I wanted to ride off into the sunset," Dr. Steele says.

"Paul was doing his own thing and was a quite well-known

spokesman for the patient-centered *medical home*, which represented exactly what we were trying to do with our community practices at Geisinger. We addressed the concept of taking a provider system that also has an insurance company and actually trying to figure out how to make it work together. I didn't know whether it was provable or not in terms of creating the sweet spot."

But the concept was provable.

He recalls that when he first got to Geisinger, the system was installing a transactional health medical record (Epic), which in those days still cost a lot of money.

Dr. Steele convinced his chief financial officer that if they were going to take the EHR to the next level, they needed the analytic capability, which required what is known as a data warehouse.

While Dr. Steele and IBM executives put together the data warehouse and analytic capabilities, Paul stepped in to help present the fundamentals of the *medical home* to the Geisinger board.

"I only asked two people during my entire fifteen-year tenure to come to Geisinger and try to explain to our board exactly what I was trying to do—Paul and Dr. Jonathan Perlin, one of the most powerful healthcare leaders of our time, who led the VA transformation."

Both international leaders provided powerful testimony that the board needed to hear.

"Paul and I both understood that primary care and a continuing relationship between a 'care giver' and a 'care getter' was hugely important. My concept at Geisinger was that we could enable caregiving with technology, we could enable caregiving with the best specialty and sub-specialty expertise, but a continuing relationship with someone, ideally in your community, who knows you not just as a patient but as a human being—that combination is the sweet spot," Dr. Steele says. "I had Paul help me try to convince my trustees that this was the way to go."

Dr. Steele says that their first big breakthrough occurred when creating the first strategic set of aspirations.

"Very clear cut, very well-socialized set of strategic targets," he says. "We tried to frame it within five years. I think that going beyond three years is a little bit of a hedge in case you don't make it."

It evolved into a fundamentally different social contract that would require a ton of effort.

"We were going to work our tails off. It meant everybody was going to work much harder. We were going to try to excel not just to have a good style of life in rural Pennsylvania, but we were going to try to excel to create a national model," Dr. Steele says.

"When I started talking about that, I assumed that probably at least a third of the audience was hoping I would just kind of go away, so they could go back to wherever they were with the original social contract."

The first test was whether Geisinger could recruit people to rural and post-industrial Pennsylvania to replace those who didn't buy into the new social contract.

"Once I found out I could do that, I felt a little bit better," he says.

Geisinger had a lot of turnover and low morale, largely due to its failed merger with Hershey, a regional medical network. The Hershey merger was scuttled due to corporate differences in July 2000 after three years. Reasons for the failure included the culture clash between an entity dedicated to research and teaching and another focused more on clinical care and the financial bottom line.

Dr. Steele started work there later that year.

"A lot of the people who could leave did leave," he says. "So, the first thing was the ability to recruit after we had socialized the new strategy, the new social contract. The second thing was to get an early win."

The first reengineering task was heart surgery. The entire process of creating the best protocols for care takes about eighteen months of very intense study.

"We got an early win on that in a number of ways. It was a substantive win and we had great leadership in both cardiology and the cardiac surgery. We had great volume. We had pretty good outcomes even before we reengineered, but we found we got even better outcomes, both in terms of quality and also in terms of cost."

—

Dr. Steele refers to *ProvenCare* as a sexy packaging label, but proudly acknowledges that it represented a fundamental change for care delivery in a whole series of acute and chronic situations. A lot of that change, particularly for chronic disease management, involved reengineering primary care.

Geisinger's hospital-based redesign pathways evolved to include a wide spectrum of high volume, evidence-based interventions. Geisinger has made these protocols and best practices available to every healthcare organization in the country.

ProvenCare® Bariatric Surgery

ProvenCare® Chronic Obstructive Pulmonary Disease (COPD)

ProvenCare® Coronary Artery Bypass Graft (CABG)

ProvenCare® Fragile Hip Fracture

ProvenCare® Heart Failure

ProvenCare® Hepatitis C

ProvenCare® Inflammatory Bowel

ProvenCare® Lung Cancer (Commission on Cancer Collaborative)

ProvenCare® Lumbar Spine

ProvenCare® Multiple Sclerosis

ProvenCare® Percutaneous Coronary Intervention

ProvenCare® Perinatal

ProvenCare® Psoriasis

ProvenCare® Rectal Cancer

ProvenCare® Rheumatoid Arthritis

ProvenCare® Total Hip

ProvenCare® Total Knee

The success of each of these disciplines is measured by patient outcomes. Each procedure begins by asking, *What would be the ideal outcome?* And with procedures come discussions about how to improve.

"Only after both the payer and provider at Geisinger each agree on what the perfect outcome should be did we decide what the technology should be to enable that. So, the technology has to be the enabler of something specific. If you simply choose technology without knowing what clinical outcome you're aiming for, you just get chaos."

Dr. Steele and his colleagues reengineered cardiology, cardiac surgery, and then orthopedics. Most other care depended on a fundamental redesign of primary care. That area was where Dr. Steele was most aligned with Paul and the *medical home.*

"With Paul's grounding at IBM and the grounding I had with my organization, we both had the ability not just to opinionate, but to actually do something."

Dr. Steele recalls his excitement after reading a 2007 *New York Times* article, which appeared above the fold on the front page and featured the Geisinger warranty.[24]

"The writer got enthused by the way we packaged this reengineering, which is a single price including our taking financial responsibility for any complications that may occur in the first ninety days," he says. "The lights went on internally as well as externally. Everybody wanted to be a part of it. The eye doctors wanted to do it for cataracts. The orthopedic physicians wanted to do it for hips and knees. The doctors who perform gastric bypass surgery wanted to do it. Everybody wanted to do it."

Dr. Steele and his team adopted the *medical home* model and added some unique features. Geisinger's version included technology-enabled communications between the *Trusted Healer* and the patient, and a care manager "quarterback" as well. Geisinger had also concluded that telephonic or distant care management did not work well. Patients benefited most from face-to-face contact with caregivers.

The sickest patients in each practice were assigned a concierge caregiver, and the 150 needing the most hands-on care were identified.

The idea behind care managers is not only to help manage chronic illness, but to make sure the patient is safe, has the necessary transportation, eats well, takes medications as prescribed and complies with their care plans.

Geisinger's advanced *medical home* program demonstrated improvement in the risk of heart attack, stroke and retinopathy in individuals with diabetes. Three-year results for 25,000 patients found that the *ProvenCare Health* prevented 305 myocardial infarctions (heart attacks), 140 strokes, and 166 cases of retinopathy. Acute care admissions decreased 27.5 percent, and 72 percent of patients said quality of care improved when they worked with a care manager. That was real transformation.

The timing of the pilot program and the fact that Geisinger garnered a huge amount of public recognition came at a time when *ProvenCare* showed significant clinical benefits.

"It was a wonderful confluence of things," Dr. Steele says.

Claims data was extraordinarily powerful in helping to redesign how to give care to specific patients. With real-time healthcare delivery data, the data can be analyzed and fed back right away to those who give the care.

The ultimate in real-time data, Dr. Steele mentions, is the concept represented by IBM's *Watson,* which adds all kinds of extraordinarily sophisticated techniques to take whatever data is flowing into Watson and improve the standards. That is the next level to what Dr. Steele and his team accomplished at Geisinger.

"Conceptually, it is very, very powerful and I understand what IBM is trying to do in creating Watson. Like everything else that's very aspirational, it's got to prove itself, and that's where we are right now," Dr. Steele says.

In 2015, *US News and World Report* cited Geisinger's commitment to refund all or part of the co-pay for spine and bariatric surgery to patients dissatisfied with their care. The magazine called it "the latest, and perhaps most radical innovation of a system recognized for continually reinventing medical care."[25]

Dr. Steele says that we are on an absolutely unstoppable course toward paying for value. Healthcare organizations clinging to fee-for-service reimbursements are going to have to create more value, no matter what. The amount providers get paid per unit of work is decreasing.

"So, I have been making the pitch now to the provider world that reengineering of care is not based on moving from fee-for-service to something else," Dr. Steele says. "It's based on the fact that we are going to have to create value, for two reasons."

Number one, all providers must have better outcomes, because there will be winners and losers in a market-based world. And to be a winner will require better access, better outcomes, and better conveniences for patients, just like in every other area of the consumer world. And secondly, providers will need to have much more cost control, because without it there won't be a profit margin, regardless of how compensated.

"I am still very positive. I think we are moving in the right direction," Dr. Steele says. "It's typical in this country to have extraordinarily uneven progress. It's very heterogeneous from market to market."

Dr. Steele has demonstrated time and again the ability to look at an organization and understand what's possible. He calls it "stretching an organization, but not fundamentally moving it away from its founding DNA." He says that as a leader you should know what you can get out of your environment, and how much you can push that environment.

"I think it's like human relationships. Basically, if you try to fundamentally change people, it usually doesn't work."

Paul, Dr. Steele and other healthcare innovators understand that all change is local. Every geographic area, every board of trustees, every profit or nonprofit organization operates from their own culture, traditions, and expectations. Any powerful new idea takes time to assimilate.

Geisinger has advanced that notion by demonstrating better ways to provide care for many chronic conditions and procedures. Yet, it will take time and local acceptance to more fully institute such change.

Large government institutions like the VA, the Defense Department, or the Federal Employees Health Benefits program can adjust more quickly because the decision to do so can be sealed with a signature. But the private sector, where many stakeholders have a say, can take years to form consensus.

The *medical home* movement offers a great example. It has been adopted in a relatively short period of time by health systems with large primary care groups. Yet, after a decade, the tipping point is just now being reached in most primary care practices. So, how do we generalize *ProvenCare* for other places that have a different fiduciary structure, a different sociology, and different market conditions?

In a way, it's the same kind of value proposition the developing *medical home* advocates offer to primary care practices:

- Here's a much better way.
- Here's the proof it will be better.
- Here's who is already doing it.
- Let us know when you are ready.

"We focused on that over the last five years of my tenure at Geisinger. And now it's my driving force. Health Transformation Alliance is one of the engines in that. It's a worthy mission, very complex. We won't have results for some period of time," Dr. Steele says.

What healthcare reform ultimately comes down to is this: "Healthcare should be available to everyone," Dr. Steele says, "because we pay for it anyway. It's not whether you are altruistic or not; it's a business case. We pay for all the care in this country. We do, one way or another. And the more people who are uninsured, the more inefficient the care is for that group. And you and I pay for it."

Paul agrees.

"When we turn away people from care or medicines because of money, when we do not help people properly care for chronic illnesses, we pay a heavy financial price when the medical crisis hits," Paul says. "We pay for too-late hospital care, surgical interventions that could have been avoided, unnecessary suffering and squandered resources. If everyone, and I mean everyone, has a *Trusted Healer*, and a *medical home*, it's a game changer."

Dr. Steele notes that change might be easier in the future because many young people have a different expectation about healthcare delivery.

"I think the next generations will be much more interested in getting their healthcare from a brand than the current setup," he says. People assume that if they go to the Mayo Clinic or the Cleveland Clinic, they are going to get the best. They are generally not going there for an individual practitioner; they are going there because of the brand.

"And these great brands, as well as three or four others, are legitimate," Dr. Steele says. "It's not hard to imagine an Amazon or CVS in that brand role."

Paul agrees, forecasting that the 10,000 CVS locations could one day become a powerful outreach for people with chronic conditions, a new resource for *Trusted Healers*, and that information flow to and from primary care could prove foundational to team care.

"It's going to be interesting," Dr. Steele concludes.

CHAPTER THIRTEEN

SPIRIT OF REFORM

atrick J. Kennedy often quotes the timeless words of the
once-enslaved abolitionist leader Frederick Douglass. In
1847, Douglass published a newspaper, *The North Star*, in
Rochester, NY, the subject of this chapter of *Trusted Healers*. As
you'll see, this city on the southern shore of Lake Ontario has been
a magnet for outspoken, values-driven, patriotic change agents.

Monuments to the city's colorful industrial heritage cluster near
the Genesee River, which flows into the Great Lake. The city flourished
with the opening of the Erie Canal, becoming a major manufacturing
center and attracting many Italians, Germans, Irish and other
European immigrants, as well as a dominant group of Yankees of New
England origin. The Yankees made Rochester the center of multiple
reform movements, such as abolitionism and women's rights.

In 1857, American heroes Susan B. Anthony and William Lloyd
Garrison spoke at a crowded abolition meeting there. Anthony,
who lived in Rochester and died there, would later be thrown in jail
for voting.

In October 1858, William H. Seward, a leading opponent of
slavery, delivered a speech to an overflow crowd in Corinthian Hall.
He argued that the political and economic systems of North and
South were incompatible, famously saying that the irrepressible

conflict between the two systems would eventually result in the nation becoming "either entirely a slave-holding nation, or entirely a free-labor nation."

In the years leading up to the Civil War, numerous locations in the Rochester area provided safe houses to shelter fugitive slaves before they snuck aboard boats for transport to safer havens.

Home to the headquarters of Eastman Kodak, Rochester became famous as the center of American photography. In the 1970s it became fashionable to call the industrial cities along the Great Lakes "rustbelt cities" following the move away from steel, chemical and other hard goods manufacturing. Rochester, with the presence of Bausch and Lomb, Eastman Kodak, Xerox, Wegmans, and other major industries, defied the trend for many decades following WWII.

The long, slow decline and ultimate 2012 bankruptcy of Eastman Kodak rocked the community, yet Rochester did not lose its resilience, continuing as a benchmark city for progressiveness.

Rochester has again defied odds with innovation. It has emerged as a place where health organizations answer to a higher calling. They work with companies large and small to address healthcare cost by stressing preventive care and aggressively treating chronic diseases.

Every community needs a common cause—a project that will improve life for everyone living there and that businesses and organizations and citizens can all get behind. For some communities, it may be the arts, or sports, or special schools for at-risk kids. For Rochester, enlightened community leaders selected healthcare.

NorthStar Network offers healthcare leadership training programs that inspire local senior executives from across the entire healthcare field to improve "the Business of Healthcare." The programs use Malcolm Baldrige-like quality management principles to help leaders identify and prioritize areas for improvement.

Linda Becker

Linda Becker founded NorthStar Network in 2010 after twenty-four years as vice president and general manager of Xerox's 2.4-billion-dollar worldwide color business. In 2001, she assumed leadership of Kodak's Health Imaging Division, now known as Carestream. Linda led a team of 4,000 people responsible for their digital business, which included computed radiography, digital radiography, picture archiving and communications system (PACS), electronic health records, as well as software and detectors for digital mammography.

In 2002, Linda joined the board of directors of Rochester Regional Health, a two-billion-dollar integrated healthcare system providing services for the Rochester and nearby Finger Lakes community. For eight years she served as chairwoman of the region's Healthcare Services Board and received the International Athena Award.

Linda has immersed herself in her community's healthcare. She quickly became passionate about making a lasting impact that radically improves the quality and cost of healthcare for those in her upstate New York community. She's bold, direct, transparent, smart, and committed to keeping the traditions of collaboration as a vehicle for improvement.

"It's a big cultural issue in our society. How can we create a culture that gives good healthcare?" she asks.

In other words, communities cannot just sit idle and wait for their healthcare to improve. Linda didn't.

NorthStar prides itself on challenging conventional thinking and thinking out of the box. Its mission is to strengthen the community by making Rochester the best, most innovative healthcare city in America.

"NorthStar Network's name came from the vision that the patient is the North Star, and we're building a network of healthcare leaders with a common vision and agreed-to goals. We could inspire community-based activities that improve healthcare quality and/or reduce costs for all," Linda says.

She started by offering yearly local, community-based healthcare events. Twice a year for the last ten years, more than 300 executives have attended a half-day session called Cracking the Code on Healthcare. Ninety-four percent of participating organizations have attended all twenty sessions to hear national thought leaders share innovative ideas for healthcare improvement.

CRACKING THE CODE ON HEALTHCARE

NORTHSTAR'S SERIES
OF EDUCATIONAL EVENTS

Topics cover a broad array of healthcare subjects, such as:

- Improving the Patient Experience
- Disruptive Innovation in Healthcare
- Moving Toward a Safer Health Care System
- A Data Driven Approach to Healthcare Transformation
- Improving Quality—Reducing Costs; Moving from Fee for Volume to Fee for Value
- Healthcare Through the Eyes of the Patient
- Employer Health Plans—Where do we go from here?
- Innovative Models for Care, Collaboration, Compensation and Reducing Costs

NORTHSTAR
HEALTHCARE BUSINESS ACADEMY
FELLOWSHIP PROGRAM

Nine full days per year. Each full day had a specific topic:

- Personal Health
- Population Health, Community Health and Public Health
- Leadership and Behavioral/Mental Health
- Improving the Patient Experience and Emotional Intelligence
- Innovation
- Process Improvement and Data Analytics
- Human Resources including Embracing Diversity
- Finance and the Hydraulics of Healthcare
- Doing the Right Things in Healthcare and the Unintended Consequences of Doing the Right Things

By 2013, Linda discovered that it is not enough to have good ideas; you need a path to translate them into action. So, a year later she created an elite year-long program called the Healthcare Business Academy Fellowship Program. The program was sponsored by twenty-six of the largest organizations in the community. Each provided a high-level executive leader to serve as a program advisor. This board of advisors met monthly to determine program content and to finalize program details.

The outcome became a twelve-month, one-day-per-month intensive leadership development program that offers unique personal experiences with nine full days of workshops and presentations, seventy online courses, and tours of local healthcare facilities.

NorthStar Network's programs have touched thousands of people within the Rochester and surrounding community—both members of the healthcare ecosystem and those receiving care.

"All healthcare is local, and we are trying to set an example for how to do it right," Linda says.

⌒‿

NorthStar is one of many organizations in the Rochester community facilitating collaborations. The result? Rochester continues to be a center for high quality, affordable care. The city was recently recognized by the Centers for Medicare and Medicaid Services (CMS) as the least expensive community in America for Medicare and fourth least expensive for commercial payers. These are just a few examples of the great work being done by so many in the Rochester community:

- Common Ground Health brings organizations together to approve any new beds or major investments in medical devices. They received a twenty-six-million-dollar federal grant from CMS for care coordination.

- The Greater Rochester Health Information Organization has built a system to enable access to all images and blood work among all healthcare organizations, reducing unnecessary tests and reducing costs. Hospitals agreed to share electronic health records. Now anyone, anywhere, from any system or any physician has access to the records and so does the patient.

- Finger Lakes Provider Performing Organizations was awarded millions to improve health of low-income citizens by redesigning Medicaid for Rochester recipients.

- The Chamber of Commerce Health Planning Committee unites large employers to work together to improve care and reduce cost. For almost a decade they have made great strides in preventive healthcare.

Ian Morrison, PhD, has lauded Rochester's trailblazing. He is a consultant, and futurist, and author of the classic book *Health Care in the New Millennium: Vision, Values, and Leadership.* In late 2017, he published a column in which he outlined all the reasons that, for more than fifty years, Rochester has had lessons to offer for health systems and businesses.[26]

In his article, Dr. Morrison notes two powerful examples of how Rochester succeeds in tackling the topic of health and healthcare to improve quality of care, lower costs and help the community lead healthier lives.

An early pioneering project in the early 2000s encouraged community members to "eat well and live well" by consuming more fruits and vegetables and monitoring their exercise, Dr. Morrison notes.

"For sixteen years, employers in the community [now a total of some 500 companies] have their employees participate in this program, which was originally pioneered by the leaders of Wegmans Food Markets." Dr. Morrison also highlights the efforts Rochester has made in the monitoring of high blood pressure, a community wide concern.

"Faith-based organizations, barbershops and other local institutions are empowered to collect the blood pressure of community members, and they have helped to build a registry of 150,000 people. Anyone, regardless of insurance coverage, who is identified as having high blood pressure is referred for immediate treatment. Ongoing financial support for such initiatives is raised through a tax on hospitals of $23 per discharge."

In 2010, he reports, the blood pressure of 62 percent of Rochester residents was under control; now it's estimated to be 78 percent.

"One of the drivers of high healthcare costs is duplication and waste," notes Linda, who recalls another innovative idea that has saved the community millions. "Community leaders discovered that when a patient goes into the hospital for care, they usually go in using a generic drug. They also discovered that they usually come out of the hospital with a brand name drug instead. By shining a spotlight on that, the community changed their behavior, and we have documented savings of seventy million dollars over the last seven years."

And several more measures such as this are on the stove.

Linda touts Paul's vision of embracing social determinants in healthcare. And she is a big believer in use of the Adverse Childhood Experiences (ACE) questionnaire developed by the Center for Disease Control.

An ACE score is a tally of abuse, neglect, and other hallmarks of a rough childhood. According to ACE, the rougher your childhood, the higher your score is likely to be and the higher your risk for developing health problems. Childhood experiences have a tremendous impact on future violence victimization, and lifelong health and opportunity.

NorthStar Network always includes the ACE initiative as part of their fellowship program, just one of the many discussions they have during the year, especially relevant to their mental and behavioral health representatives.

(Take the ACE Test: see Notes in Guides and Resources in the back of *Trusted Healers*.[27])

"The charity care in our community hospitals is outstanding, complemented by excellent federally qualified health centers [FQHCs] and one of the most unique 'free clinics' in the country," Linda says. "One of our FQHCs specializes in speaking the language of the patient. There are twenty-two languages spoken in Rochester, and there is a large and growing immigrant population."

Another FQHC occupies a niche with expertise in caring for people with Hepatitis C and HIV/AIDS.

"And St. Joseph's, a role model for the *medical home*, is in a league all by itself," Linda says. "You will find at St. Joseph's a group of people that embrace social determinants like no other place in America."

St. Joseph's Neighborhood Center, rooted in the caring tradition of the Sisters of St. Joseph, provides comprehensive physical and mental health services to uninsured and under-insured people in and around Rochester. The Sisters of St. Joseph have been active in mission and ministry in the Greater Rochester area for over 150 years, continually responding to the needs of the people of the region.

St. Joseph's was established in 1993. One of the sisters heard from the people in the neighborhood that there was a lack of access to primary care, mental health, and social services. So, they opened this neighborhood center in a small house to address these needs for the uninsured. Twenty-five years later, the Sisters of St. Joseph have created a unique and powerful example of a *medical home*.

"Sister Chris" Wagner

Underpinning it is "Sister Chris" Wagner's philosophy of life, which is to "work the best way possible and pay attention to the needs of neighbors and the community." One of the five founders, two of whom are still active staff, Sister Christine C. Wagner, SSJ, PhD, recently stepped down after a quarter of a century as CEO to assume development responsibilities.

In 1992, Sister Chris graduated from the Maxwell School of Citizenship and Public Affairs at Syracuse University with a doctorate in social science. In addition to contributions to numerous publications, she serves on a variety of community boards, including the Greater Rochester Health Foundation, the Rochester Regional Health Information Organization, the Excellus Blue Cross Blue Shield Regional Board, Venture Capital Foundation, and the

University of Rochester Institutional Review Board.

"We ban the use of the word 'clinic' here," Sister Chris says, "as that denotes a drop-in, disjointed model of healthcare." She explains that their vision is to operate a *medical home* that finds out what problem the patient presents, asking questions about the social determinants so they get a full picture of what their life is like: What is going on with the patient? What about a job? Transportation? Living conditions? Violence? Emotional issues? Domestic issues?

If you don't, you are leaving 90 percent of a person's life behind, Sister Chris says. "You can get their blood pressure under control with medications, but the cause is left unattended."

This way, "we can then address intervention for all the things they are struggling with. We can address them here—every one. Social determinants are just as important as the medical," Sister Chris says.

She notes that they used to separate counseling and behavior health patients from social services patients. Now, they do not, recognizing that the patient's social situation and their mental health is the same issue, no doubt something to be applauded by Patrick Kennedy.

We can find no place in America like it. There's no "free clinic" in the nation that has been in operation this long with such a comprehensive package of services.

When they bring in master's students, or young professionals in family therapy, clinical social work, and other clinical fields, Sister Chris gets to them before they get in the door.

"We say to them right from the beginning, you are not coming in here as only a mental health therapist; you are also social workers and you listen with all of those ears. They may have a housing issue. It's not yours to solve; it's yours to find out. You need to pick up on it. Tell somebody. Let us know so we can work as a team to get people what they really need," she says. "We make that connection with every student that comes in here. Listen with your whole self."

The only money St. Joseph's will gratefully accept comes from donations and the modest fees for service. They do not take third-party payments or insurance of any kind, nor do they seek state or federal funds.

Here is what you have access to for a $20 fee-for-service:

- Primary healthcare
- Physical examinations
- Work physicals
- School physicals
- Specialist consultations
- Lab work
- Eye and hearing screenings
- Nutrition education
- Diabetes education
- Smoking cessation counseling
- Gynecology
- Chiropractic, physical therapy, and therapeutic massage
- Restorative and preventive dental care
- Mental healthcare for individuals, families, and group counseling
- Psychiatry
- Social services advocacy
- Legal and financial counseling
- Healthcare access—insurance eligibility screening, application assistance, Medicaid and New York State Exchange enrollment

"We are a primary care office with extensive services," she says. "We are not free. Long ago, we figured out that it is a therapeutic necessity to pay, even a little, for the services. The services have to have a value to the patient."

In fact, almost every "free clinic" has learned that lesson and now asks for small co-pays. There are more than 1,200 free clinics in America, taking care of over five million people.

For medical or dental visits, the patient always sees the same professional, a concept aligned with Paul's *Trusted Healers* model. For mental health, the patient will always be scheduled with the same counselor.

"We have about three thousand patients, making around fifteen thousand visits per year. Of our almost three hundred volunteers, one-third are licensed, administering some of the highest quality care available. From both provision of service to funding sources, we have kept ourselves purposely unencumbered by red tape and administrative burdens so we can help people with a model of care that works," Sister Chris says.

There is no doubt that America's preoccupation with third-party payers, Medicaid and Medicare red tape, and insurer paperwork gets in the way of proper patient care. It's expensive to accept either federal program. A free clinic would have to hire trained people to administer the system, add new equipment, work longer hours, and the paperwork and the regulations would choke a horse. If they were to begin this, they would need to qualify as a "look-like" to the FQHC program.

Why do all that when there are two fabulous clinics already in the community?

"The neighborhood center model is a safety net," Sister Chris explains. "While our sister healthcare organizations in the area provide valuable service, we can do what they might not be allowed to do by state and federal funding regulations.

"We have been getting more and more attention for doing what we do. We are very careful about where money is coming from, keeping ourselves in the driver's seat in terms of any restrictions on patient care," she says.

"Here and there, our good friends with the state of New York try to figure out how to support us. The irony of this is that they look at us as the gold standard of how they want to transform the care in New York State, but they don't have a definition for this neighborhood center.

"Some think that this nation has solved the problem in healthcare. But we have not. Many of our patients work, have insurance, but cannot afford to use it. With mental health, the new parity law is wonderful and a step in the right direction, but the high co-pays disable the ability to get care." Sister Chris adds that many patients are uninsurable, some because of immigration status. "You put premiums, deductibles and co-pays together, they are spending their food money."

About 70 percent of St. Joseph's patients are working poor. Ironically, many are employed by area hospitals.

"What I found after the implementation of the Affordable Care Act is that when people get insurance on the Marketplace, they pay for insurance they cannot afford to use. Mental health parity disappears with fifty-dollar co-pays for every mental health visit. People cannot afford it. We see all of our patients for twenty-dollar co-pay, the same for chiropractic, and all other services. For those underinsured for any reason, we will see them."

How does this *primary care home* afford to provide such a comprehensive array of services for such a small co-pay? Hundreds of dedicated volunteers staff the center. They have no insurance paperwork and minimal governmental directives. Many of the pharmaceuticals are donated. And finally, they have a powerful coalition of corporate and philanthropic support behind them.

The services are so comprehensive at St. Joseph's that they had to develop a custom EHR with Greenway Health in Tampa. A standard medical record system just did not offer the ability to include dental, medical, mental health and other services under one patient record.

"They worked with us for months and months to devise how to include all of our disciplines in the same record—primary care, dental, mental health, social determinants, chiropractic, complementary medicines, and acupuncture, and all caregivers here can see what everyone else is doing."

Here is the illuminating part of this story: Sister Chris and the four other sisters who created the St. Joseph's Neighborhood Center did so without regard to any input beyond what the patients needed and asked for. They just listened to the patients and adjusted. And they did that for twenty-five years.

"We pretty much winged it," she says. "We listened to what people said they needed. We developed significant, strong partnerships in the community. We continued to grow these partnerships. Just by listening to the patients, treating people holistically, and following what we were hearing, we somehow naturally landed on the *medical home*."

The *medical home* takes many forms.

CHAPTER FOURTEEN

INNOVATION

Innovation is the most important ingredient in social change and transformation. This timeless truth does not have to play out with nations, or massive industry. It can happen with a small business. It can happen with a civic organization or in our personal lives.

Nick Donofrio, a brilliant mind in creating global change, stood watch over the center of gravity for change for four decades as executive vice president of innovation and technology at IBM.

Nick breathes innovation. He's retired from Big Blue but still very active in corporate leadership positions.

We catch up with Nick as he prepares for a board of directors meeting at a conference center in the Northern Virginia countryside. We ask Nick to tell the IBM healthcare story because he exemplifies how a leader makes decisions, uses innovation and creates change that matters to people worldwide. We still hear the historical echoes of his journey through the last forty years of high-stakes technological revolution. His aspirations come from the heart.

Did the company's goal to transform global healthcare seem a bit ambitious? Not to Nick. Not to anyone around Nick.

During his tenure, he worked for seven of IBM's eight CEOs. In 1967, when Nick joined the company, Thomas Watson, Jr., was

CEO and named among the "100 Persons of the Century" by *TIME*. Watson was called "the greatest capitalist in history" and one of "100 most influential people of the 20th century."

Nick led IBM's technology and innovation strategies from 1997 until his retirement in October 2008. His responsibilities included research, governmental programs, technical support and quality, corporate community relations, as well as environmental health and product safety. In 2008, IBM honored Nick as an IBM fellow, the company's highest technical honor.

Nick holds seven technology patents and membership in numerous technical and science honor societies. His honors include fellow of the Institute for Electrical and Electronics Engineers, fellow of the UK-based Royal Academy of Engineering, a member of the US-based National Academy of Engineering, and fellow of the American Academy of Arts and Sciences. He serves as a director for many corporations.

"Why would we not want to transform global healthcare? We are the founder of 'World Peace through World Trade,'" says Nick. "It's no accident that IBM innovates itself into residing at the center of gravity for changing 'healthcare' into the bright new future of 'life sciences.'"

IBM's global impact began with corporate diplomacy in the decades surrounding World War II, which marked a shift in the company's relations with international organizations. Before World War II, the work of charismatic chairman Thomas J. Watson, Sr., for the International Chamber of Commerce suggested that free trade and reduction of tariff barriers would create a peaceful global order independent of intergovernmental organizations. After the war, Watson sought the support of intergovernmental organizations such as the United Nations for regulatory frameworks that enabled the pursuit of international corporate operations. Thus, the meaning of the slogan *World Peace through World Trade* subtly shifted to *World Peace for World Trade*.

"In the old IBM, the IBM I joined, we did everything ourselves. It's hard to believe, but IBM in the United States employed more tool and dye makers than any other company when I joined the firm in the early 1960s," Nick says. "The tools we needed, we made—on our own machines. We made the machines that made the machines. You talk about artificial intelligence, you know, and bots and robots making robots—we made machines that make machines."

As the new millennium approached, the company was determined to figure out what connectivity and technology it could provide for healthcare. It soon realized that it would have to team with people outside the company to figure out the best ways to leverage its expertise.

"We know that *life sciences* is the science for the twenty-first century. Just as computer science was the science of the twentieth century," Nick says. The interesting point here, Nick says, is that you cannot do *life sciences* without computer science. "So, from a business perspective, we were in a pretty good position to really make a difference."

IBM had the tools to make a huge contribution. It had data and computational skills that could be used by scientists.

"We were not good biologists. We were not life scientists," he says. But the company was perfectly suited to give those in the medical field the support and technology to advance healthcare. The move helped IBM transform itself from a technology company to an innovations company.

"We had to remember to start with the problem, not with the answer," Nick says. "Because we are engineers and scientists, we tend to start with the answer. We start with what we know. Don't ask, 'What is the opportunity?' Ask, 'What is the problem?'"

The company responded by building a collaborative, open, global, and multi-disciplined environment.

"We did not allow anyone to make assumptions about people," Nick recalls. "We welcomed everybody to participate because we were not smart enough to know who doesn't matter. And we recognized that going in. So, we built environments all over the world that supported this, that enabled this."

Nick says this inclusivity is critical to becoming an innovative company, or an innovative force in the life sciences marketplace. "We fold it in, fold it up, and fold it under. We built stronger and stronger research teams, with people who knew what they were talking about. We started to make medicine a real science. A real engineering science, where we could put discipline and structure to it, and aspire to global leadership," Nick says. "The word global is in there deliberately, because it says that you aren't the only smart people in the world. There are other people. There are other opportunities."

The result was the first InnovationJam in July 2006. It was arguably the largest online brainstorming session ever held. The event attracted more than 150,000 participants from 104 countries and 67 different companies over the course of two seventy-two-hour sessions.

IBM's then CEO Sam Palmisano's objective was to develop and bring to market the best ideas from the event. The InnovationJam yielded tens of thousands of creative and far-reaching ideas, many of which have made an impact on business and society today.

"We opened up our labs, and we said to the world, 'Here are our crown jewels, have at them,'" Sam said at the time.

He had good reason to share. An earlier visit to the company's labs had convinced him that many great ideas were percolating, but behind closed doors. In his mind, they weren't going to escape into the market using traditional development methods. As it turned out, this instrumental event guided the company's future. From those brilliant ideas, IBM selected the top ten innovations and earmarked $100 million to develop them.

"That's how we tried to get synergistic here, how we gave ourselves a jump start."

One of the discussion initiatives was healthcare for the world, Nick says. "We got all kinds of good ideas out of that. Two or three of the ten that we picked were related to healthcare."

Nick realized that he couldn't rely on insular thinking. "You have to have other people's work in front of you—what can you build on as standard? You have to be willing to be collaborative. You have to be global in your thinking, both for opportunity as well as resources and skills, realizing that you only have a limited amount of capability. You have to keep broadening and deepening yourself, bringing multiple skills to bear and orchestrate."

That's the core around which Nick Donofrio and top leadership helped remake IBM into a global innovator and enabler.

~~

Quietly, behind the scenes, IBM helped John Craig Venter with sequencing the second human genome and assembling the first team to transfect a cell with a synthetic chromosome. Venter became world famous.

"When we helped map the human genome, the energy around all that felt right. We were destined to play a big role in future healthcare," Nick says. "Our mammoth agenda around life sciences showed where the world was going and helped create new directions for our clients."

Nick is most fond of IBM's contributions to the University of Pittsburgh Medical Center. That collaboration over the last two decades helped the organization evolve from a single hospital into a sixteen-billion-dollar integrated global health enterprise.

The word *global* at that time did not have a very positive connotation in major business circles. But IBM saw that differently. Globalism and globalization were proudly used terms. The company promoted global involvement at every turn. As a public service, the company counseled the president of India on the global innovation outlook, both in healthcare and education.

"We did a big virus pandemic exercise," Nick recalls. The exercise was led by Paul and Dr. Martín-J. Sepúlveda, who served as vice president of Global Well-Being Services. The operational questions were, "How will it hurt? Where will it hurt? Are we ready?"

IBM was.

"We did all kinds of global plans, because of Paul and Martín, and we took that service and offered it to other people. But that was the kind of company we were. You have a good idea. It makes sense. It's relevant in the environment. We'll back it and we'll support it," Nick says.

Innovators like Nick Donofrio never lost sight of the fact that healthcare is one of the most important concerns of the twenty-first century. This journey is one of the most important we will ever take.

DR. PAUL GRUNDY PUTS HIS STETHOSCOPE BACK ON:

GUIDELINES ON WHAT QUESTIONS TO ASK ABOUT YOUR DIAGNOSIS

When you have been told you have a medical problem, be sure to ask these questions about your diagnosis:

"What are the different treatment options?"
"What outcome should I expect?"
"Do we have to do this now, or can we revisit it later?"
"Is there anything I can do on my own to improve my condition?"
"What are the side effects?"
"How will I hear about my test results?"
"How much will this cost me?"

CHAPTER FIFTEEN

24/7

I magine this. A healthcare system with *no waiting, no schedulers, no intermediaries.* Patients can call, they can text, and they can use any of the technologies available to contact their own primary care physician.

That physician answers his or her phone 24/7. *No time limits. No backup* of other patients in the congested waiting room. Patients have unlimited primary care services, complete access to their physician directly with *no co-pays or deductibles. No impossible demands* of the doctor while being force-fed the misery of volume-based compensation.

Sounds like a fantasy, right?

In New Jersey, some are living the dream.

Enlightened leaders there are testing an innovative employee benefit program, where families can opt in to a primary care program designed to deliver the right care, at the right time, in the right location.

They pose this question: If a *Trusted Healer*, working in an environment where he or she can practice the best medicine possible, becomes totally available at no cost 24/7 to the patient, will that result in an increase in quality of care, patient satisfaction and a decrease in overall costs?

It's called *direct primary care*, and it brings a new dimension to the idea of a *Trusted Healer*. But does it work clinically, and does it work financially?

The state, through a company called R-Health, offers state workers the option of choosing this new form of primary care. Basically, anyone who is part of the state health benefits program or the state educational health program is eligible for New Jersey's direct primary care pilot program. It's a broad cross section of people—everyone from university professors, teachers, to state troopers and firefighters. The state would like to have around 60,000 people enrolled by the end of the pilot.

Employees still have insurance, but this special *direct primary care* is fully paid for by the state as an additional benefit. The goal is to measure the cost savings, the quality of care, and the patient perceptions.

Hopefully, the results will show that even though the state pays more for the primary care benefit, other healthcare expenses reduce significantly as quality of care improves. The goal is to eliminate barriers to *Trusted Healers*, leading to happier, healthier patients, and reduced healthcare costs.

When the primary care physician gets a new patient, a careful assessment starts the relationship. The provider schedules at least an hour, and often more, to conduct an initial wellness exam. There are no co-pays and no cost sharing. Patients arrange appointments by calling the office, or using the secure app, and time is reserved each day to accommodate walk-ins and members who need to be seen immediately.

Each physician sees between 500 and 1,000 patients—less than a third of a typical primary care physician panel. The doctor is not compensated based on the volume of patient visits racked up.

Marion Ball

Studying this alternate universe is one of the top medical researchers in the world, Dr. Marion J. Ball, who probably has more initials after her name than anyone: EdD, FLHIMSS, FCHIME, FAAN, FMLA, FACMI, FIAHSI. Working in tandem is IBM's Research Division team. Paul and other IBM executives have had the privilege of working with her for many years.

"We seek to unlock the value of this form of primary care, and we are collecting the data now, as our research is in progress," Marion says.

Marion's distinguished career has included being professor emerita of Johns Hopkins University School of Nursing, and affiliate professor in the Division of Health Sciences Informatics for Johns Hopkins School of Medicine. She is a visionary in the field of health informatics with experience in the federal, academic, and private sectors. She has published some of the core texts in the field of health informatics and has thirty-five years of experience in the healthcare IT community.

She is a member of the Institute of Medicine, has served on the Board of Regents of the National Library of Medicine, and is the author and editor of twenty-seven books and over two hundred articles in the field of health informatics. Her nursing books have been translated into Chinese, Portuguese, Japanese, German, Korean, and Polish. Two of her latest books, published in 2015 and 2016, are entitled *Health Information Management Systems: Cases, Strategies, and Solutions* (Fourth Edition) and *The History of Medical Informatics in the United States* (Second Edition).

We've all experienced the classic scenario of seeking an appointment with the doctor.

It's a call—well, maybe several calls because it's busy, maybe a recording, and a dozen callbacks before the busy signal morphs into voicemail, then a return call. "What's the problem? What's your name again? May I have your date of birth? Let me see . . . your doctor is doing physicals today. How about tomorrow or Friday?"

The mounting obstacles make the ostensibly simple process of seeing your doctor seem like crossing a bridge guarded by a troll who asks you a riddle to pass, all for probably less than ten minutes with the physician or provider.

Marion and her team are working to evaluate how breaking down those barriers facilitates a personal relationship between physician and patient, improves outcomes, lowers costs, and improves everyone's satisfaction.

"The best way to describe it is like in the olden days when you have a doctor who was a friend of the family; the doctor was a valuable member of the whole community, in a different way, because everybody would know that person."

The team is studying communication technologies that work best, such as cell phone, text messaging, and wearables. She tells the story of a site visit she made to one of the New Jersey *Trusted Healers*.

"We went to New Jersey to see a specific practice with R-Health, the company providing the organization for the study. The physician asked me to follow her around, saying 'Let me show you how things work.'

"So, we were in her office, and she got a phone call. Because of privacy issues, she asked the caller if it would be okay to discuss this with a visitor in the room. He said yes. He said he had been 'bitten by a bee right under my eye.' He said, 'I am worried about my eye.'"

Marion recalls that the physician pulled up his record while he was on the phone. She asked him to take a picture with the secure app that was already installed on his phone and share it with her. He did. She evaluated the picture, prescribed a medication that was stocked in the office, and asked him if he could stop in to pick it up.

The patient stopped by a few minutes later, and his doctor took a quick look at him, confirmed that the medication prescribed was appropriate, gave it to him and asked that he message her with any changes or problems. The physician scheduled a follow-up message to be automatically sent to the patient in two days and documented the encounter in the EHR. The entire event was handled efficiently and effectively, and prevented what would have likely been an emergency room visit in a practice without the capacity to immediately respond to a patient.

This robust approach to primary care is very much about the personal aspect—how important it is to know the patient well, have a relationship with the patient.

"So, it's not a new idea," Marion says. "But it certainly is one that we are hearing more and more about now as we move into this whole new world of getting the patient involved in their care, in prevention, and taking a stake in taking care of themselves."

Patients in the study are largely under the age of sixty-five, and all are state employees or their dependents.

"Patients sixty-five and older present a whole different ballgame," Marion says. "They need to have a close personal relationship with their caregiver, but that is not what we are studying right now. What's important to this study is that you have a population of consumers who were covered in the old way and now we are looking at their healthcare coverage in the new way and we hope to see the difference in outcomes, costs and all of the other things that go along with this.

"We are beginning to see, for instance, that patient satisfaction is really high, as you would expect. But we still must see if it's cost effective. Everything comes down to *show me the money*. But if we can show that our chronic disease patients, people who have asthma or diabetes, for instance, are staying out of the emergency room, we may then show that patients are not going to the emergency room because of the direct relationship with their doctor."

The physician she accompanied on the tour had been doing this for a year and a half.

"Did she get any sleep?" we ask Marion.

"You would be surprised. She has gotten five calls in the middle of the night. Four of them, she was able to take care of on the phone. The other case went directly to the emergency room. So, in a full year, that's a pretty good record."

Marion tells us about Sasha Ballen, chief technology officer for the project in New Jersey.

Sasha Ballen

"She actually is on the front lines. None of this research study would be possible without her."

We contact Sasha at R-Health to learn more. Sasha is an expert in healthcare data analytics. She is adept at harnessing technology to drive clinical improvements and practice efficiency. Her breadth of experience in medical data spans across government, private practices, accountable care organizations, and hospital systems.

Sasha predicts that this powerful experiment will be celebrated.

"Direct primary care, to me, means a primary care relationship that is entirely divorced from volume-based incentives," Sasha says. "So, philosophically, our goal is to allow physicians to be properly compensated so that they can spend appropriate time with their patients without regard to the overall volume of their practice.

"We don't think physicians, particularly primary care physicians, should receive rewards for seeing more people. They should have incentives for helping people maintain optimum health."

Sasha says that it is really important to define that.

"That really drives my thinking, when I am trying to consider how I want to direct or develop our programs. My background is not clinical, so I am just considering what tools can I build or provide the physicians and the care teams so they can have a deeper, more meaningful connection with their patients. We want to deliver better support, help them become healthier, better utilizers of the healthcare system, to save money, and achieve their health goals."

People often talk about direct primary care in terms of *concierge care*, so it's important to talk about the definition, Sasha says. The program in New Jersey provides incentives for patient satisfaction, better health outcomes, and lower costs.

"When you take those three objectives and put them together, you are starting to approach a reasonable proxy for quality in healthcare. Quality in healthcare is so hard to define—from whose perspective are you calling something high-quality healthcare?"

Sasha explains that if you join all those elements, if you take the patient experience, the empirical data (their actual outcomes, things like their lab values, clinical information) and the total cost of care, if all three of those things improve, then you have a reasonable statement of quality.

"This is really about a physician who has enough time to really listen, take a good history, talk to people and understand what is happening in their broader life. And this is appropriate for primary care," Sasha says. "You actually don't need to encourage office visits. What you want to encourage is engagement. So, our goal is to give the right care, at the right time, in the right place. When you visit us, you will feel like it is less busy, less frantic, calmer than typical practices."

Because the physicians have fewer patients, they have enough time for longer office visits. Not every patient needs a half hour visit for an upper respiratory infection, but the half hour is reserved.

"We call it the reception area. We don't call it the waiting room."

Sasha says that traditional primary care physician's office revenue hinges on the volume of office visits. Where office visits are needed they should be easily accessible.

"Not only do we not have barriers to office visits, R-Health staff does everything they can to make the interaction between the physician and member as frictionless as possible," Sasha says.

A traditional office, out of necessity, sets up a kind of a gatekeeper, or barrier system between the patient and the physician—layers of people who are stopping the patient from getting to the physician.

"This time-honored tradition takes you further away from your physician, and the feeling that your physician is someone that you can go to for help and advice. We try to remove as many of those barriers as possible, so people get access to their physician day and night through an app on their phone.

"They call in the middle of the night if they are scared, if they think they may need to go to the emergency room, or if they are worried about some kind of acute issue," she says. "Our physicians always say, 'Yeah, they might call me in the middle of the night, but really when they do, it is because they need me. People don't call frivolously.'"

Primary care providers generally don't enter practice to become rich, Paul reminds us. They go into primary care because they love to help people and they want to treat their patients, he says.

Sasha agrees.

"Generally speaking, the doctors who sign on to our model of care are the folks who want the time and space to deliver that kind of care to their patients. It's really not appropriate for every single physician. For the physicians who went to medical school to be this kind of doctor, this model really changes their professional experience."

～～

The New Jersey study has been ongoing since January 2017 and has provided great feedback from participants. Early indications reveal significant savings by a reduction in ER utilization and hospital readmission rates.

"It's not that the physicians in a traditional fee-for-service practice don't want to deliver excellent care. I feel sorry for the physicians on the treadmill," Sasha says. "It's terrible for them. Dr. Grundy will tell you that. They are often not enjoying their work. I think our healthcare system is built upon perverse incentives. The role of primary care in this country has been just absolutely destroyed over the past forty years."

New Jersey could help correct course.

"I think that when we show results, the state will roll this out on more than just a pilot program; they will build it into the plan design. There are a lot of things that an employer group can do that will motivate engagement in a program like this," Sasha says.

"Their employees still have traditional insurance. They might need specialist care, but they contract with us to deliver the primary care piece of the puzzle, so the state pays a bit more for their enhanced primary care, and the overall spending goes down because patients are better managed.

"I spent a lot of time working in a *medical home* environment. One of the things I took away was how the cards are stacked against the primary care physician. You take the *medical home*, fundamentally a wonderful concept—then you have the underlying fee-for-service volume-based nightmare. We just have to get rid of the fee-for-service system. It's a terrible system for primary care," Sasha says.

That's one of the things we hope could result from the innovations here. If we could find a way out of volume-based medicine, everyone would look like what Marion and Sasha Ballen's clinical teams are doing.

Sasha offers a parting thought. "One of the things that we talk about internally is that we need to reeducate everybody. We need to tell the patient to expect more. Patients don't really expect much from their primary care physician at this point. I think that just like physicians want to deliver more, patients have to be educated on expecting more," Sasha says.

CHAPTER SIXTEEN

RIGHT, NOT PRIVILEGE

Approximately 70 percent of health center patients have family incomes at or below 100 percent of the poverty level; 40 percent are uninsured; 36 percent depend on Medicaid; approximately 66 percent are racial and ethnic minorities.

Caring for this patient demographic requires greater resources and more challenging work environments. Dr. J. Nwando Olayiwola leads a crusade to rectify the gaping disparities in healthcare.

Dr. Olayiwola is a family physician and the inaugural chief clinical transformation officer for RubiconMD, a leading provider of electronic platforms that improve primary care access to specialty care for underserved patients. As a clinical transformation specialist, she champions quality, equitable healthcare for disadvantaged citizens and those who are socioeconomically deprived.

She also provides clinical care at the Zuckerberg San Francisco General Hospital and Trauma Center and is an associate physician and clinical instructor at the University of California, San Francisco. She teaches at the Center for Family and Community Medicine at the Columbia University Medical Center. Her resume includes stints as director of the University of California San Francisco's

Center for Excellence in Primary Care, and the chief medical officer of Connecticut's celebrated Community Health Center, Inc., which received the highest level of *medical home* accreditations in the US. She is an expert in the areas of health systems reform, practice transformation, health information technology, and primary care redesign.

"Social injustice and social inequities invariably impact health and healthcare. First, we have got to accept and believe that. Then we can do something about it," Dr. Olayiwola says.

Her mastery of social equity and quality healthcare derives in part from traveling the world with Paul and from her career experience leading the transformation of twelve federally qualified health centers (FQHCs) into the highest level of accreditation for *medical homes* in America.

"It's a badge of honor to say your organization is a *medical home*. It makes the statement that you provide high-quality care, organized around what care delivery should look like, and that you put a lot of thought into how healthcare should look into the future," she says.

"However, the recognition or certificate is not enough. You have to really make the fundamental changes that this requires. Part of the challenge is how to actually redesign a ship that is already in motion. People are still coming for care. You cannot stop seeing patients to reengineer the system. You've got to do it in real time, while they are there."

When Dr. Olayiwola assumed the FQHC chief medical officer post in Connecticut, she reached out to Paul.

FQHCs are community-based healthcare organizations that provide services to patients regardless of their ability to pay. The federal government first funded them as part of the War on Poverty in the mid-1960s. For more than fifty years, these health centers have delivered affordable, accessible, quality, and cost-effective primary healthcare. During that time, health centers have become an essential primary care provider for millions of people across the country.

FQHCs must meet a stringent set of requirements, including operating under a governing board that includes a majority of patients. They may be community health centers, migrant health centers, or healthcare for the homeless.[28]

Today, nearly 1,400 health centers operate more than 11,000 service delivery sites. More than twenty-seven million people from every US state, the District of Columbia, Puerto Rico, the US Virgin Islands, and the Pacific Basin rely on these health centers for care.

FQHCs integrate primary medical, dental, mental health, substance use disorder, vision care, and patient support services such as medical transportation and education. They are also increasingly becoming the first line of defense in combatting the nation's opioid epidemic.

In 2017, nearly 90 percent of health centers provided mental healthcare to more than two million people nationwide. Additionally, nearly 70 percent of health centers offered substance use disorder services, including medication-assisted treatment.

The FQHC clinics provide an enormous amount of primary care to disadvantaged populations all over the nation. While the degree of difficulty to transform to a *medical home* seems, at first glance, much higher for these centers than a typical primary care practice, the movement Dr. Olayiwola helped inspire in Connecticut has spread throughout the nation.

"How do you take a living, breathing institution and change it so radically while you are delivering care and trying to make sure you don't make any mistakes? Our team found the way," Dr. Olayiwola says.

Challenges include the physician culture, recruitment of doctors, a lack of uniformity from state to state, and greater demands on information sharing, teamwork and documentation.

"The *medical home* model requires a strong healthcare team working together to ensure that patient education, care coordination, and preventive care are all provided," Dr. Olayiwola wrote with co-author Dr. Daren R. Anderson in a 2012 issue of *Journal of Health Care for the Poor and Underserved*.

"Such a team requires physicians to function more as leaders and delegators, sharing responsibility for many routine tasks that previously they would accomplish themselves. This represents an important change in physician culture and personal identity that sometimes presents a major challenge for practices going through redesign."[29]

So, in this regard, Drs. Olayiwola and Anderson suggest, FQHCs already have a shared leadership culture, which is less hierarchical than traditional practices, and therefore more easily make this cultural transition.

Dr. Olayiwola has traveled the world to expand the reach of the *medical home*, to build awareness, and to consult on its adaptation. She has participated in workshops with Paul in Australia, Ireland, Denmark, and Singapore, as well as countless presentations in the US.

She says that other countries are wisely embracing the *medical home* model, molding it into their cultures, and coming up with some really innovative, provocative shifts in the way they deliver care. She is currently collaborating on such *medical home* adaptations in Australia and New Zealand.

Dr. Olayiwola and Paul have become a powerful combination. They have inspired the transformation of clinics and systems across the country. While doing so, she makes sure that the voice of the disadvantaged is always represented.

In early 2019, Paul's colleagues, inspired by the work of Dr. Olayiwola with FQHC *medical homes*, began helping a major American healthcare corporation in Tuba City, Arizona. This organization serves rural and school-based sites throughout the Western Navajo chapters and individuals who live in a 6,000-square-mile region that's also part of the Navajo, Hopi and San Juan Southern Paiute reservations.

Long-term colleague Bert Miuccio, HealthTeamWorks' chief executive officer, notes that Tuba City Regional Health Care Corporation will be earning *medical home* recognition to take advantage of Arizona's new Medicaid American Indian *Medical Home* designation and greatly improve access and quality of care.

"Paul has a tremendous amount of emotional intelligence and cultural sensitivity. We have collaborated on work in so many countries. It's an amazing experience to see his level of awareness, sensitivity, and respect—with humility and also authority," Dr. Olayiwola says. "Paul drives the momentum around it, creating buy-in, changing payment structures, and bringing people around the table. What's better than that representative and inclusive combination?"

On one memorable trip, Paul and Dr. Olayiwola met in Copenhagen, Denmark, one of Dr. Olayiwola's many stops in Europe while she was a Marshall Memorial fellow of the German Marshall Fund of the United States in 2014.

"I wanted to learn how the healthcare and social services needs of new immigrants and first-generation families were met in various European contexts," Dr. Olayiwola says. "In addition, because first and second-generation immigrants are often marginalized, I took advantage of the opportunity to explore public policy issues to achieve health equity."

One of the common threads in how these countries provide for their underserved populations—whether it be indigenous Basque communities in Spain, refugees in Bosnia, or Senegalese immigrants in France—is that everyone views healthcare as a fundamental right for all, she says.

In between meetings in Copenhagen, Paul and Dr. Olayiwola took a bus to visit a neighborhood with a predominantly immigrant population from North Africa and the Middle East. Dr. Olayiwola recalls watching Paul and his way with the strangers he met. Paul asked residents there about their medical care: "How do you get your healthcare? Do you know your GP?"

Dr. Olayiwola shares the story of one Danish resident in a department store who told Paul about his great relationship with his doctor.

"So, there we are at a department store, talking to this man at the suitcase counter about his great GP," she says. "That conversation underscored for me the fact that our work cannot be just about the system we are changing—we cannot just change the structure of things; it has to be about the relationships because this is what makes people light up. They are not thinking about the building and the care model. They care about the relationships, and we have got to make sure we don't lose that in this. Watching Paul make that connection was just outstanding.

"He really is a global citizen, like my father," Dr. Olayiwola continues. "You could just plop them in any country. They don't have to speak the language; they don't have to know anything about it. They will find a way to connect with people and to have the people trust them. People feel comfortable doing that with Paul. That is not something that you can just do. You have to have a certain gift. Observing that little session in Denmark, this guy just trusted Paul, not knowing him at all. He believed in him. Without any question."

Dr. Olayiwola knows the importance of listening to and *hearing* patients, especially the disenfranchised or impoverished.

"We do not have a healthcare system in America that has achieved real equity," she says. "We have a lot to do in the sense that we don't even yet agree that health disparities exist, that disparities are real for groups of people, based on their zip code, the color of their skin, their sexual preferences, their religion, their ethnicity or their status, whether immigrants or citizens. People don't yet believe that this has an impact on their health and their healthcare in America.

"We need a new awareness, a shared agreement that aligns around the fact that social injustice and social inequities invariably impact health and healthcare. We have got to believe it. Then we can do something about it. Because if we tried to just fix the problem with healthcare, that may not be enough," Dr. Olayiwola says.

She tells a story from her FQHC experiences in the state of Connecticut.

"We built a beautiful flagship community health center in central Connecticut, right there in Middletown with a rooftop garden and probably the most aesthetically pleasing healthcare site you have ever seen in your life. It's great. The patients would come in and feel, 'Wow, I can get healthcare in this type of setting?'

"But if you are getting healthcare from somewhere like that, though it's a beautiful place, but you can't drink clean water in Flint, Michigan, or if gang violence is disrupting your city or threatening your life, or you don't have any fresh produce because there are only bodegas around and you cannot actually access a grocery store with fresh produce—you will still have the structural, environmental, social ills and challenges that keep people from being healthy."

Dr. Olayiwola says the biggest challenge for this next generation is working to build a good society—a healthy, safe, equitable society that will then be a foundation for good health.

"If we go the other way," she says, "where we just keep building healthcare system structures and hope the other issues will just get fixed, we won't get much. It's been great to see that in England, for example, where Paul has done a lot of work. They believe that social care and medical care are not separate. Here in the US, many times when I start to talk about the importance of social justice, to care for patients' larger social needs, I hear the pushback, 'Well, we are already asking doctors to do so much. Why do we have to have that in healthcare?' That's often what you get unless you're preaching to a choir that understands.

"In England, Australia, and many other developed nations,

the social impact on health is very well believed and understood. Something as vital as good healthcare should never be a victim of zero-sum thinking. If one stakeholder wins, another does not have to lose. We do not have to continue to believe that there is not enough to go around. There is."

Dr. Olayiwola predicts that the US will get to a place where we agree that healthcare is a right and not a privilege, and more than that, *equitable* healthcare is a right and not a privilege.

Or simply, *everyone matters.*

"The kind of healthcare that I get in my socioeconomic bracket with my brown skin should be the same as someone in another socioeconomic bracket with another color skin. This should be the same. And that should be the same as someone in another socioeconomic bracket with a different identity. Whether or not I choose to access it or tap into it is another thing," Dr. Olayiwola says.

She says, as does Paul, that everyone should have access to the same thing at a bare minimum, and that bare minimum should be high quality.

"We can decide what are the bells and whistles to add on top of that. In the future, that's what we will get to, because we will get past this argument that healthcare is a right and we will believe that. And then we will believe that equity in healthcare is important. We will get there."

Dr. Olayiwola also hopes to see in her lifetime healthcare included in social and environmental contexts. For example, people need to understand that gun reform is healthcare reform. Everything that has a social, environmental, or political nuance has implications for healthcare.

"If we can say that we view youth and gang violence as a threat to healthcare, that it's a public health crisis that perpetuates cycles of poverty and disenfranchisement, then we have arrived. If we can draw these parallels and be comfortable addressing those parallels .. . if we can see that, then I see great things ahead," Dr. Olayiwola says.

CHAPTER SEVENTEEN

A BETTER PLACE

Hope Mills is a small country town near Fayetteville, NC. It's a friendly, family-oriented community with little violent crime, lovely neighborhoods, and it's convenient to military bases and a good place to start a business. Ample hospitals are nearby with good primary healthcare. There are great parks and lakes, and involved citizens watch out for each other—a trait important to surviving and recovering from hurricane-induced flooding, which happens more frequently than anyone would like. It's home to Josh Hair, national champion watermelon seed spitter, second in renown to one of the nation's chief healers, Dr. Douglas E. Henley.

You can guess his origin from his slight Southern drawl, quite charming for the No. 1 statesman of family medicine in America. He is known for his keen intelligence, matched with a unique ability to listen, to collaborate, to bring people together.

Dr. Henley very much misses his patients and practicing medicine in Hope Mills.

But now, as CEO of the American Academy of Family Physicians (AAFP), he brings great minds together running the nerve center for primary care in America.

AAFP is the national specialty society of family doctors. It is one of the largest national medical organizations, with 131,400 members in fifty states, Washington, DC, Puerto Rico, the Virgin Islands, and Guam, as well as internationally. Its doctors are on the front lines of a suffocating healthcare system in desperate need of reform.

⌒

As you would expect, Dr. Henley's resume is extensive. Prior to his career with AAFP, he served in private practice for twenty years in his hometown of Hope Mills. He is a current and founding member of the board of directors of the Patient-Centered Primary Care Collaborative and served as its chairman. He was a founding member of the Ambulatory Care Quality Alliance Steering Committee and serves on the steering committee of the Core Quality Measure Collaborative and has been a commissioner on the American Health Information Community and the Certification Commission for Healthcare Information Technology. Other past appointments include serving on the editorial boards of *Family Practice News* and *Journal of Family Practice* and as a member of the board of directors of the *Annals of Family Medicine.*

Dr. Henley holds an MD from the University of North Carolina Chapel Hill School of Medicine and the university's family medicine residency program. He is board certified by the American Board of Family Medicine.

Meeting with Dr. Henley on a hot summer afternoon in Washington, DC, we talk about the early days of primary care transformation working with Paul. They first met in 2006, when the gathering began to form the Patient-Centered Primary Care Collaborative.

"We learned so much from Paul, watching him work and advocate all over the world," Dr. Henley says. "He steadily showed us lessons we need to remember here every day."

One of Paul's many lessons was to let physicians initiate changes.

"Let's experiment there. Show outcomes. Show improvement. It will take care of itself," Dr. Henley says. "The term I use for that is *cheerful persistence*. It's not going to happen overnight. You've got to continue to look to the future to what you want the outcome to be. Don't take your eye off the target."

Dr. Henley and his colleagues carefully monitor medical innovations from around the world. They contemplate whether what they see can be woven into our system, whether they are government or private-sector initiated and managed. Dr. Henley says he is convinced that the US must have primary care as the core of its solution. If it's all about consolidation or market share, then it is about saving money. The answer is in the *medical home* and foundational primary care and the value and impact of continuous healing relationships over time.

While those in *medical home* practice still feel the pain of fee-for-service structures and volume-based compensation, overall Dr. Henley views the nation's journey to the *medical home* as a triumphant affirmation.

"Two years ago, we did one of our family medicine member surveys and adoption was at 45 percent," he recalls, "and it's better than that today. We knew then as we know now—primary care also has to stand up, improve, and march toward team-based, patient-centered care. In my view, if you look at our beginning, and look at where we are today, I think we are in a different and better place, even with all the struggles, challenges and frustrations that we have with the current system."

Dr. Henley observes that the high adoption rate of the *medical home* is true for primary care practices, independent or employee situations, or even in academic situations, residency programs and everywhere there is primary care.

He says that primary care physicians, in general, have stepped up to the plate, and are working hard to continue to improve and transform.

"I think there continues to be a need for employers and insurers to know that a practice of medicine has standards. So that's very important. It's time consuming and costly for practices to go through *medical home* transformation and designation, and I know many of them feel that there has not been enough payment reform to support and sustain it. So therein lies some tension. But everyone is working hard to demonstrate improved patient outcomes, better management of overall healthcare costs, and improved physician satisfaction and patient experience.

"I am very pleased with where we are," he continues. "It's not that we shouldn't continue to talk about it, we shouldn't continue to emphasize it—we should do all those things." But the issue of increasing regulatory and administrative burden, especially prior authorization, presents a huge challenge and needs attention by employers, policy makers, and payers. Additionally, dysfunctional and clunky EHRs have only added to this burden by making all physicians—especially primary care doctors—very expensive data entry clerks, taking precious time away from patient care and the important connection between patient and physician.

It has become "the death of the healing relationship by a thousand clicks," Dr. Henley says. And the result has been the erosion of trust, quality of care, and patient and physician satisfaction.

"Unfortunately, our primary care doctors still struggle with burnout—not just physicians, but other clinicians as well. We need to solve some of the technology problems we face with the EHR. It's just wearing people out," Dr. Henley says.

———

Among Dr. Henley's many allies is Dr. Michael Barr, who helped lead the American College of Physicians to join the other primary care associations in the reform effort. Today the ACP has more than 154,000 members internationally—the largest medical-specialty society in the world.

"We met in Philadelphia in April 2006. Joining Dr. Paul Grundy was IBM's Dr. Martín-J. Sepúlveda as they presented the idea of uniting what Paul calls the 'House of Primary Care,'" Dr. Barr recalls. "Yet even then, the large corporations loved the principles we developed, but emphasized that there would be no additional remuneration for practices unless we created an assessment process to identify exactly what is a *medical home.*"

Today, Dr. Barr carries that flag for the *medical home,* helping to develop the accreditation standards for medical practices seeking *medical home* designation. He is executive vice president of quality measurement and research for the National Committee for Quality Assurance (NCQA), which recognizes about 85 percent of *medical home* practices in the US.

Many federal, state, and commercial payers offer incentive programs to practices that achieve NCQA recognition, which offsets some of the costs of the process. The vast majority of the costs are associated with elevating and improving primary care operations. That leads to the gap between what primary care practices get paid (and how they get paid) for routine services versus the additional costs and support necessary to perform (and sustain performance) as a patient-centered *medical home* (PCMH.)

Dr. Barr explains that newer *medical homes* look a little different. Some have established mental health services. Others have extended hours and access.

"We continually seek the advice of our practice community. To become a recognized PCMH under the NCQA 2017 program, practices need to meet all forty core criteria and achieve twenty-five credits from the menu of elective criteria," Dr. Barr says.

"The way we accredit a *medical home* has completely changed since the early days, where there were three different recognition levels. We have streamlined everything while holding the standards quite high. Every practice needs to get ready for value-based compensation, and the PCMH model helps prepare practices for this challenge."

Championing that effort is Ann Greiner, president and CEO of Patient-Centered Primary Care Collaborative. We meet her just prior to the 2018 Annual PCPCC Conference in Washington, which draws healthcare stakeholders from all over the world and features some of the most powerful and influential healthcare leaders in America.

Ann Greiner, Dr. Paul Grundy, and Dr. Doug Henley

Ann agrees with Dr. Henley that primary care is warming up for a victory lap.

"I do feel that there has been widespread adoption of the *medical home* by commercial plans, the federal government, and by states—both Medicaid and in their capacity as purchasers of healthcare for their employees," Ann says.

"In addition, the military has embraced the *medical home*. Its *medical home* model— I'm thinking particularly about the VA and Navy—is particularly robust and does a fantastic job of integrating mental health into primary care. They are a single payer and have made decisions to create an expansive care team and have made the investments to support team-based care. Overall, the *medical home* model is very successful," she says.

Ann is the energetic voice of the PCPCC, responsible for leading organizational strategy. At a critical time in US health policy, Ann works across a diverse stakeholder group of more than seventy executive member organizations to direct PCPCC policy. They collaborate to advance an effective and efficient healthcare system built on the strong foundation of primary care and the patient-centered *medical home*.

Prior to leading the collaborative, she served as vice president of public affairs for the National Quality Forum, and as deputy director at the Institute of Medicine (now the National Academies of Medicine). She also held leadership positions at NCQA and the American Board of Internal Medicine and served in the Jesuit Volunteer Corps (JVC), working in the ghetto in Los Angeles, an experience that has guided her professional aspirations ever since.

"The JVC's slogan was *ruined for life*; I was ruined in a good way," Ann says.

Like Dr. Henley, she is deeply concerned about physician burnout.

"We are focused on getting more resources into the *medical home* and other advanced models of primary care so that the full model can be implemented and move primary care away from fee-for-service payment."

Ann says progress has been made, but not every patient-centered *medical home* across America is fully developed. Many *medical home* practices have not yet added behavioral health to help address mental health and big societal issues like substance abuse disorder and addiction. And not every PCMH has a full-fledged team.

"There are many models where we've got physicians, medical assistants, aides and nurse-practitioners on the primary care team. But in others, we don't have a behavioral health resource. We don't have someone who can guide you in terms of your diet or help you achieve other healthy habits. Many *medical homes* still do not have well-developed links to the community to help address the social determinants of health," Ann says.

The US health system is moving away from a payment system that rewards providers for doing more and toward population-based models that lead to more investment in primary care as health systems are paid to keep people healthy and effectively manage their chronic conditions, but many analysts think the evolution has been too slow.

Ann offers another solution. States can compel health plans to invest more in primary care and *medical homes,* to move from an average of 5 to 8 percent of total healthcare dollars spent on primary care to 10 to 12 percent.

Ann says that this has happened in Rhode Island and Oregon. Other states have introduced such legislation, including Delaware, Colorado, California and Vermont.

The PCPCC's aspiration is to nurture a budding movement on the part of the states to start investing in advanced models of primary care as a wildfire strategy, leading to a national discussion about greater investment in primary care in time for the next presidential administration. Ann also aspires to become a beacon for innovative employers and insurers that want to design benefits that support robust, patient-centered primary care.

Dr. Henley alludes to a larger story in America: The increasing consolidation of hospital and healthcare systems, supposedly to improve quality, has in reality resulted in a focus on increasing market share and greater bargaining power for higher payment.

As these healthcare systems intentionally employ primary care physicians, they establish payment models that encourage volume over value and financial incentives to keep referrals and diagnostic testing within the system.

This not only increases overall costs, especially to patients, but it also creates potential ethical conflicts when the most appropriate referral may be outside the system to a more qualified specialist or less costly diagnostic testing.

Ann concurs, noting that *trust* is a big topic in healthcare. The American Board of Internal Medicine held a three-day meeting on trust in medicine. Like every other institution in America, trust seems to be suffering.

Dr. Henley addresses those headwinds.

"Artificial intelligence and machine learning have great potential to reduce the administrative burdens I noted before, as well as simplifying documentation in EHRs. There is great hope for advancing appropriate clinical decision support information at the point of care, including quality and cost data for patient referrals when appropriate. But the implementation of these evolving technologies needs to occur carefully and properly and with a focus on the needs of primary care and its workflow."

While some key indicators are trending well for primary care, more people are becoming uninsured again, Dr. Henley laments. Or if they are insured, it is likely that their deductibles and co-pays are sky-high on the healthcare exchanges and increasingly in employer-sponsored health plans as well.

"Because of that, people are not accessing primary care. This is a big leap backward away from supporting foundational primary care, and I worry about the future of our country in this regard," Dr. Henley warns.

Ann notes that the *medical home* may not spread as rapidly as it could unless we change payment and change benefit designs. If I have a $1,500 or $5,000 annual deductible, it's a cash decision to go to my *Trusted Healer* until I have spent that down, and some families do not have that cash on hand. That's not in the spirit of where we need to be," she says.

In developed nations where, as a society, they believe that *everyone matters*, healthcare is smoother, not as expensive, more accessible, more appreciated, and produces better outcomes.

Ann says, "There are also countries that use private entities to deliver care. It doesn't necessarily have to be a public model. I am thinking about the Dutch. They have private plans, but they also have a social construct that healthcare is a right. So, they have a very different point of view and they have government policies that reflect that.

"In the Netherlands, the private plans operate within agreed-upon swim lanes. I don't think they would ever tolerate not providing care to someone who has a preexisting condition because that would go against their societal norms. It's not like the government has to be in charge of everything," Ann continues. "There are systems where private entities have a significant role."

Like Ann, Dr. Henley wishes the US would replicate Denmark. But, he says, there are real differences between the nations that must be acknowledged. "It's a small country, small population, very homogenous. For centuries, they have made the social choice that they are going to support each other and will pay for that through taxes or whatever the structure may be."

Denmark spends about 19 percent of total healthcare spending on primary care.

"They have that commitment to each other. Our country, like many others around the world, is much more diverse than Denmark and more challenging in terms of variations in economy, income level and things like that," Dr. Henley says. "So, how do we get to a better place? Like Denmark, we can go to the same starting place— robust, enduring foundational primary care."

We ask Ann what advice she would give today's American healthcare consumer about a *medical home* and getting to that "better place."

"We really need to get our care from a practice that understands how important it is to work with patients to do all we can to avoid getting sick in the first place. We want a partner who knows us, a practice that partners with us, encouraging healthy behaviors, such as diet, exercise, and proper sleep. We want a *Trusted Healer* who not only understands what our medical needs are, but our mental health needs and what our preferences are for the kind of care we receive.

"And that should be our patient-centered *medical home*. We should want a care team that will help keep us healthy, help us manage chronic or acute situations that arise, and also interpret all this information that is coming at us from the Internet—we really need help in how we navigate healthcare."

Donald M. Berwick, MD, MPP, president emeritus and senior fellow at the Institute for Healthcare Improvement, has shown that 15 to 30 percent of the healthcare spending in this country is unnecessary, duplicative, or doesn't lead to better outcomes. That's a large amount of a 3.6-trillion-dollar healthcare economy that could be redirected to primary care without increasing overall spending.

According to a Kaiser Foundation analysis for 2017, other wealthy countries spend about half as much per person on healthcare as does the US.[30]

US $10,348
Switzerland $7,919
Germany $5,550
Netherlands $5,385
Austria $5,227
Average $5,169
Belgium $4,839
Canada $4,752
Australia $4,708
France $4,600
Japan $4,519
UK $4,912

Over the past four decades, the difference between health spending as a share of the economy in the US and comparable countries has widened. In 1970, the US spent about 6 percent of its GDP on health, similar to spending by several comparable countries, where the average was 5 percent.

The US was relatively on pace with other countries until the 1980s, when its health spending grew at a significantly faster rate relative to its GDP. In 2016, the US spent nearly 18 percent of its GDP on health, whereas the next highest comparable country, Switzerland, devoted less than 13 percent of its GDP to health.

One of the most outspoken physicians on this issue is Dr. Ted Epperly, past board chair and president of the American Academy of Family Physicians, and author of *Fractured: America's Broken Health Care System and What We Must Do to Heal It.*

We meet with Dr. Epperly in Chicago. He offers urgent words that Paul knows all too well—that the arrival of social unrest has already happened in America.

"We're really dealing already with the have and have-not system of rationing care. It gets rationed to the rich, who over-utilize, and kept away from the poor, who are priced out of the market. So, in some ways, I think we are already doing that; we're just using the capitalistic model to do it, versus a socialistic model, which other countries are grappling with."

Dr. Epperly says the Canadian system is so much better than ours, and they ration it based on time. Everybody can get access, but there are certain people who go to the front of the queue based on urgency. The US's financial system of rationing foments inequity and social unrest.

"I think it will only get worse, and my sense is that we have already seen the early warning symptoms of it. I think it can lead to continued social unrest in our nation, because of the unjustness of it."

Dr. Epperly reminds us that Martin Luther King, Jr., once said that of all the forms of inequality, injustice in healthcare is the most shocking and inhumane.

"I think there is a lot of truth to that, in the sense of what it means to the poor and underserved. If you are living sick and dying younger, you are never achieving what you could achieve in terms of educational potential. You'll never achieve the job income you could have achieved. It almost locks in our social system," Dr. Epperly says.

"It's sad to see a nation that touts itself like ours does around 'freedom for all,' social justice issues around 'everybody should have a shot'—that we have actually put a system in place to keep that from happening."

We are in crisis and don't know it, he says.

"I will go as far to say that many just don't care. It's not their fight. It's 'pull yourself up by your bootstraps,' and if you can't do it, then so be it. *C'est la vie.* At some point, what is our obligation to be a brother to our fellow man?"

Dr. Epperly points to a lurking danger to those between the ages of fifty and sixty-five. "We have gotten old enough that we start to develop chronic diseases. It could be the early emergence of cancer. It could be late emergence of bad health behaviors catching up with us. If you are underinsured in that age group, or you lack insurance before you get to the Medicare age of sixty-five, then you live sicker and die younger. You actually have diseases that get out of control because you can't get the care needed to get them under control—rheumatoid arthritis and diabetes are classic examples of this. And so, you actually get sicker in the process. You then crash into age sixty-five with a whole lot of badness on your health plate and all of a sudden the system is trying to play catch up with you, at high cost."

Dr. Epperly suggests that the US offer Medicare to those age fifty and older. That would create a healthier society and lower healthcare costs by keeping this aging demographic healthier.

"We are evading our responsibility in particular to that age group. If you retire early, or you just can't afford the premiums on your healthcare policy at that age, it's a critical time period. I see that happening now in many of my patients in the fifty to sixty-five-year-old age group. They hold on, almost until they can't hold on any longer, and then they turn sixty-five and then I see them and I look at a lengthy list of problems. So, I ask, 'Mr. Smith, why didn't you address this sooner?' 'I didn't have the resources to do it.'"

Dr. Epperly offers a true example of a recent case.

"A wonderful sixty-year-old woman. She developed an abdominal mass in the fall of 2017. She had a six-thousand-dollar deductible, and she couldn't afford what she perceived to be the workup for this. She just hoped against hope. She got a new health plan in January.

Her company was sold and she shifted to a new, lower deductible plan. So she went in on January 4 and was seen. On January 5, she received the diagnosis of metastatic pancreatic cancer. She died on February 23.

"I share this tragedy to illustrate that even for those insured, you can be so underinsured that it drives your healthcare behaviors in negative ways."

He laments the confusion over healthcare in America.

"Most people, unless they know this business, don't know which way is up on a lot of this stuff. It's just become a morass." Sometimes the only way to know, he suggests, is to have a family member who has gone through it or to be in it yourself.

"We want to try to educate as many people as possible and try to have them understand what in the hell is going on here. I hate to see this happening. It really is a problem. The leading cause of bankruptcy is health bills."

⌐⌐

Like Dr. Epperly, Dr. Robert Juhasz has seen the consequences of inaccessible or unaffordable healthcare on the aging population. He's an osteopathic pioneer of the *medical home* movement. He helped guide the transformation of primary care to *medical homes* at the Cleveland Clinic, where he has practiced for the last twenty years.

Dr. Juhasz (pronounced You-haz) served on the Accreditation Council for Graduate Medical Education board with Paul. We interview him in Chicago. He has a calming influence and obviously loves the art of medicine and his leadership roles.

Dr. Juhasz reflects on the last three decades of change he has experienced as a physician.

"The pace of change in healthcare has continued to accelerate. That being said, some ideas rejected in the past, such as prepaid capitated care, have again taken a foothold. Today, we are trying to improve the care, making sure we have time to do the right things for the people we are privileged to see. That's the physicians' struggle today—making sure you take care of people, not just problems."

Dr. Juhasz notes that primary care is still challenged to improve care of chronically ill patients.

"Today's patients are sicker. Unfortunately, we are in a position now where the data entry person is the provider. When you go home at night and spend two or three hours at home doing documentation, or you stay an extra two or three hours at work doing medical records, you get burned out. You're not quite ready the next day," he notes. "If we could find a solution to that, I think it would be a huge leverage point to make a practice more joyful."

Part Three

INSPIRING A
COURSE AHEAD

CHAPTER EIGHTEEN

MENTORING

S ince the earliest records of civilization, mentors have carefully passed down knowledge and skills for survival to the younger generations. *Mentor* entered the language through Greek mythology in the *Odyssey* as the name of a character who advises Odysseus's son. One of the underlying themes of *Trusted Healers* is that we can manifest almost any societal change with the steady, unconditional love and counsel from a mentor.

Janine Tatham

Megan Pelino

We meet with two very bright, motivated young executives in healthcare who are benefiting from a mentoring relationship with Paul.

One is Janine Tatham, whose corporation, NexJ Health, provides powerful tools for strengthening primary care and improving population health management around the world. Another is my daughter Megan Pelino, who first met Paul when she was in high school contemplating a career in medicine. Paul coached her journey through college, her decisions about graduate school, traveling abroad, and her eventual career track. He has also encouraged Janine's academic pursuits.

"Being mentored by Paul is like an open door to the world. After my first meeting with him, I had a three-inch-thick binder full of the names and contact points of people all over the planet. After the meeting, he pulls me aside in the boardroom and says, 'Janine, you need to get an MPH [master of public health].'"

Paul told her it would be a good move to go back to school. "The world needs that," Paul said.

Janine says that Paul completely sold her. She is excited about pursuing that advanced degree, but would like to accomplish a few career goals first.

Viewing the world through the eyes of two extraordinary young people gives us a renewed sense of confidence in the future. Listening to the stories of the mentorship with Paul illustrates the impact of unconditional mentorship.

We will be handing off this healthcare reality to a generation of bright, motivated, inspired young people. How they are developing their values and their passion for shaping the future is one of the most promising messages in *Trusted Healers*. Mentoring the next crop of leaders is as important as forging new policies.

"There is nothing better than building a non-transactional friendship which evolves over shared experiences," Paul says. "True friendship is the best mentorship of all."

~

Janine is the director of strategic accounts at NexJ Health, where she is responsible for developing, executing, and delivering on global go-to-market strategies to grow strategic business.

NexJ Health is a Toronto-based technology company specialized in delivering patient engagement solutions for population health management. With her passion for bringing disruptive technologies to market for healthcare transformation, coupled with her success in selling patient-facing solutions to healthcare providers and payers, Janine is an invaluable part of the NexJ Health team. Janine holds a bachelor's degree in honors economics with a minor in gerontology from the University of Waterloo in Ontario, where she was a member of the women's varsity golf team.

Founded by William Tatham, a successful technology entrepreneur with expertise in developing customer-centered software applications to influence positive behavior change, NexJ offers evidence-based programs, such as NexJ Connected Wellness, for preventing and managing chronic disease. The virtual care platform extends the *Trusted Healers* relationship beyond the bricks and mortar of the clinic.

We meet with Janine in Washington following a series of conferences she attended surrounding NexJ's project in the Isle of Jersey and Great Britain. Janine is in her twenties and already a key part of the executive team of this very exciting new company.

"When we were starting up, our executive team met with IBM's Dr. Michael Weiner, who became so engaged with our presentation that partway through he was finishing our sentences, and by the end of it, he was presenting it to us," Janine says.

Dr. Weiner told Janine that what she is working on was the subject of his dissertation ten years ago. "It's the right thing, but I was ten years too early! The time is now. The world needs this now. We need to partner with you," Dr. Weiner told Janine. He added that Dr. Paul Grundy needed to see this right away. Two weeks later, Paul came into the office.

"We offered Paul the same presentation and we went on for hours and hours! At the end of the three-hour meeting, I have a long list of people to meet around the world who have the same vision, and Paul was connecting us. Connecting us with gifted professionals in the UK, Ireland, Singapore, in Vermont and Utah. And he has in-depth stories about changing the way healthcare is delivered in each of these systems," Janine says.

"Who is this guy, this Dr. Paul Grundy? Where did he come from? I was thinking. It was enlightening and refreshing, I would have to say. We know that we need to connect with the right people around the globe who 'get it.' And to have Paul support us with that, well, it's been helpful!"

⌒

The Jersey project is one that Paul spotted when it first began in 2013. Paul heard about a new healthcare innovation occurring on the channel island of Jersey, near the coast at Normandy. He flew there and accompanied a postal worker on daily rounds with Joe Dickinson, inventor and head of the innovative *Call & Check*, an award-winning service developed by Jersey Post.

That's right—a healthcare innovation that involved the postal delivery staff for the island's population of about 100,000. Paul, quite excited about this bright new service, told everyone in the world about it.

Joe Dickinson

"Paul resonates across people and cultures, because he is a people person," Janine says. "Paul passed us along to Joe Dickinson of Jersey to support his groundbreaking work," and, quickly, NexJ prepared to go live with the system in Jersey and the United Kingdom.

The *Call & Check* innovation leverages a virtual care platform for very progressive population health management.

"Our first pilot on Jersey involved a population of people sixty-five or older. These citizens are socially isolated, live alone, and may be in need of some additional support. The average home care visit costs somewhere between seventy and one hundred dollars per hour," Janine says. "Alternatively, for the cost of a registered letter, they could have a trusted, familiar face, that's known to them in the community—a postal worker—check in on them twice a week."

Janine says that the postal worker, a person the resident has probably known forever, asks a few questions (they always chat anyway) at the doorstep. How are you feeling? Have you taken your medication today? Do you need any medication refills? Do you need any social services support? Do you have any messages you would like passed on to your care team?

They also notice things that might need repair or attention—fall hazards, unsafe conditions, litter, and unkempt property.

"They record their answers on the same handheld device that they capture signatures on when they deliver a package, with NexJ's software running seamlessly on it. It's easy to use. If the individual needs a prescription refill, help with the groceries, or has any safety concerns, that information is shared in real time with their personal circle of care. That might include family who live out of town, a trusted neighbor, family physician, or social worker, and the appropriate support is triggered from the appropriate *Trusted Healer*.

"In Paul language, it's moving away from episodic care and towards preventative and community care. And so, it's changing the landscape of care," Janine says.

That pilot program succeeded, and the entire island now is offered the *Call & Check* program.

Paul saw the program was in need of a technology platform and he fell in love with the concept. The program, expanding in Great Britain, is called *Safe and Connected*, and supports Prime Minister Theresa May's cross-government loneliness strategy.

Subsequently, eleven other nations, as well as several large cities in the States, have expressed interest in *Call & Check*.

Joe Dickinson says, "It's a simple solution to help address the world's rapidly aging demographic problem. We can provide much-needed support to people who live alone and potentially find themselves socially isolated plus many other groups within our communities."

Call & Check aims to help people stay in their homes longer.

"Those being monitored are surrounded by their family and friends, which is proven to have mental and physical benefits," Joe says.

—

Paul notes that NexJ senses healthcare's biggest untapped opportunity for improving the overall health of populations and the patient experience while reducing the cost of care.

"Health systems across the world should look at this model as something to replicate, leveraging a virtual care platform with artificial intelligence and transforming a community-based resource to support people to live at home longer," Paul says.

Janine describes the three primary issues that healthcare faces globally as quality of care, patient safety, and cost and scope of services.

"To me, the system needs to transform to a people-centered model in order to effectively address these issues. The Canadian Association of People-Centred Health defines the principles of people-centered health. Every person in the system should be informed as to their health status, educated as to their alternate courses of treatment, and encouraged to be responsible for their own wellness," Janine says.

"In this model, you share access to the patient's health record and test results across providers and with the patient, eliminating redundant tests. This makes care more collaborative. In a 'siloed' system, you can't do that. A people-centered model creates better care, for a lower cost. And the best and fastest way to achieve that transformation is with disruptive innovation.

"So, I would contend that in order to achieve that, the system needs a virtual care platform to extend the reach and efficiency of advanced primary care, and for that matter, all healthcare," she says.

Janine explains that the NexJ virtual care platform enables healthcare professionals to deliver team-based and collaborative care that is coordinated and integrated across all elements of the broader healthcare system. The evidence-based programs encourage patients to become active participants in their care and adopt healthy lifestyle behavior changes to prevent or manage their chronic disease.

"Patients with chronic disease generate more than three-quarters of healthcare spending in North America. Their outcomes are mostly driven by how attentive they are with their medications and their lifestyle behaviors," Janine observes. "NexJ Health strives to enable *patient activation,* which is defined as having the knowledge, skills, and confidence to manage one's own health and wellness."

Compelling evidence connects these attributes with improvements in population health and patient experience and lowered costs.

"In our view, this is healthcare's biggest untapped opportunity for improving the overall health of populations, and patient experiences, while reducing the cost of care," Janine says. "It's all about engaging patients to participate in managing their chronic conditions."

Family and friends are enlisted to support the healthcare team.

"This is a natural extension of the *medical home* model," she says. "Our virtual care platform extends the reach and efficiency of advanced primary care and strengthens the relationship between the patient and the *Trusted Healer.* This is clearly a next step needed globally."

Janine refers to this concept of augmenting advanced primary care with a virtual care platform as *advanced virtual care.* It leverages artificial intelligence to support care teams in delivering more personalized care and precision medicine.

"Today, there is really no way to capture data between prescription and outcome. Did the patient take the medication? Did they follow the care plan? Did it work? Through a virtual care platform, we can capture all of this valuable patient-reported data, as well as capture every interaction with the patient across all aspects of the healthcare system and the associated outcomes."

We do this, she explains, so you can easily see what interactions result in the best outcomes. Once you apply machine learning to that data, you can then tailor the care plan to the specifics of each individual patient. And that becomes precision medicine.

"We are working on this right now," Janine says. "That's where the 'patient-facing virtual care platform' comes in—to gather all that data and then use artificial intelligence to connect those dots." This happens in the environment of a *Trusted Healer* and with care interventions shared across all providers, Janine says.

Examples of where NexJ Health is delivering advanced virtual care include hypertension prevention with the Heart and Stroke Foundation, mental health support with the Canadian Armed Forces, complex care coordination with the Hospital for Sick Children, and cancer coaching with Prostate Cancer Canada.

Canada has universal healthcare, introduced by Tommy Douglas, known as the father of socialized medicine (also the grandfather of actor Kiefer Sutherland).

"He almost had his leg amputated when he was young. His hospital experience led him to come up with this: that no Canadian should have to go bankrupt to pay for the acute care services they need to live. It's a social safety net that a lot of people feel is a social responsibility. So, people listened. We changed our healthcare system," Janine says.

"Tommy Douglas realized that we will go bankrupt if we [Canada] do not develop a robust focus on preventative care and wellness. We believe this can be made clearly possible by looking upstream and activating people to become involved in their care, so they can share in decision making and advocate for their own health. This can all be encouraged and coordinated by the familiar physician in an advanced primary care model —a system where we can integrate mental health, social services, preventive measures and acute care all in a comprehensive record, accessible to all caregivers on the team.

"Our generation is very open and embracing to disruptive innovation and disruptive technologies. We will get it there—with the right people and the right innovators willing to embrace it and run with it," she says.

While there will always be the vital trust relationship with *Trusted Healers*, the future is moving toward virtual-assisted advanced primary care supported by artificial intelligence. "A lot of it will be virtual. It will be very efficient. Every single interaction along your personal roadmap to health will come from an evidence-based care plan that is tailored specifically for you. Everything you see in medicine in this society will be precision medicine delivered to you virtually, as much as possible to maximize efficiency and minimize cost," she says.

We ask Janine what she would tell the generation that follows her journey.

"I probably won't have to; they will be able to know what I am thinking," she says. "Things changed so rapidly for us. Lightning speed. We've become quick at adaptation. We keep learning. We keep growing. The tools will be different, that's all. I think our generation is very adaptable—whatever flies at us, we kind of roll with it."

Such nimbleness can be seen at Cancer Treatment Centers of America (CTCA), which has a two-year leadership development program that enables recent graduates to gain skills related to multiple facets of business in healthcare. Fellows work closely with CTCA executives and clinicians, rotating through various departments in order to gain a comprehensive perspective on their integrative care model, as well as healthcare and business in general.

This fast-paced, rotational experience at CTCA develops young entrepreneurs into thoughtful and strategic thinkers, preparing fellows to be future leaders in healthcare. Megan, my daughter, was one of them.

Megan graduated from Notre Dame with a degree in sociology and from Columbia University with a master's in public health. She studied abroad and interned with the Kennedy Forum and Patrick J. Kennedy, sharing his conviction for taking care of those suffering from mental illnesses. And she immersed herself in one of the top posts in healthcare for recent master's program graduates.

"Being at Cancer Treatment Centers of America as a management fellow was exactly where I needed to be to start my career. I am truly so lucky to have had the opportunity to be surrounded by such brilliant people working towards such a noble cause at this stage in my development," Megan says.

"I was able to be really challenged in terms of why I was making the decisions I was making, what the implications would be for the hospital and patients, and how we can continue to do better and strive for better. I really enjoyed learning how to build a strategy, how to structure an appropriate analysis, how to communicate that analysis to various audiences, one being clinical and one being more of a strategic focus. I view my experience at CTCA as getting my MBA in healthcare on the ground. It completely shaped my view of leadership and teamwork and positive impact I strive to make."

Today, she has a new role with a Chicago-based biotech company focused on clinical cancer research and diagnosis. They gather and analyze clinical and molecular data through the power of artificial intelligence.

"The fellowship was a perfect launching pad to strengthen my skill set and problem solving, and now I get to apply that in a creative way to the future of healthcare: data and precision medicine," Megan says. "One of my goals in my career is to learn as many healthcare *languages* as possible. I learned *business, provider* and *oncology* while I was a fellow, and now I get to learn *data, pharma,* and *tech* through the lens of a start-up. I really can't wait to see what this next chapter has in store and where it will take me next. All I know is I'm on the right path to learning the most I can and creating the biggest impact that I can."

We catch up with Megan in Washington, DC, to discuss Paul's mentorship and her career goals.

"I think Paul likes where I am right now. Because he knows I have all of these dreams like he did when he was starting out, and he knows I want to make an impact. I want to create change," she says. "One thing Dr. Grundy and I share is the servant leadership and service mentality. I met him when he and my dad started working together, in high school at the time, trying to decide whether I want to go to medical school.

"This is when he became a mentor figure in my life. Paul helped me think about what it means to go to medical school, what it means to have a career in medicine. He became even more of a mentor when I entered college. He would always come to me to help me think about all the options in healthcare. Now, he comes to me, I go to him, we talk on the phone, we email each other."

Megan was more inclined to the mechanics of healthcare than practicing as a physician.

"I was thinking policy—my perspective of how I could affect change in healthcare, and not be a clinician. I wanted to be a policy maker, a policy analyst. That's what I learned—that my ambition lies outside the clinical space," Megan says.

Paul inspired and encouraged that.

"I see Paul as a master networker and visionary. I experienced some of my favorite things abroad when I followed Paul's advice. He gives me the best restaurants and coffee shop recommendations. I am happiest and most at peace with a really good cup of coffee. I went on this pilgrimage, as he would probably call it, for the best cappuccino in London."

Megan tells one of her favorite stories, which occurred when a couple of friends joined her in catching a very cheap flight to Split, Croatia, not even knowing where that would be. They went for the weekend.

"When we got there, we stumbled into Diocletian's Palace," she recalls—an ancient palace of the Roman emperor Diocletian from the turn of the fourth century AD. "Admiring this historic site, I texted Paul to see if he had any suggestions while we were there."

What happened next illustrates Paul's amazing worldly knowledge. He didn't suggest museums or monuments or specialty restaurants. He sent them to a remote corner of Diocletian's Palace.

"Paul said to look for a small sign reading 'Academic Ghetto' and go get their absinthe," Megan says. "We went up and down stairs surrounding a courtyard covered in vines. Cats everywhere.

"We found a small sign: 'Academia Club Ghetto.' Here were three American college students walking into the best-kept secret in Western Europe like we owned the place. We walked in and were blown away by the hundreds of baubles hanging off the ceiling, cats climbing on everything, video projections, not to mention some super hip art décor on the walls and semi-Bohemian furniture—an unconventional, avant-garde oasis in the heart of the classic Diocletian Palace! We kicked back to world music as the daylight faded, and then the music and lights turned electro after dark," she recalls.

"Thank you, Paul. He connects me with heads of state and then tells me where to get the best entertainment in Split, Croatia. That's Paul. Empathic. We end every conversation on the phone 'How are you doing? How's school?' He genuinely cares about how I am doing as a person.

"I came back from London with a deep interest in public health. I feel a very spiritual calling to serve others. I could learn about communities, about vulnerable communities, at-risk communities, and use my knowledge to help them find solutions. And this connection of the scientific, the spiritual, the well-being and the ethical—this mental health space—I wanted to explore that further, so I sent an email to Patrick J. Kennedy at the Kennedy Forum."

Megan got his attention with that. She accepted the offer to work with the Kennedy Forum and his team in that summer between Notre Dame and grad school. There she experienced exactly how policy is made.

"And how policy is a growing, living, breathing thing," she says.

She watched Patrick preparing to testify in front of Congress as to why a bill needed to pass. She learned how to network in this space, to meet leading visionaries, and work alongside the leadership of the National Institute of Mental Health.

Patrick makes a broad observation about Megan's internship. "This stuff is the future. She'll have had a chance to get acquainted with it early on in her life's journey, wherever it takes her. Because there is undoubtedly going to be intersections between what she ends up spending her time and energy with and this movement—because it's a movement far beyond the medical side of it. It's a movement for acceptance," Patrick says.

"I view the population with mental illness as a population that needs advocacy, that needs leaders to speak for them," Megan says. "And it's such an invisible illness that affects so many, and if you look at it from a public health perspective, for example, if you have both cancer and a mental illness, you have a lower rate of surviving. If you have diabetes and mental illness, the same exact thing."

As Patrick J. Kennedy reminds us, mental illness and behavioral health affect everything: education, medical care, business, law enforcement, imprisonment, family relationships, community violence, social services, everything.

Megan says, "At Notre Dame and Columbia, with the help of some fantastic professors, I started to tie together some of my interests in terms of sociology, mental health, public health, and the ethics of science and technology. My professors helped me to understand the intersection of all my interests is actually somewhere in the mental health space. I had always been passionate about it. I led retreats all through college on mental health, well-being and spirituality."

"Megan, this is where your skills, your interests and your passions lie," they advised.

"From a long-term perspective, if you asked me, where do you want to go in your career, I would say I am still figuring that out. It's figuring out how you get people to change their thinking. How do you get people to change their behaviors? It all leads to Paul's *Trusted Healer.*"

That curiosity, the birth of innovation, forms the basis for leadership.

CHAPTER NINETEEN

SELF-DISCOVERY

O ne certain place to see leadership is wherever there is notable innovation. The scaffolding of innovation strengthens with leadership. And leadership comes from within. It requires a level of courage, strength, and determination to match the conviction. Leadership creates a culture that drives, leverages, and motivates.

The quest for innovation has roots in curiosity. As IBM's Nick Donofrio says, at the root of all this is a problem, not a solution. Leadership is about falling in love with the question, not the answer. On this *Trusted Healers* journey, we have felt the passion and the strength of great leaders. At the core of great leadership is a cause, one that *matters* to others. That cause spins off a problem, a question, a quest, and a conviction to create something better.

You can hear the voices of Nick, of Patrick J. Kennedy, Dr. Glenn Steele, and Dr. Mike Roizen, resonating with purpose. Mission matters; leadership matters.

Championing mental health and solving the opioid abuse crisis, transforming the way we deliver acute and chronic disease care, changing the world with wellness—it all starts from something that matters because you have a belief, a desire, a need to change something. In a way, the cause becomes a gravitational force. It takes on a life of its own, fueled by sincerity, emotion, and enthusiasm. Cause finds its own place. We listen, we share, and we tell the stories. We all have stories. Here's mine.

※

I spent my childhood in Fairport, NY, a beautiful little village of about 5,000 people east of Rochester, New York.

I did what most kids do. I had good friends, we played sports, and I did homework. My sister, Sue, is seventeen months younger; we had dogs, my parents both worked, and I was a paperboy.

Yes, a paperboy. With pride, I would carefully and expertly roll, fold, and then hurl the Rochester *Democrat and Chronicle* morning paper. Walking, running, biking, then driving the route up and down hills, usually in the dark, I was a paperboy!

Morning came early and, yes, it was every day, 365 days a year. The district manager dropped off the papers, so the garage door was my alarm. It went off without fail at 5 a.m., and my day began. My papers, my customers' papers, were here.

I started my paper route career substituting for another paperboy, and really admired that kid. I wanted the route as my route. No more subbing. I was ready! Learning the trade, my route was about average in size: twenty-two dailies, fifty-four Saturdays and one hundred Sundays. Dad helped often, especially on Sundays.

At night and weekly, I had to collect payment. No credit cards, mail payments or auto-pays. We paperboys, in those days, kept a small notebook with a page for each subscriber. I would tear off a small square receipt when they came to the door with the forty-five cents due. The receipt was imprinted with the date, and this postage-stamp-sized document offered positive proof that my customer paid for that week's newspapers.

I loved being a paperboy, so I learned something very special: what it feels like to love a job. I carried newspapers from age eleven until I turned eighteen.

At first, I walked the route. Later, I figured out the bike was better. When I learned to drive, I based my operation from the family car, a green Chevy Nova stick. The green was not a good green.

I became a pretty good paperboy. Customers appreciated me. I had pocket money. My best buddies also had paper routes. Our small fraternal order of paperboys would compare newsprint on our hands when we arrived at school. A badge of honor! It was cool to be a paperboy!

I learned mastery. I learned accountability. I learned about *everyone matters*—that all of my neighbors counted on me to bring them the news. Dry. Neatly folded, on time, every day. I learned a little about image. My customers all knew my name was Dan and greeted me in the store or out in the community at an event. I was somebody important to them. I was "their" paperboy!

I learned about discipline. This responsibility happened every day. I could not ignore the route even if I was sick. I carried papers in the dark, in the snow, and in the rain. If I was late, my customers let me hear about it. If I missed a house, I got a complaint call. If I tossed the paper too hard and it hit the bottom of the aluminum screen door, *Bang,* the dogs barked and the lights went on and I had a very unhappy customer.

Hitting the door with an aggressive or errant toss was the cardinal sin, ranking just below being late or just flat out missing a house. You see, every customer had my house phone number and, well, every day was a pass-fail test. They either had a paper or not, and if I hit the door and the dogs barked, no one was ever shy in calling Mom or Dad to report my failure or my errant toss.

Maybe all of us have not been paperboys, but all of us as kids may have laid back, looked at the sky, watched the clouds and imagined who we were and how we could make a difference.

In a spiritual way, the experience of walking or biking alone at age thirteen through your world in the darkness somehow invites you to think. You begin your morning in the silence of the full night.

Papers are delivered, lights go on, and people stir, shuffling along, readying to go to work or school. There's a rhythm here of working in America. You understand that you are standing on an orbiting thing as the sun magnificently peeks over the horizon. I learned far more about myself in those days than I realized at the time. What was important in life, what it would take for me to find a job one day—the questions never stopped as I walked, biked and tossed my papers. You think about everything delivering papers at 5:30 in the morning in the dark.

I learned about the exchange relationship. I collected from my customers to pay the *Democrat and Chronicle*. I delivered the papers, making a little more than I owed. I kept about fourteen cents per customer—more for Sunday delivery.

I learned to be an opportunist, and I learned the power of feedback. Tips were good, although not expected. However, not waking up barking dogs at 6 a.m. was even better—at least to my customers! I learned the art of collection and how to offer the next year's *Democrat and Chronicle* calendar during the week of Christmas. Yes, tips were good!

I learned a little about marketing and persuasion, knocking on neighbors' doors and pitching them on the idea of subscribing to the *Democrat and Chronicle*. "The grocery store coupons alone will pay for the cost." You see, if you have one hundred Sunday customers and only twenty-two daily customers—well, you get the idea.

I was also an altar boy. And yes, I had the daily 6:30 Mass plus the 11:15 Sunday mornings, and most funerals and weddings. Father Kelly was the pastor of Assumption Catholic Church. He was a big man, kind, and he expected me to ring the bells at the appropriate time without his glaring and encouraging eye signaling. I think he stills holds the record for saying the quickest Mass—seventeen minutes.

Dad drove me to my daily Mass responsibilities. He and his two brothers, Don and Doug, were also altar boys. Being an altar boy was a rite of passage in our family. After Mass, Dad would take me to a village diner for breakfast. He instilled in me that he would support me in anything that I wanted to do if I was committed 100 percent. Those days and moments were special to me. I miss those moments, and today my favorite meal is taking my grown kids and Anne to breakfast. I hope they will do the same with their kids. Maybe they will invite me.

So, my day started delivering papers, followed by serving Mass, then going to breakfast with Dad. I would not have changed a thing.

I learned about timing, always making sure I visited every house the week of Christmas to collect. Not the week before that or the week after that—the week of holiday bliss. I enclosed a Christmas card greeting in every paper, personally signed, *Your Paperboy, Dan.*

I learned about savings. I put that money away.

Maybe all this set the stage. Many successful business leaders and celebrities, such as Walt Disney, Tom Cruise, and Warren Buffet, started out in life carrying newspapers. Warren still stages a newspaper rolling and throwing contest at his annual meeting in Omaha each year. I bet he is tough to beat.

My college experience at Western Kentucky University was enriching and culminated in two undergraduate degrees and a master of arts in organizational communications and behavioral sciences. I joined a fraternity and made lifelong friends. My college mentor is my mentor today. Along the way, leadership skills enabled me to develop some mastery in communications and public relations, so I won the election to lead the national collegiate public relations organization (PRSSA) as a junior. I served as the chairman of the University Center board on campus and the tutor for our fraternity. Lifelong friends, experiences, and a great education served me well.

Today, I continue to teach leadership to graduate and doctorate students. I fund a leadership program and scholarships. Applied leadership still drives my passion.

My fascination with the art and science of leadership paid off. I found myself with an opportunity to work for IBM.

I know now that the paperboy experience was Little League

baseball, the college experience was important in developing my skills, and IBM was, well, IBM—the big leagues. I was so excited for this opportunity and felt that I was prepared. I knew this organization would lead the way to a new era and that computers would change people's lives, forever.

So I did everything I could to get IBM to hire me, and they did, and I spent an incredible career among a collection of brilliant people generating about eighty billion dollars annually in transformational societal change around the world. Now the coaches were handing me the ball. There was a level of responsibility, commitment, and mastery that built on everything that came before.

I am deeply in debt to those who believed in me and worked with me in our pursuits. From those early mornings walking and biking delivering papers in the dark, to working for IBM alongside the many gifted colleagues supporting terrific clients, helping to solve many of the grand challenges of our world, I feel very blessed.

A lifelong student of leadership and transformational change, I love and respect education. When Mom went back to school to pursue her master's degree, I tagged along. I sat with her in the back of the lecture halls listening, watching, and curious. (I think I was supposed to do my homework.) That experience of being in the advanced learning class influenced how I read, what I think, and why education became a very personal experience. When I decided to pursue my graduate degree, it was Mom that said, "They can take everything away from you, but they cannot take your education."

My IBM journey spanned thirty-six years. Now, as I look at it in the rearview mirror, I hunger to share the stories of leadership that I witnessed as we navigated a world embracing exuberant change, a world awakening to new ways of doing things, and discovering that there is a brighter future.

As I look back on four decades of being immersed in social change and transformation at IBM, one thing I can clearly offer is to break all this down, illuminating the necessary stages of an advancing world.

As Nick says, start with the problem.

Our problem was not that we aspired to greatness in healthcare. There is no aspect of life on earth that needs data and computing more than healthcare. Our problem was that we had not yet amplified our presence there.

Our aspiration to transform global healthcare led to the inspiration of a global vision and the commitment and the discipline to change course and speed as called for along the way.

If we aspired to global leadership, then of course we needed to involve ourselves in the global pandemic threat, or genome breakthroughs, just like we did the mission to put a man on the moon. We must live our *aspiration*. We must become our aspiration, one that inspires greatness. An aspiration is something that you believe you can go do.

Aspiration oftentimes comes from *curiosity*. Most of the powerful leaders I know are endlessly curious. They have a profound need to pick decisions apart, see how things happen, learn why people make the decisions they do. Paul's endless curiosity led him to find the one solution for healthcare crises all over the world: the *Trusted Healers*, and the *medical home*.

Curiosity always leads to *empathy*, a trait almost everyone on earth wants to experience from leaders. Everyone needs to know the leader pays attention, cares, understands, and shows awareness, sensitivity to what team members feel.

Paul empathizes with physicians—he is a doctor.

He empathizes with global leaders—he is a diplomat.

He empathizes with corporate leaders—he is one.

He empathizes with other cultures—he grew up in foreign cultures, served his country in other cultures, opened clinics in other cultures.

⌐⌐

Think about the great leaders that inspire you. If you are a true leader, you want to inspire. You believe in the power of *inspiration*, as the leader. Inspiration is how you bring people along. You inspire them. There is nothing greater than inspiring people. Spell it out in neon. I had the opportunity to be inspired by Nick Donofrio. I have the honor of inspiring Paul, and he in turn inspires me.

Find and keep a *mentor*. As leadership roles grow, you will have less and less feedback from people who work with you. Rely on your punch-in-the-gut-if-necessary mentor to help you make the course corrections and speed adjustments that invariably will be needed.

Paul inspires a world of primary care to believe that things can become much better if we bring the primary care practice into a *medical home* environment. And he inspires entire nations to base their healthcare system on a core of robust primary care.

Exercise *discipline* to control your speed and course. There is little room for making a mistake. If you're on the right path, go faster. Paul has a different pace for every culture that comes to him for guidance. He moves with the pace of that culture, respecting their traditions and taboos, and asking the questions that will help them make good decisions about their healthcare future.

You need to have all four of these things to succeed:

- Command (mastery of your mission)
- Control (of your business—speed and direction)
- Access (knowledge of how to reach and influence the right people)
- Influence (respect of people who matter)

If you have those, you can go to the top. Access and influence are not enough. Unless you have muddy boots, have the responsibility of a deadline, you will struggle.

There's no better way to deflate a poor leader than to ask, "Are we going the right way, navigating through this exasperating situation? Are we going fast enough?" If that leader cannot answer those questions, you've lost all aspiration and inspiration. You better know the answer. Know it, and not just say it.

Become the leader who creates something based on an *aspiration*, and who believes so strongly in that intent that everyone involved becomes *inspired.*

Few on my healthcare reform quest have embodied the arts of aspiration and inspiration more than Jeremy Hunt, who led the UK's health and social care. Jeremy awakened in people their ability to make a change, make something better, to move away from being trapped in a rabbit hole of their own making. His *aspiration* was to fix the brokenness of England's once beloved GP-centered healthcare.

Jeremy listened intently to his critics and all of his constituents, not pretending to have all the answers, but with every bone in his body he shared his desire to make it better. He defied the dour expectations.

This *empathy*, like his *aspiration* to transform the nation's healthcare system, cannot be faked.

Jeremy's *curiosity* motivated him to seek out Paul, who became a key mentor. Paul traveled to England a dozen times, guiding the pilots in primary care, explaining the *primary care home* to any group of physicians or political leaders ready to listen.

Paul never asked for a thing in return. He was just fulfilling his own destiny.

Jeremy Hunt provided *patience* and *inspiration* to his country, staying steadfast to his discipline and determination, altering the speed and direction of a nation's quest to heal their *Trusted Healers.*

"I get a rough time . . . from the GP community," Jeremy admits during our interview in Parliament. "I am sort of the whipping boy in our system—every single problem in the health system comes to the health secretary. I kind of have gotten used to it over the years."

This is a leader who understands leadership.

As I ponder the complex, often emotional challenges that at times seem irreversibly entrenched or frustratingly convoluted, I often long for the simplicity and solitude of that newspaper route again. I wish for those mornings when I could think, wonder, and dream; when I would pause my bike, lean it up against a big tree and just watch the edge of the rising sun.

Our lifetime calls upon us to navigate a spiritually advancing era. We benefit from the lifework of some of the greatest, most inspiring leaders the world has ever seen. We remember words like "Ask not" from JFK, "I have" from Martin Luther King, Jr., "Tear down" from President Ronald Reagan. These hallowed challenges echo still today, pointing to a hope felt around the globe.

None of these gifted people would have been successful without the belief that *everyone matters.*

Playing back this fast-paced leadership experience of constantly wrangling change and transformation, the fullness of time leaves me with one certainty. The one thing that never changes—the idea of being willing to change the world, make a difference, to believe that *everyone matters.* This ideal should guide us all.

EPILOGUE

At the beginning of *Trusted Healers*, we suggested that by the end of this book, the realization would strike you that there are some secrets here.

Leadership is not something that individuals proclaim about themselves. You can proclaim you are a *manager,* but you can't proclaim yourself a leader.

There are secrets in this book on how to approach communities, organizations, companies, states, or countries to create change, and make a difference. The global leaders we meet in *Trusted Healers* either consciously or unconsciously follow a process of societal change. Now we can look back to see exactly how and why their leadership connects with societies. Or we can watch the news and see why change is blocked when a shared value that *everyone matters* is missing. This is usually fueled by a false belief that there is not enough to go around.

One secret is that in order to create a desired change among a population, we must first accept the worldwide fact that all change is local and all beliefs are rooted in painfully earnest tribal beliefs.

People will weigh the idea of a change against their world, not ours. Unless we can suggest that the change is beneficial to their customs and practices, we will not succeed.

Our shared journey has taken us into the motivations and capable minds of some very powerful leaders—past, present and future.

None of these leaders underestimate the tiger and try to muscle it back in the cage. As we have demonstrated, they move with the flow of their culture. They start with an *aspiration*. Then they provide *inspiration*, which flows from their inner spirit. They believe that *everyone matters*.

You can't fake this. This must come from the heart. We call this standing on the high ground. Living your aspiration.

We hope *Trusted Healers* illuminates the unblinking commitment to that idea made by each and every global leader we have met on this journey. None of these gifted people would be successful without that belief.

We hope you can sense the energy of their passion. We hope you close *Trusted Healers* with a better idea of how leadership works and how to create change that matters to the people of the world.

Paul understands his destiny. Paul epitomizes and demonstrates how to move societies, how to nudge cultures into a better direction for healthcare. When he reaches out and talks to these communities and helps them change, we see better outcomes and people leading better lives. At IBM, he was the Johnny Appleseed of global change and the worldwide champion of the *Trusted Healers*. His work now bears fruit in many nations. And even in retirement, his work continues.

Paul has reunited with one of his best friends, Dr. David Nace, one of the top innovators in population management in the world. Dr. Nace worked with Paul in the earliest days of the crusade.

Paul was in San Francisco when he learned that Dr. Nace had joined Innovaccer as a consultant. They got together and Paul asked him to drive him to Napa. Paul wanted to see his uncle, who lives there. On the way to Napa, Dr. Nace described the scientists he met from India whose passion for problem solving was unbelievable. He became exuberant and animated describing how these young IT executives had decided to tackle the problem of healthcare with Google and Amazon technologies, and that they were going to solve it.

Dr. Nace, who was driving, was gesturing with both hands. The road to Napa has a lot of twists and turns. Paul tapped him on the arm and gently said, "Hey, David, could you put your hands back on the steering wheel?"

Two world-class innovators, veterans of the journey, saddled up again together. They continue the crusade to save healthcare. Together, they will be assisting Innovaccer, Inc. with clinical applications for the new technologies. Paul will focus on *Trusted Healers*, helping primary care physicians around the world get acquainted with this next generation of information technology. Dr. Nace is the new chief medical officer. Paul's new title—chief transformation officer. A storybook ending, or beginning?

Hans Christian Andersen began his fairy tale writing career by retelling folk tales he had heard as a child. Andersen published a number of volumes of fairy tales, and his last works of this type appeared in 1872. Among his most popular tales are *The Ugly Duckling, The Princess and the Pea,* and *The Little Mermaid.*

While some of his tales exhibit an optimistic belief in the ultimate triumph of goodness and beauty, like *The Snow Queen,* others are deeply pessimistic and end unhappily. Why would this brilliant storyteller create gentle and noble creatures as well as frightening images of trolls and monsters? What can we learn?

One reason for Andersen's great appeal to both children and adults is that he was not afraid of introducing feelings and ideas that were beyond a child's immediate comprehension, yet he remained in touch with the child's perspective.[31]

There are trolls guarding the bridge on our journey; there is great goodness and beauty in healthcare, yet our journey is incomplete. People are being left out. There is a lot of pain, and those who are disenfranchised from help wonder why.

The trolls in Hans Christian Andersen's stories asked questions. The Scandinavian people carefully listened to the trolls, and they have crossed the metaphorical bridge. Now, to us, three questions are presented:

What are your secrets to better health?
Who matters?
Shall we share healthcare with everyone?

To pass over the bridge, answers are required.

WHAT ARE YOUR SECRETS TO BETTER HEALTH?

Our journey has taken us through a centuries-long struggle to answer this first question in the trolls' repertoire. Our forebearers drank and smoked themselves to death. That was the rhythm of the healthcare culture. They had few secrets to health. Life expectancy was low. They did not listen to warnings.

Now, our journey has taken us to a place where we are beginning to learn, share, and benefit from the secrets. The *Age of Healthcare Information* drove in our golden spike and made the answers possible.

Patrick J. Kennedy embodies the belief that *everyone matters* as he tackles America's inability to see the truth and recognize the damage our taboos and stigmas have caused. We are enduring the biggest public health crisis of our time with suicide, violence, opioid addiction, and substance abuse.

Dr. Paul Grundy's crusade for the *medical home* and *Trusted Healers* leaves us more determined and encouraged to continue this journey.

Dr. Glenn Steele has been boldly reinventing healthcare, designing life-saving procedures and protocols based on proven methods, revolutionizing the quality and cost of healthcare.

Dr. Michael Roizen is creating our wellness curriculum. He shows us what health is, on television, in newspapers, and in best-selling books translated into dozens of languages. And by his personal example.

The dawning *Age of Healthcare Intelligence* will bring us more brilliant innovations. It's an exciting moment in our journey.

Bright new generations will enhance the answers to the trolls' riddle. Young professionals, some of whom Paul has mentored, like Megan Pelino and Janine Tatham, will accelerate this journey as they envision an inclusive world of personalized precision medicine.

WHO MATTERS?

The second question asked by the trolls has an obvious answer. Some nations, including the United States, are slow to answer.

Trolls block the bridge. We cannot cross.

Escaping a culture boxed in by racism and bias, led by a series of powerful national leaders, a movement has begun, guided by the belief that *everyone matters.* This thread has been common on our journey.

All *Trusted Healers* we interviewed, our trusted voices, demonstrate with their life, their work and their heart that *everyone matters.* Recall the work of Sister Chris in Rochester with the St. Joseph's Neighborhood Center.

And there are so many more powerful, enlightened professionals working in healthcare today. It's a profession that draws those who share these beliefs. Our journey has touched on the work of just a few of the devoted, innovative, tough, resilient healthcare leaders that are among us today, working to better our future. Sometimes against tough odds.

The *Trusted Healer*, by definition, embodies this.

Dr. Paul Grundy, by his life's work, is the epitome of a champion for this belief.

In our discussion of societal change and leadership, at the core of great leadership is a cause, one that matters to others. That cause spins off a problem, a question, a quest, and a conviction to create something better. That cannot happen unless you believe that *everyone matters.*

SHALL WE SHARE HEALTHCARE WITH EVERYONE?

The answer to the trolls' third question is different in many countries. In the United Kingdom, Ireland, Canada, in Scandinavia, in Western Europe, the answer is a huge part of national pride. *Everyone matters.* No one is left behind for any reason. The trolls have allowed passage.

UK secretary of state for health and social care Jeremy Hunt reminds us of the reverence the people of England have for their GPs, their *Trusted Healers.* In London, where 140 languages are spoken in a single school district, *everyone matters.* And Professor James Kingsland and his colleagues join Paul in guiding a rescue of the struggling GPs with the *primary care home.* Prof. Kingsland urges his nation to "not try harder at what has failed."

Above all, like Canada, they cling tightly to their universal care. As Dr. Nwando Olayiwola says, equitable healthcare is a right. Dr. Glenn Steele, one of the leading healthcare administrators in the world, reminds us pragmatically that everyone should get the best of our healthcare, if for no other reason than that we are paying for it anyway.

Dr. Ted Epperly and Dr. Michael Roizen worry that this disparity will not end well. T. R. Reid reminds us that no country has ever been successful with a healthcare system like ours. Including us.

Those nations who answer the trolls satisfactorily may cross the bridge.

The US is not one of them. Yet.

The United States of America, as a country, continues to struggle to adequately answer the three questions. Many of us have progressed along our healthcare journey. Many of us have made our way past the trolls.

Unfortunately, many have not. Some are left standing and staring at the trolls. To them, the answers are not obvious. Where's the path? The commitment to the answer defines the path.

The answer that we can provide is that the evolution of primary care, the creation of the *medical home,* and the *Trusted Healers* revolution provide momentum for the journey. They are supplying encouraging, effective, and compassionate answers so we can cross the bridge to better health and care, get past the pesky trolls and accelerate our journey.

We hope you can see that healthcare now moves on a good and noble trajectory around the world, responding to cultural challenges and yet moving forward, powered by thoughtful leaders, advanced by clever innovations and fueled by the belief that *everyone matters.*

Paul is optimistic.

"The latest figures are that 48 percent of all US primary care doctors are now practicing in a *medical home* environment. The quality of the care we receive will keep getting better and better around the world, and in America, we will eventually have a healthcare system that includes everyone," Paul says.

We need to melt the layer of protective ice over our hearts to make it happen.

When we set out on this journey, our simple aspiration was that, as Patrick J. Kennedy says, "You will never look at healthcare the same way again."

As we conclude this together, we pose one last question and a possible answer.

Who is your *Trusted Healer*?

Dr. Paul Grundy helps us begin our journey by addressing that question:

> It's somebody who could give you guidance on what happens to you in your afterlife. It's somebody who you turn to when the chips are down. We all know instinctively that we are going to get sick; we all know we are going to die. We try to deny that, but we know it.
>
> There arises the power of that person in that position in society, the traditional healers, *Trusted Healers*. In every culture on earth, the healer and the preacher are held in highest esteem.

Paul knows we hold our *Trusted Healer* in the highest regard. He reminds us that we have moved into the new *Age of Healthcare Intelligence*. We are newly empowered to influence our own health and well-being.

In a *medical home*, our *Trusted Healer* can focus on what they were trained to do—as Paul would describe, "difficult diagnostic dilemmas and patient relationships."

Assisted by a care team, our *Trusted Healer* has more time to get to know us, to learn what motivates us, to watch for early warning signs, to isolate our health weaknesses and prescribe changes to our lifestyle and diet, to keep us up-to-date on medical science, curating and distilling new findings to update our care plan.

In turn, we get to know our *Trusted Healer* as a person. We collaborate. We discuss options, costs, and urgency. Now there is quality time to get the best of medicine.

Trust is a magnificent thing.

We knew that when we reached the completion of this journey there would be a realization that we each have a greater role to play now. Can we accept this new opportunity? Can we accept this challenge?

⌒

We close with these words from Frederick Douglass:

> *If there is no struggle, there is no progress.*
>
> *Those who profess to favor freedom, and yet depreciate agitation, are men who want crops without plowing up the ground.*
>
> *They want rain without thunder and lightning.*
>
> *They want the ocean without the awful roar of its many waters.*
>
> *This struggle may be a moral one; or it may be a physical one; or it may be both moral and physical; but it must be a struggle.*
>
> *Power concedes nothing without a demand.*
>
> *It never did and it never will.*

ACKNOWLEDGMENTS

*T*rusted Healers is intended to explore the continuum of care through the intersection of societal shifts, the impact of primary care, and the importance of leadership in creating positive outcomes.

In our world today, *Trusted Healers* give us confidence to care for ourselves and by doing so improve the quality of our lives. These individuals are committed to making a difference, strengthening the fabric of society in our homes, in our workplace and in our communities.

I would like to thank the many friends and colleagues who inspired the content of this book, especially co-author Bud Ramey and the gifted team at Koehler Books, including John Koehler and editor Joe Coccaro.

A special note to IBM leadership and the 137 IBMers who came together in 2006 and believed that with aspiration, clarity of mission, health expertise and the application of technology we could make a difference in the continuum of care. Stated another way, we believed that integrating best medical care with technology that was centered on the patient would be a catalyst for improved quality and outcomes. These IBMers reassembled in communities around the world, working side by side with medical professionals, health plans and life sciences leaders who likewise had this common aspiration.

To my dedicated leadership team who lived this journey with me every day—thank you.

My sincere thanks to Dr. Paul Grundy and his tireless efforts to promote the importance of primary care and the *medical home.* To Patrick J. Kennedy, my appreciation for lending his voice and leadership to create parity for mental and behavioral health and an end to the opioid crisis.

To Dr. Glenn Steele, Dr. Mike Roizen, the Honourable Jeremy Hunt, and our other featured worldwide healthcare leaders, your own stories and personal leadership serve to inspire this book and set an example for future generations.

To my mentor of more than forty years, Dr. Randy Capps of Western Kentucky University, your support, encouragement and confidence has been a guiding force throughout my professional life. And to my IBM mentor, Nick Donofrio, your wisdom and the occasional "Get Out of Jail Free" card showed me the path to success.

Randy Capps

To my parents, Dick and Pat, thank you for supporting me and instilling that anything is possible with commitment, perseverance, education and faith.

To my daughters, Kathryn and Megan, every day I am reminded through your actions and endeavors just how bright the future will be for this rising generation. Kathryn, Megan, Anne—I love you.

Thanks to Hank and Mary Altman for their support. Hank's fifty years of experience and total mastery of the art of editing was invaluable, humbling and very much appreciated! And to Anne Altman, for your encouragement; when others said it was not possible, you believed.

Why do we do what we do?
Because *everyone matters.*

GUIDES AND RESOURCES

MY SIX PROMISES

I want to offer everyone who has read *Trusted Healers* six promises we should all make to ourselves as we go through life.

I originally created *Six Promises* as good coaching for tomorrow's leaders in my classes for PhD students at Western Kentucky University. Our society needs a different kind of leader, with a more precise ethical compass, in the coming years.

Then I realized that, you know, when we view these things together, it's more than that. A career should be more than ingenuity and ambition.

These are six ways to amplify a good life, six ways to leave behind a legacy, six ways to make a difference—promises we should make to ourselves no matter what role we play in the culture.

•1•

Learn to look for and judge goodness and harmony in people, in society, and the events around you.

Have you directed your energy toward goodness? Do you have the patience to allow harmony to evolve? Does your aspiration line up with the idea of making a difference, recognizing that *everyone matters*?

•2•

Grasp the essence of every decision
in your life or career.

Grasping the essence means looking behind the simple act of making a decision. What lies behind the situation? What are the consequences of the decision? What is your vision of the future once this is done?

•3•

Create meaningful relationships, adding value and
substance to your organization or those around you.

In today's world, as soon as you say something, it's out. We have been getting too comfortable with instantaneous, shallow communications with each other. Think about that as a leader, a parent, and a friend. Be in the moment. Go meet with someone instead of texting. Build real relationships and networks of people you value, people willing to share mutual confidence and understanding.

•4•

Your words matter.

Rhetoric counts. People listen to what you say. It is not only what you say that matters; it is what people hear. Rhetoric matters. Ralph Waldo Emerson once said, "What you do speaks so loudly, I can't hear what you're saying." A leader takes responsibility for not only what is said, but also what people hear. If you have to make a speech, write it down. Know that it can be enduring.

•5•

Wise leaders understand political power.

Ask three questions before you compose your thoughts for public consumption: How can this message spur action? What are the means available to me to do that? Have I taken in all the viewpoints and emotions of others?

•6•

Foster practical wisdom in others.

Your organization is a living, breathing entity. Give it a pulse. Listen to the people around you. Create mentoring relationships. Give people around you a sense of being a part of something greater than their day-to-day tasks may afford. Become a philosopher. Express random thoughts and ideas. Be the idealist. Be the politician. Be a novelist; tell stories, use metaphors, analogies, conjure something in people around you. Be a teacher. Live by your code.

⌒⌒

There is no better tool for teaching leadership than learning by example. *Trusted Healers* is rife with many who personify dedication, vision, and an ability to inspire others.

As we have seen throughout, Dr. Paul Grundy is a leader's leader, a man who inspires and emboldens others. Here is a list of ten qualities to which I attribute Paul's leadership success:

1. **He UNDERSTANDS the importance of his adversity in defining his purpose and who he is.**

Paul Grundy did not blink when his family encountered extreme poverty. He went to work. Instead of being crushed by the death of his beloved big brother, Paul set his sights on changing the world. Everyone who has ever been with Paul for an extended amount of time remarks that he is absolutely, totally fearless.

2. He CREATES clarity from complexity, seeing what others cannot see.

Paul figured out quickly how the HIV/AIDS pandemic would spread throughout South Africa. He studied the plight of American healthcare and saw a way out—the *medical home*. He sees primary care doctors struggling, spending too much time typing into a computer, and then he champions solutions.

3. He LISTENS, RESPECTS AND RESPONDS to tribal tendencies, customs, and beliefs in communities.

Paul respected the traditional healers' beliefs and helped them find an acceptable way to fight the HIV/AIDS pandemic. He counseled Secretary of State for Health and Social Care Jeremy Hunt to empower the general practitioners to create their own *primary care homes* rather than legislate a solution. He gently coaches the leadership of Ireland, understanding that they have their own cultural way of changing things, enabling them to see the solutions to their crisis at their own pace.

4. He MAKES AN OFFERING of hope and inspiration to society and never gives up.

Paul spent thirteen years nurturing the *medical home* throughout America and other cultures, traveling anywhere he could find a willing group of doctors to present his stories and his data. He still does.

5. **He COLLECTS practical data as well as personal stories and enthusiasm.**

Everywhere Paul goes, he gathers stories—from taxi drivers, from clerks, from physicians and patients, and applies them toward his message, combining these first-person accounts with a wealth of studies and experiences around the world to support the *medical home*.

6. **He GUIDES efforts with principle-based organization. He creates an aspiration, proclaims it and then inspires people to do great things, and has the discipline for course correction and speed adjustments.**

Paul's entire career with IBM epitomized this process. He led the executive team in their aspiration to transform healthcare around the world. He inspired European nations, most notably Denmark, to create a system of robust primary care to become the best in the world. Then he inspired both America and Denmark to share what they do best. He paced his advocacy by creating "big successes" with the VA, government employee healthcare, and military healthcare systems, adjusting his speed for political realities and cultural tendencies. The tipping point is being reached, and *medical homes* are blooming all over America and the developed world.

7. **He CREATES meaningful networking, never letting go.**

Paul's network has been accumulated over his entire career and reaches into hundreds of countries. Once he finds global expertise, he connects that expertise with leadership around the world that needs that talent. He curates the latest technology and shares that view with leading healthcare organizations worldwide.

8. He IS ACCESSIBLE, always.

Paul has been to Great Britain and Ireland dozens of times in the last few years, always going out into the communities, experiencing patients, talking to *Trusted Healers* and inspiring leadership to stay on course. If any group of doctors in America wants Paul to come speak to them, he goes. If any nation is struggling with their healthcare, he arrives to help.

9. He RECOGNIZES that the world will be better because of our next generation of leaders. He believes in them and nurtures them.

The active list of people Paul has mentored goes back to the beginning of his career. Paul has mentored many notable international leaders in healthcare and government. Many of the brightest young people coming out of college today are under his mentorship. He knows that society thrives if the next generation learns from the current generation.

10. He ATTRACTS the best quality people in his world, where *everyone matters*.

Paul attracts people who think like he thinks. Sean Hogan remarks that Paul has a knack for drawing really good, sincere, thoughtful, talented people to him. He also notes that this is not just a trait, it's a phenomenon. And once Paul sees that in a person, they become part of his network.

RECOMMENDED READING

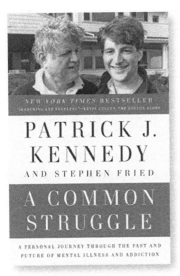

A Common Struggle: A Personal Journey Through the Past and Future of Mental Illness and Addiction

by Patrick J. Kennedy, Stephen Fried
A *New York Times* Bestseller

Patrick J. Kennedy, the former congressman and youngest child of Senator Ted Kennedy, details his personal and political battle with mental illness and addiction, exploring mental healthcare's history in the US alongside his and every family's private struggles.

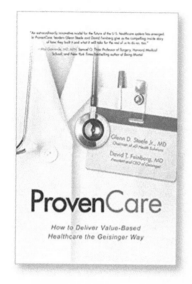

ProvenCare: How to Deliver Value-Based Healthcare the Geisinger Way

by Glenn D. Steele, Jr., MD, PhD, David T. Feinberg, MD

When it comes to providing high-quality care in the most efficient, cost-effective way possible, *ProvenCare* is the gold standard in the industry. Developed at Geisinger Health System and praised by healthcare leaders worldwide, this pioneering approach provides an essential blueprint for healthcare executives who want to provide higher levels of care for their patients, greater incentives for practitioners, and smarter solutions at lower costs.

This Is Your Do-Over: The 7 Secrets to Losing Weight, Living Longer, and Getting a Second Chance at the Life You Want

by Michael F. Roizen, MD,

Mehmet Oz, MD (Foreword), Ted Spiker (Contributor)

From the best-selling co-author of the YOU series, this is the ultimate guide to reversing damage, optimizing health, and living a life filled with energy and happiness. No matter what kind of lifestyle you lead, no matter what your bad habits, whether you're a smoker, a couch potato, or a marshmallow addict, it's never too late to start living a healthy life. You do not have to be destined to a certain health outcome because your parents were on the same path, or because you think you've already done the damage. And you can even change the function of your genes through your lifestyle choices.

What to Eat When: A Strategic Plan to Improve Your Health and Life Through Food

by Michael Roizen, MD, Michael Crupain, MD, Ted Spiker

New York Times best-selling author Dr. Michael Roizen reveals how the food choices you make each day—and when you make them—can affect your health, your energy, your sex life, your waistline, your attitude, and the way you age.

What if eating two cups of blueberries a day could prevent cancer? If drinking a kale-infused smoothie could counteract missing an hour's worth of sleep? When is the right time of day to eat that chocolate chip cookie? And would you actually drink that glass of water if it meant skipping the gym? This revolutionary guide reveals how to use food to enhance our personal and professional lives—and increase longevity to boot. *What to Eat When* is not a diet book. Instead, acclaimed internist Michael Roizen and preventive medicine specialist Michael Crupain offer readers choices that benefit them the most—whether it's meals to help them look and feel younger or snacks that prevent diseases—based on the science that governs them.

The Familiar Physician: Saving Your Doctor In the Era of Obamacare

by Peter B. Anderson, MD, Bud Ramey, Tom Emswiller

Powerful forces of change are at the core of Obamacare—and they could either strengthen or destroy our family doctors. It's a perfect storm that threatens our hope for more effective and personalized medical care, and it holds the potential to drive our trusted *Familiar Physicians* toward extinction. In the midst of the storm is a new and promising approach called the *medical home*.

Learn what you can do to help assure that the *Familiar Physician*, the basis for a strong physician-patient relationship, survives the approaching storm.

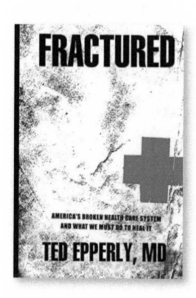

Fractured: America's Broken Health Care System and What We Must Do to Heal It

by Ted Epperly, MD

In the United States, we spend over $2.6 trillion on healthcare each year, yet we rank thirty-seventh in the world for outcomes. Even more shocking, millions of Americans don't have any sort of health insurance. These harrowing statistics reflect that, as a nation, we focus more on disease and sickness than on wellness and health, creating a society where many are living sick and dying young. The reality is clear: we suffer from a dysfunctional, have versus have-not healthcare system where medical miracles are performed for some, while access to care is denied to others. In *Fractured*, Dr. Epperly draws on his decades of experience as a family physician to identify the system's gaps and disparities and propose a compelling strategy to mend them, with the goal of creating an integrated, accessible, patient-centered approach to health and medicine.

NEW YORK TIMES BESTSELLER

THE HEALING OF AMERICA
A GLOBAL QUEST FOR BETTER, CHEAPER, AND FAIRER HEALTH CARE
T. R. REID

WITH AN EXPLANATION OF HEALTH CARE REFORM

The Healing of America: A Global Quest for Better, Cheaper, and Fairer Health Care

by T. R. Reid

Bringing to bear his talent for explaining complex issues in a clear, engaging way, *New York Times* best-selling author T. R. Reid visits industrialized democracies around the world—France, Britain, Germany, Japan, and beyond—to provide a revelatory tour of successful, affordable universal healthcare systems. Now updated with new statistics and a plain-English explanation of the 2010 healthcare reform bill, *The Healing of America* is required reading for all those hoping to understand the state of healthcare in our country, and around the world.

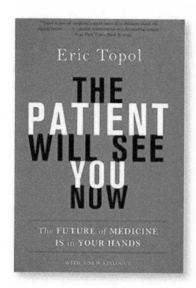

The Patient Will See You Now:
The Future of Medicine Is in
Your Hands

by Eric Topol, MD

In *The Patient Will See You Now*, Dr. Eric Topol, one of the nation's top physicians, shows why medicine does not have to involve long waits and impersonal care. Instead, you could use your smartphone to get rapid test results from one drop of blood, monitor your vital signs both day and night, and use an artificially intelligent algorithm to receive a diagnosis without having to see a doctor, all at a small fraction of the cost imposed by our modern healthcare system.

The change is powered by what Dr. Topol calls medicine's "Gutenberg moment." Much as the printing press took learning out of the hands of a priestly class, the mobile internet is doing the same for medicine, giving us unprecedented control over our healthcare. With smartphones in hand, we are no longer beholden to an impersonal and paternalistic system in which "doctor knows best." Medicine has been digitized, Dr. Topol argues; now it will be democratized. Computers will replace physicians for many diagnostic tasks, citizen science will give rise to citizen medicine, and enormous data sets will give us new means to attack conditions that have long been incurable.

DISCUSSION QUESTIONS

What is the one thing that is most important in your family's healthcare future?

How many different fundamental models of healthcare delivery are deployed in the US?

What one fact about societal change is universal around the world? All change is _____.

What country's healthcare is the US Medicare system modeled after?

What part of our healthcare system is considered a universal care model?

Does universal care look easier to manage than other models?

Why do citizens in Great Britain favor their healthcare system so strongly?

In leadership, what is the one thing you cannot fake?

Why is Denmark so far ahead of the rest of the world in primary care development?

What nation sports the most robust primary care in the world?

What benefits do you gain by having a *Trusted Healer*?

What does *everyone matters* mean to you?

The breakthroughs in quality and cost at Geisinger Health System stunned the country. When will these evidence-based practices be adopted in your community?

Why do US free clinics feel they must charge for a visit?

What was "extreme consensus" and why was that so destructive to fighting HIV/AIDS in South Africa?

Why do the federally qualified health clinics find the *medical home* relatively easy to adopt?

How would you define the "high ground"?

What do you think Dr. Paul Grundy learned from the traditional healers in Africa?

CONTINUUM
OF CARE

T he *medical home* conceptually works. Dr. Paul Grundy teaches that healthcare is not a silo; it is an ecosystem called the *continuum of care*, and it's as wide as it is deep. And it has to be transformed—from birth to death, for every kind of care, coordinated and guided by a *Trusted Healer*.

Continuum of Care is a concept involving a system that guides and tracks patients over time through a comprehensive array of health services spanning all levels and intensity of care.

The Continuum of Care covers the delivery of healthcare over a period of time, and may refer to care provided from birth to end of life. Healthcare services are provided for all levels and stages of care.

Services and Mechanisms
Continuum of Care includes both services and integrating mechanisms.

The *services* can be broken down into seven basic categories:

- Extended care
- Acute hospital care
- Ambulatory care

- Home care
- Outreach
- Wellness
- Housing
- The four basic *integrating mechanisms* are:
- Planning and management
- Care coordination
- Case-based financing
- Integrated information systems

Array of Healthcare Services

The Continuum of Care can include a wide set of services and does not usually refer to a formal system of care delivery. The following are examples of the types and settings of healthcare services that are regularly connected through the Continuum of Care.

- Acute healthcare services
- Hospitals
- Emergency departments
- Inpatient services
- Outpatient services
- Urgent care
- Physician practices
- Long-term care
- Assisted living
- Skilled nursing facilities
- Rehabilitation centers
  - Home care
  - Visiting nurse services
  - Hospices / Palliative care
  - Behavioral health
  - Wellness care
  - Government / Public health services

        °   Care management
        °   Research

In addition to these healthcare settings, the Continuum of Care may also extend to include:

- Home care
- Homeless patients (street or shelter)
- Domestic travel
- International travel

Characteristics and Conditions

The Continuum of Care will vary for each patient depending on his or her unique needs. Common characteristics and conditions include:

- Prenatal care
- Genetic birth defects causing pre/post-natal morbidity/mortality
- Genetic anomalies that increase risk of physical or behavioral illness
- Newborn care
- Healthy patient / Preventive care
- Healthy lifestyle counseling
- Unhealthy lifestyle / High risk factor care
- Acute illness
- Acute injury
- Chronic illness or morbid conditions
- Recovery from physical illness
- Recovery from mental illness or addiction
- Rehabilitation for physical injury
- Imminent death
- Deceased—care for the emotional, financial and societal needs of the family, as well as public health and research

Used with permission by the Healthcare Information and Management Systems Society (HIMSS), an American not-for-profit organization dedicated to improving healthcare in quality, safety, cost-effectiveness, and access through the best use of information technology and management systems.[32]

TEN QUESTIONS TO ASK YOUR PRIMARY CARE PRACTICE

Here are questions Dr. Paul Grundy says you should ask during an appointment. It will not take long to have this discussion, but will set the stage for a great relationship with your care team.

- Will your team let me know when screening tests are needed?

- Will you remind me if I fail to get an appointment when I should have?

- How would you describe your communication style? And do you welcome me to ask questions and express my opinion?

- Is someone on my care team available 24/7? Am I able to call you directly in case of emergency? How does your office handle emergencies if I cannot get in touch with you?

- Am I able to call or email you with non-emergency questions? If so, how long should it take for a response?

- If I am ill, how long should I expect to wait for an appointment after calling to schedule one?

- If I need to seek a specialist, will you collaborate with me to select the right person? Will you follow my care?

- Do you provide post-visit reports that summarize what occurred?

YOUR ACE SCORE

F irst, remember that the ACE score isn't a crystal ball; it's just meant as guidance. It tells you about one type of risk factor among many. It doesn't directly take into account your diet or genes, or whether you smoke or drink excessively, to name just a few of the other major influences on health.

There are ten types of childhood trauma measured in the ACE Study. Five are personal: physical abuse, verbal abuse, sexual abuse, physical neglect, and emotional neglect.

Five are related to other family members: a parent who's an alcoholic, a mother who's a victim of domestic violence, a family member in jail, a family member diagnosed with a mental illness, and the disappearance of a parent through divorce, death or abandonment. Each type of trauma counts as one. So a person who's been physically abused, with one alcoholic parent, and a mother who was beaten up has an ACE score of three.

There are, of course, many other types of childhood trauma: racism, bullying, watching a sibling being abused, losing a caregiver (grandmother, mother, grandfather, etc.), homelessness, surviving and recovering from a severe accident, witnessing a father being abused by a mother, witnessing a grandmother abusing a father, involvement with the foster care system, involvement with the juvenile justice system, etc.

The ACE Study included only those ten childhood traumas because those were mentioned as most common by a group of about 300 Kaiser members; those traumas were also well studied individually in the research literature.

The most important thing to remember is that the ACE score is meant as a guideline: If you experienced other types of toxic stress over months or years, then those would likely increase your risk of health consequences.

Prior to your eighteenth birthday:

Did a parent or other adult in the household often or very often . . . Swear at you, insult you, put you down, or humiliate you? or Act in a way that made you afraid that you might be physically hurt?

No ___ If Yes, enter 1 __

Did a parent or other adult in the household often or very often . . . Push, grab, slap, or throw something at you? or Ever hit you so hard that you had marks or were injured?

No ___ If Yes, enter 1 __

Did an adult or person at least five years older than you ever . . . Touch or fondle you or have you touch their body in a sexual way? or Attempt or actually have oral, anal, or vaginal intercourse with you?

No ___ If Yes, enter 1 __

Did you often or very often feel that . . . No one in your family loved you or thought you were important or special? Or, Your family didn't look out for each other, feel close to each other, or support each other?

No ___ If Yes, enter 1 ___

Did you often or very often feel that . . . You didn't have enough to eat, had to wear dirty clothes, and had no one to protect you? or Your parents were too drunk or high to take care of you or take you to the doctor if you needed it?

No ___ If Yes, enter 1 ___

Were your parents ever separated or divorced?

No ___ If Yes, enter 1 ___

Was your mother or stepmother:

Often or very often pushed, grabbed, slapped, or had something thrown at her? or Sometimes, often, or very often kicked, bitten, hit with a fist, or hit with something hard? or ever repeatedly hit over at least a few minutes or threatened with a gun or knife?

No ___ If Yes, enter 1 ___

Did you live with anyone who was a problem drinker or alcoholic, or who used street drugs?

No ___ If Yes, enter 1 ___

Was a household member depressed or mentally ill, or did a household member attempt suicide?

No ___ If Yes, enter 1 ___

Did a household member go to prison?

No ___ If Yes, enter 1 ___

Now add up your "Yes" answers: ___

This is your ACE Score: _____

The CDC's Adverse Childhood Experiences Study (ACE Study) uncovered a stunning link between childhood trauma and the chronic diseases people develop as adults, as well as social and emotional problems.

This includes heart disease, lung cancer, diabetes and many autoimmune diseases, as well as depression, violence, being a victim of violence, and suicide.

The first research results were published in 1998, followed by more than seventy other publications through 2015. They showed that:

- Childhood trauma was very common, even in employed white middle-class, college-educated people with great health insurance.

- There was a direct link between childhood trauma and adult onset of chronic disease, as well as depression, suicide, being violent and a victim of violence.

- More types of trauma increased the risk of health, social and emotional problems.

- People usually experience more than one type of trauma—rarely is it only sex abuse or only verbal abuse.

Two-thirds of the 17,000 people in the ACE Study had an ACE score of at least one—87 percent of those had more than one. Thirty-six states and the District of Columbia have done their own ACE surveys; their results are similar to the CDC's ACE Study.

The study's researchers came up with an ACE score to explain a person's risk for chronic disease. Think of it as a cholesterol score for childhood toxic stress.

You get one point for each type of trauma. The higher your ACE score, the higher your risk of health and social problems. (Of course, other types of trauma exist that could contribute to an ACE score, so it is conceivable that people could have ACE scores higher than ten; however, the ACE Study measured only ten types.)

As your ACE score increases, so does the risk of disease, social and emotional problems. With an ACE score of four or more, things start getting serious. The likelihood of chronic pulmonary lung disease increases 390 percent; hepatitis, 240 percent; depression 460 percent; attempted suicide, 1,220 percent.

(The study's participants were 17,000 mostly white, middle and upper-middle class college-educated San Diegans with good jobs and great healthcare—they all belonged to the Kaiser Permanente health maintenance organization.)

Source: Center for Disease Control

BOOKS BY
MICHAEL ROIZEN, MD

The Great Age Reboot, Coming in 2020

What to Eat When: A Strategic Plan to Improve Your Health and Life Through Food by Michael F. Roizen, MD, Michael Crupain, MD, Ted Spiker

This Is Your Do-Over: The 7 Secrets to Losing Weight, Living Longer, and Getting a Second Chance at the Life You Want by Michael F. Roizen, MD

RealAge: Are You as Young as You Can Be? by Michael F. Roizen, MD

The RealAge Diet: Make Yourself Younger with What You Eat, by Michael F. Roizen, MD, John La Puma

Cooking the RealAge Way: Turn Back Your Biological Clock with More than 80 Delicious and Easy Recipes, by Michael F. Roizen, MD, John La Puma

The RealAge Makeover: Take Years off Your Looks and Add Them to Your Life, by Michael F. Roizen, MD

The RealAge Workout: Maximum Health, Minimum Work, by Michael F. Roizen, MD, Tracy Hafen

YOU: Being Beautiful : The Owner's Manual to Inner and Outer Beauty by Michael F. Roizen, MD, and Mehmet C. Oz, MD

YOU: Staying Young: The Owner's Manual for Extending Your Warranty, by Michael F. Roizen, MD, Mehmet Oz, MD

YOU: On A Diet: The Owner's Manual for Waist Management, by Michael F. Roizen, MD, Mehmet Oz, MD

YOU: The Smart Patient: An Insider's Handbook for Getting the Best Treatment, by Michael F. Roizen, MD, Mehmet Oz, MD

YOU: The Owner's Manual: An Insider's Guide to the Body that Will Make You Healthier and Younger, by Michael F. Roizen, MD, Mehmet Oz, MD

AgeProof: Living Longer Without Running Out of Money or Breaking a Hip by Jean Chatzky, Michael F. Roizen, MD with Ted Spiker, Mehmet C. Oz, MD

RealAge: Are You as Young as You Can Be? by Michael F. Roizen, MD

ENDNOTES

[1] "The Oprah Winfrey Show Finale," Oprah.com, accessed February 19, 2019, http://www.oprah.com/oprahshow/the-oprah-winfrey-show-finale_1/8.

[2] Jane O'Brien, "The Time when Americans Drank All Day Long," *BBC News, Washington* March 9, 2015, accessed March 1, 2019, https://www.bbc.com/news/magazine-31741615.

[3] "The Study That Helped Spur the US Stop-Smoking Movement," American Cancer Society, January 9, 2014, accessed March 1, 2019, https://www.cancer.org/latest-news/the-study-that-helped-spur-the-us-stop-smoking-movement.html.

[4] "Building the Transcontinental Railroad Digital History ID 3147," Digital History, accessed February 10, 2019, http://www.digitalhistory.uh.edu/disp_textbook.cfm?smtID=2&psid=3147.

[5] "Outcomes of Implementing Patient-Centered *Medical Home* Interventions." A Review of the Evidence from Prospective Evaluation Studies in the US (PCPCC, October 2012), accessed February 24, 2019, http://dvha.vermont.gov/advisory-boards/9-18-13-grundy-presentation.pdf.

6 "Blue Cross Blue Shield of Michigan Marks 10 Years of Health Care Transformation with Patient-Centered Medical Home Designation Program," MI Blues Perspectives, accessed February 10, 2019, https://www.mibluesperspectives.com/our-news/.

7 Mitchell Bard and Howard Lenhoff, "America's Role in the Rescue of Ethiopian Jewry," *The Jewish Virtual Library, Ethiopian Jewry*, accessed November 27, 2018, https://www.jewishvirtuallibrary. org/america-s-role-in-the-rescue-of-ethiopian-jewry.

8 Bill Moyers, "Argentine Human Rights," *CBS Crossroads Argentina* Part 1, 12:51 and Part 2, 2:50, accessed February 12, 2018, https://www.youtube.com/channel/UCAaQKFvHE3LudcIPJM-roPIw, and https://www.youtube.com/watch?v=H3BC5phpyqw.

9 Thair Shaikh, "Q&A: Is Fukushima as bad as Chernobyl?" CNN, April 13, 2011, http://www.cnn.com/2011/WORLD/asiapcf/04/12/japan.nuclear.disaster.fukushima/index.html.

10 Charlie Rose, *PBS Charlie Rose*, "IBM's Rometty: 'Health Care Will Be Our Moon Shot,'" April 16, 2015, https://www.youtube.com/watch?v=46MYhalt7EU.

11 "The Physicians Foundation's Sixth Biennial Survey Finds Physicians are Pessimistic About the Future of the Profession as Burnout Rates Continue to Rise," The Physicians Foundation, accessed February 7, 2019, https://physiciansfoundation.org/press-releases/the-physicians-foundations-sixth-biennial-survey-finds-physicians-are-pessimistic-about-the-future-of-the-profession-as-burnout-rates-continue-to-rise/.

[12] "Crossing the Quality Chasm: A New Health System for the Twenty-First Century," NCBI, Institute of Medicine (US) Committee on Quality of Health Care in America, accessed February 5, 2019, https://www.ncbi.nlm.nih.gov/pubmed/25057539.

[13] Mark A. Schuster, et al. "How good is the quality of health care in the United States? 1998," *Milbank Quarterly* vol. 83,4 (2005): 843–95, accessed February 5, 2019, https://www.ncbi.nlm.nih.gov/pmc/articles/PMC2690293/.

[14] "Reducing Waste in Health Care," *Health Affairs*, December 13, 2012, accessed February 5, 2019, https://www.healthaffairs.org/do/10.1377/hpb20121213.959735/full/.

[15] "Defining the *Medical Home*," PCPCC, accessed January 13, 2019, https://www.pcpcc.org/about/medical-home.

[16] "The Shared Principles of Primary Care," PCPCC, https://www.pcpcc.org/about/shared-principles (accessed January 13, 2019).

[17] "Understanding the Basics of the Patient-Centered *Medical Home*," PCPCC, accessed January 13, 2019, https://www.pcpcc.org/2015/02/27/understanding-basics-patient-centered-medical-home.

[18] Ibid.

[19] "Health Care Costs and Election 2008," Henry J. Kaiser Family Foundation, October 14, 2008, accessed February 5, 2019, https://www.kff.org/health-costs/issue-brief/health-care-costs-and-election-2008/.

[20] Peter B. Anderson, MD, with Bud Ramey and Tom Emswiller, *The Familiar Physician*, (New York, Morgan James Publishing), 2014, 49.

[21] "2017 Snapshot of Health Care," Kaiser Family Foundation, accessed February 11, 2019, https://www.kff.org/health-costs/report/2017-employer-health-benefits-survey/.

[22] **Medicine Honors Dr. Paul Grundy**
> **2008 Honorary Membership, the American Academy of Family Medicine**
> The honorary membership in the AAFP has been awarded forty-four times over seventy years in the organization. Paul is honored for his efforts to inspire positive change in the US healthcare system by emphasizing the value of family medicine and primary care as the foundation of a better medical system.
> **2012 Member of the National Academy of Medicine**
> **2012 National Committee for Quality Assurance (NCQA)**
> **2012 Health Quality Award**
> NCQA presents Health Quality Awards to individuals and organizations that both highlight the need for and drive healthcare improvement. Past recipients include former Pennsylvania governor Edward Rendell, former California governor Arnold Schwarzenegger, the Honorable Hillary Rodham Clinton, former US surgeon general David Satcher, and Senator Edward Kennedy of Massachusetts.
> **2012 New Jersey Academy of Family Physician**

Edward Schauer, MD Health Policy Award
2014 Ambassador of Healthcare DENMARK
Honored by Her Royal Highness Princess Mary.
2016 The Barbara Starfield Award
This was awarded in recognition of exceptional
work toward advancing the *medical home* and
person-focused care, advancing the PCMH model
as a vehicle for transformational change, not only
in the United States, but also around the world.
2016 Honorary Lifetime Member of the British
National Association of Primary Care
The first international lifetime member.
2016 Honorary Lifetime Member of the Irish
National General Practice Association

[23] "Global Conference on Primary Health Care," World Health
Organization, accessed February 5, 2019, https://www.who.int/
primary-health/conference-phc.

[24] Lindsay Abrams, "Where Surgery Comes with a 90-Day Guarantee," *The Atlantic,* September 26, 2012, https://www.theatlantic.
com/health/archive/2012/09/where-surgery-comes-with-a-
90-day-guarantee/262841/, (Accessed February 3, 2019).

[25] Steve Sternberg, "Unsatisfied with Your Surgery, Get Some of
Your Money Back," US News and World Report, Nov. 11, 2015,
accessed February 4, 2019, https://www.usnews.com/news/ar-
ticles/2015/11/11/unsatisfied-with-your-surgery-get-your-money-
back.

[26] "Community Collaboration for Health Care," Ian Morrison, PhD,
December 1, 2017, accessed January 11, 2019, http://ianmorrison.
com.

27 "Adverse Childhood Experiences (ACEs)," Center for Disease Control, accessed November 27, 2018, https://www.cdc.gov/violenceprevention/acestudy/index.html.

28 "What is an FQHC?" FQHC.org, accessed February 4, 2019, https://www.fqhc.org/what-is-an-fqhc/.

29 Daren R. Anderson, MD, and J. Nwando Olayiwola, MD, "Community Health Centers and the Patient-Centered *Medical Home*: Challenges and Opportunities to Reduce Health Care Disparities in America." *Journal of Health Care for the Poor and Underserved* 23, no. 3 (2012): 949–957, accessed January 3, 2019, https://www.researchgate.net/publication/258428952_Community_Health_Centers_and_the_Patient-Centered_Medical_Home_Challenges_and_Opportunities_to_Reduce_ Health_Care_Disparities_in_America.

30 "Health Insurance Coverage of the Total Population," Henry J. Kaiser Family Foundation, accessed January 11, 2019, https://www.kff.org/other/state-indicator/total-population/?dataView=1&currentTimeframe=0&sortModel=%7B%22colId%22:%22Location%22,%22sort%22:%22asc%22%7D.

31 Encyclopedia.com, "Fairy Tales," accessed February 13, 2019, https://www.encyclopedia.com/people/literature-and-arts/scandinavian-literature-biographies/hans-christian-andersen.

32 "Continuum of Care," Healthcare Information and Management Systems Society, accessed February 10, 2019, https://www.himss.org/definition-continuum-care.

CPSIA information can be obtained
at www.ICGtesting.com
Printed in the USA
FSHW020250260419
57586FS